UNIONS

OF

THEIR OWN CHOOSING

AN ACCOUNT OF

THE NATIONAL LABOR RELATIONS BOARD

AND ITS WORK

BY

ROBERT R. R. BROOKS

ASSISTANT PROFESSOR OF ECONOMICS

WILLIAMS COLLEGE

NEW HAVEN

YALE UNIVERSITY PRESS

LONDON · HUMPHREY MILFORD · OXFORD UNIVERSITY PRESS

To

JAMES AND RUBINA

Employees shall have the right . . .
to bargain collectively through representatives *of their own choosing.*

ACKNOWLEDGMENT

THE author wishes to express his obligation to Mr. Malcolm Ross, Director of Publications of the National Labor Relations Board, for his endless labors in collecting material, much of which would have been unobtainable without his assistance; for his cheerfulness during a very hot summer in replying to innumerable questions; and for his trust in providing the author with valuable memoranda in advance of their publication.

To Mrs. Elinore Morehouse Herrick, Director of the New York Regional Office of the National Labor Relations Board, the author is similarly obliged for materials, for advice, and for access to the files of informally settled cases upon which Chapter I is largely based. To Mr. John Carmody and Mrs. E. T. Kerr of the same office the author is grateful for reading and suggesting improvements in Chapter I.

Mr. Nathan Witt, Secretary of the National Labor Relations Board, very kindly consented to read the entire manuscript and thereby placed the author deep in his debt.

To many students who have acted as catalytic agent for the formulation of opinions expressed in this book, to Mr. and Mrs. Henry A. Storer for providing the seclusion necessary for its completion, to Mr. Eugene Davidson of the Yale University Press whose constant guidance through two manuscripts has proved indispensable, and to Professor Max Lerner of Williams College for reading and suggesting improvements in Chapters VIII and IX—to all of these the author expresses his gratitude.

None of those who have had a hand in this work assume any responsibility for its shortcomings except the author.

R.R.R.B.

CONTENTS

ACKNOWLEDGMENT ix

LIST OF ILLUSTRATIONS xiii

I. THE BOARD AT WORK 1

II. THE BACKGROUND 23

III. ANTIUNIONISM 45

IV. COLLECTIVE BARGAINING 81

V. INDUSTRIAL PEACE 118

VI. INTERUNION CONFLICT 140

VII. THE UNFAIR PRACTICES OF LABOR . . 171

VIII. THE BOARD AND THE COURTS . . . 202

IX. THE N.L.R.B. AND DEMOCRACY . . 236

NOTES AND BIBLIOGRAPHY . . . 258

APPENDIX: NATIONAL LABOR
RELATIONS ACT 275

INDEX 287

ILLUSTRATIONS

Tripping on His Own Mantle 7

We Need a New Officer on That Beat . . . 16

The Umpire Begins to Get What He Had Coming 21

Worth Looking Into! 43

Careful There, Where You're Shooting! . . 50

The Modern Joshua: Stand Still! 78

It's Full of Termites! 97

Making It Legal 115

We Can Settle It Out of Court, Judge! . . . 128

His Decisions Are Questioned 156

Somebody Stole My Gal 158

You Gave Him the Most Icing! 165

To Spite His Face 170

Slightly Warped! 181

Parental Authority 206

"Gosh! and I Made It Myself!" 227

UNIONS
OF THEIR OWN CHOOSING

CHAPTER I

THE BOARD AT WORK

IN the autumn of 1937, five shoe-manufacturing companies located within a few blocks of each other in New York City decided to move out of town. When the flight was over, the five companies had all settled down in small towns in New York and New England. Before they moved, each of the companies had an agreement with the Shoe Workers' Union covering wages, hours, and other conditions and granting the closed shop. On resuming operations in their new locations, the companies found themselves amply provided with nonunion labor at lower wages than in the city. The shoe workers of New York City were left without jobs during a period of rapidly increasing unemployment, and the union's strength and prestige were seriously threatened.

There were three possible courses which the union might pursue. It could desert its members in the city, follow the companies into the small towns, and attempt to organize the workers there as a basis for renewing agreements with the companies. It could sue the companies for breach of contract since the flight took place before the expiration of the agreements.[1] Or it could charge the companies with violation of the National Labor Relations Act in attempting to evade collective bargaining. The union decided upon the third course of action.

In February, 1938, the union filed a formal charge against all five companies asserting that the employers left the city for the "sole purpose of evading collective bargaining," that they had locked out their employees, that it was "almost impossible for these locked-out workers to obtain employment," and that the situation required that "this case be tried at an early date." Written upon forms provided for this purpose by the regional offices of the National Labor Relations Board, this charge was duly notarized and turned in at the New York Regional Office on the fifth floor of the Woolworth Building.

Immediately upon its arrival, the charge was turned over to a field examiner for the board. The field examiner separated the five cases, assigned a case number to each, and wrote to each of the employers asking that they come into the office to discuss the situation with him and with a union representative in an effort to reach an understanding which would make formal action unnecessary. From this point on we shall follow the course of only one of the five cases, since all were handled in a similar manner.

On February 21, Mr. Feldstein of the Black Shoe Company, Mr. Blomberg of the Shoe Workers' Union, and a field examiner for the New York Regional Office met together in a room in the Woolworth Building. Mr. Blomberg restated the union's charge that Mr. Feldstein had deliberately locked out his workers on November 1 in spite of an agreement which did not expire until January 15, 1938. Although Mr. Feldstein had stated at that time that he was going out of business, by the first of January he was shipping machinery to New England and by the end of the month had resumed operations and was selling to his old customers. The sole reason, said Mr. Blomberg, for this move was that Feldstein, along with other shoe manufacturers, wanted to beat the union and evade collective bargaining with his workers. This was clearly a violation of the act. Blomberg then demanded that the Black Shoe Company either move back to New York or offer reëmployment through the union to as many of the former New York employees as now wished to work in the New England shop.

"Well, Mr. Feldstein," said the field examiner, "what is your side of this story? You realize, of course, that the board has ruled on several occasions that employers cannot legally move plants into nonunion territory if their intention is to interfere with the workers' right to self-organization. They must either return and fulfil their agreements, or offer reëmployment to the displaced workers. The board has even ordered that the employer pay transportation expenses of his former workers to the new shop. In the present case it is peculiar, isn't it, that all five employers under agreement with the union, all located within a short distance of each other, moved out of the city almost simultaneously before the expiration of their contracts?"

"I can't speak for the other companies which moved out of the city but I can tell you," said Mr. Feldstein, "why I closed my plant. I speak of 'closing' my shop rather than 'moving' it for reasons which I shall try to make clear. My parents were both Russian, but I was born in this country forty-one years ago and I've tried all my life to be a law-abiding citizen. I first went into the shoe business back in the war days as a production manager. I worked hard, saved a little money, and in 1920 went into a partnership. But the shoe business is a pretty competitive affair. My company failed in 1922, and so did another firm of which I was a partner between 1923 and 1925. In 1926 I started my own company. For a while I did pretty well. Then came the depression and the bottom fell out of the business. But I managed to survive and by 1936 was on my feet again. I had a partner, Mr. Rikornik, who bought from me, little by little, a 10 per cent share of the business. In the summer of 1937 the 'recession' hit me hard and I decided to liquidate. I'd had enough of the business and decided definitely to get out. My wife was in very bad health as a result of a sinus condition and we thought that perhaps a change from the city would do her good. I turned over to Rikornik the trade name and good will of the company and split the lease of the machinery with him in proportion to our shares. I had no idea at the time what I was going to do next except to get my wife out of the city."

"I suppose that by pointing out that Rikornik got the trade name and good will of the company, you mean to prove, Feldstein, that you were definitely out of the business. Well, what good was the trade name of the company if Rikornik only got 10 per cent of the machinery?"

"You know as well as I, Blomberg, that we did a retail business in addition to the manufacturing end, and the company's good will was valuable in the retailing that Rikornik planned to go into, and did."

"Well, how did it happen that if you were really going out of business, you didn't sell your machinery and divide up the proceeds on a cash basis?"

"As a union business agent, you ought to know that most of the shoe machinery in this country is leased, not sold. We *couldn't* sell it and our lease hadn't expired."

"Tell me," said the examiner, "how, after having closed your shop, you happened to resume operations in Massachusetts within three months of laying off your workers."

"Well, Mr. Examiner, first of all I had to do something. I couldn't retire at the age of forty-one on the small savings

I'd made. Second, I had my share of the machinery. I knew the shoe business and it was the logical thing for me to go into. But the important thing was that by going out of business I'd left my salesmen and agents high and dry. They began to press me to resume operations on whatever basis possible in order to keep them going until better times came. Then this town in New England offered me low rents and taxes and a labor force from which I could easily train skilled operators. So I agreed to do it. At the present time, business is going very badly and I don't know how long I can go on."

"Now, Mr. Feldstein," continued the union representative, "I'm sorry about your wife, but this story of yours just won't do. First, if you were so sorry for your salesmen and agents, why didn't you think of your hundred workers who are now pounding the pavements, many of them on the verge of starvation and unwilling to apply for relief? Second, how do you explain that all five companies moved at the same time? Were five wives ill? Sinusitis isn't epidemic, you know. Third, I have here a report from Dun & Bradstreet which flatly says that your former company was successful, that you were able to accumulate considerable means, that the net worth of your company was over $60,000, and that you moved to Massachusetts 'in order to take advantage of a more favorable labor market.' "

"As I said before, Blomberg, I can't speak for the other companies that moved out of town. My own story is just as I've told it. That report from Dun & Bradstreet is based on figures up to July 1, 1937. We *were* successful up to that time. But I have here a certified copy of an accountant's report showing that between July 1 and October 1, 1937, the firm lost $12,884.69. With a net worth of less than $50,000 on October 1, it's pretty obvious that I couldn't go on long at that rate. As for the workers who are out of jobs, I *am* sorry for them. But the best that I can offer is to take them back individually if business picks up and if they will come up to Massachusetts and settle down in the community."

"Mr. Feldstein," said the examiner, "what were your relations with the union at the time that you closed your New York plant?"

"Very satisfactory, sir. Blomberg will bear me out that we never had any difficulty. We operated under a closed-shop contract and got along O.K. In fact, when the union called a general stoppage in September, 1937, against employers who were violating the code of fair practices set up by the Stabilization Commission in the shoe industry, we were allowed to continue operations because we had always lived up to the code. We had no reason for trying to escape the union. I say as strongly as I can that we did not close down in an effort to evade collective bargaining. I'm willing to tell Blomberg, with you as a witness, Mr. Examiner, that whenever a majority of my present employees wish to bargain with me through the Shoe Workers' Union, I'll be willing to comply."

"I think I have the important aspects of this case pretty well in mind," concluded the examiner, "and if neither of you gentlemen have anything to add, we'll send a memorandum to the National Board and let you know the results as soon as possible. Thank you both for your courtesy."

On April 5, 1938, a memorandum from the Secretary of the National Board to the director of the New York Regional Office advised that the charges brought by the union be dismissed and that no complaint against the company should issue since there was no evidence that the company's move was made to defeat the union. The

Courtesy of Parrish and the *Chicago Daily Tribune.*

TRIPPING ON HIS OWN MANTLE

regional director immediately sent the company and the union a formal notice of this dismissal. The field examiner wrote the union a note explaining the notice, and the case was transferred from the "Open" to the "Closed" files of the New York office.[2]

Of the thousands of cases handled by the National Labor Relations Board through its offices all over the country during the first three years of the life of the act, 16 per cent of the cases resulted in dismissal of the charges brought by unions against employers.[3] Unions are invited, if they wish, to appeal these dismissed cases to the National Board, but only in very few cases have they done so. Almost no public notice has been taken of this phase of the board's work.

ON September 30, 1937, an officer of the Leatherworkers' Union Local 401 wrote a letter to a regional office saying that five of its members had just been discharged "without cause and undoubtedly for union activity" by the Monumental Manufacturing Company. On receipt of this letter, the regional office promptly sent the union blank forms on which to state the charge as specifically as possible. These forms were attested by a notary public and returned in quadruplicate to the regional office. The union charged that the company had violated the National Labor Relations Act: (1) by refusing to bargain collectively; (2) by interference with and restraint and coercion of the workers in their right to join unions of their own choosing; (3) by discriminatory discharge of five workers.

On October 8, a field examiner of the regional office wrote the company requesting that a representative of the company meet with him and the union officer on October 14 to discuss the union's charge. The company willingly agreed.

After postponing the conference once, at the company's request, Messrs. John and Louis Bottle (for the company), Messrs. Kemoroff and Nosta (for the union), and the field examiner met on the afternoon of October 25.

Field Examiner: "Mr. Nosta, will you be so kind as to restate the charges which the union is making against the Monumental Manufacturing Company?"

Mr. Nosta: "On September 30, I was told that five members of the union employed at Mr. Bottle's company had been fired. Since we had an organizing campaign on at the time and these men had been working faithfully for the company for a long time, it seemed obvious to us that these men were being victimized for their union activity. On investigating further, I found that one of the men, Marvin Gloss, had been let go earlier, before he joined the union, so we are dropping the charges in his case. But the other four were fired in a bunch and at a time when it would act as a check to our organizing campaign."

Field Examiner: "Mr. Bottle, what information can you give us about this situation?"

Mr. Louis Bottle: "After you wrote me about the union's charge I checked up with my brother, who is in charge of production and shipping. He said that we had been getting a lot of complaints from customers about the condition in which our goods arrived. We've brought with us fifteen letters from customers making these complaints. We have a system, which I'll explain in detail if you like, that makes it easily possible to find out who's responsible for bad work. We found that all of the poor work was coming from these four men: Rubin, Sidney, Frank, and Fernschuss. So we had to let them go."

Mr. Kemoroff: "But, Mr. Bottle, the men say that they did this work at the order of Mr. John Bottle and that he assumed responsibility for the way in which it was done."

Mr. John Bottle: "I know that's what they say, Mr. Kemoroff. But you know how people try to blame things they've done on somebody else. The fact is that the cases these men shipped were ruined because the screws they used were too short and of too heavy a wire. They split the wood on the lower sides of the cases where it didn't show. The proper screws were available in the shop. The men were too slack to go and get them. We couldn't afford to lose customers by having men like that around so we let them go—and we can't possibly take them back."

Field Examiner: "Have you any evidence, Mr. Nosta, that these men were discharged for union activity, rather than for incompetence?"

Mr. Nosta: "I'm afraid that we haven't a very good case, Mr. Examiner, but I'd like a little more time to refer back to the men, and to talk to Mr. Louis and Mr. John about the possibility of a union contract."

Field Examiner: "Suppose we adjourn, then, until we have more information."

After a series of subsequent conferences between union and company representatives, Mr. Nosta, on December 10, wrote the regional office formally withdrawing the charge.

Of the total number of cases handled by the National Labor Relations Board's organization in the first three years of its operation, 24 per cent were settled by the withdrawal of charges brought by unions against employers.[4] Many of these cases were similar to the one detailed above; that is, cases in which the union thought it had a grievance but discovered, on attempting to state it before a government official, that it really had nothing to go on. Other withdrawn cases have occurred when the union really had a valid grievance against an employer, but could not hold its membership in line against the employer's attack long enough to prosecute the case. In these instances, when the union is in effect dissolved, the board cannot itself act as prosecutor. Still other withdrawn cases result when unions advance charges against an employer which they might be able to substantiate, but later withdraw because the employer makes amends without further action by board officials. And finally, there is a group of cases in which charges unauthorized by the union are made in the name of the union, but are withdrawn by union officers as soon as they learn of the action.

To repeat briefly: Sixteen per cent of the charges brought by unions or workers against employers are dismissed by board officers. Twenty-four per cent of the charges brought under the act are withdrawn by unions or workers because, for various reasons, they have no case. As far as the board's records and actions are concerned, therefore, 40 per cent of the total number of cases are settled without gain to the workers or their representatives, and to the relief and satisfaction of employers.

I, THE undersigned swear that I heard the foreman Louie tell Pete Remarck that he was fired for talking about more money, shorter hours, better conditions and a union, he also said "we don't want any of them union guys around here."

[*signed*]   PAUL OCCHIO.
FRANK LADRONE.

This affidavit, written in longhand on a crumpled scrap of paper, was received by a regional office on April 30, 1937, and was duly filed together with the accompanying charge. After a series of conferences between representatives of the Sands Point Neckwear Company, the United Neckwear Workers' Union, and a field examiner of the New York office, the regional director sent the following letter to the Sands Point Neckwear Company:

. . . We have carefully checked the facts surrounding Pete Remarck's discharge. We have witnesses whose stories stand up under the strictest examination which bear out the Union's contention that Remarck was discharged in an effort to check unionization in your plant. . . .

It is our earnest desire to work this out in an amicable way and without having recourse to legal action. Will you, therefore, attend a conference on May 21 at 10 A.M.? . . .

Please come prepared to make a decision as to whether you will reinstate Pete Remarck with back pay to April 12, the date of his discharge.

Promptly at 10 A.M., May 21, 1937, representatives of the company and the union sat down with a field examiner.

Mr. Thomson (for the company): "You know, sir, just because two things happen together, it doesn't prove that one is the cause of the other. If it did, just as soon as a union started organizing, we couldn't discharge anybody, regardless of how inefficient he was."

Field Examiner: "I'm perfectly aware of that, Mr. Thomson, but if you didn't discharge Pete because he wanted a union, why *did* you discharge him?"

Mr. Thomson: "Well, in our shop we have a rule against running the electric irons at high speed, because they burn the ties. Pete broke this rule and burned a lot of ties. So we let him out."

Field Examiner: "What do you mean by high speed?"

Mr. Thomson: "Our irons are adjustable. They can be run at different degrees of temperature."

Mr. Hastings (for the union): "Come on now, Mr. Thomson, you know as well as I that all of the good pressers in your place break that rule. They're all on piece rates. They can work faster if their irons are hot. If they are going to make a decent living, they have to run the irons at high speed and all the foremen know it. They wink at the breaking of the rule as long as the ties are not obviously burned. When the ties are scorched too bad, the pressers are docked. Why pick on Pete? The fact is that the foreman fired Pete because he talked union during lunch hours. The sooner we get that straight the further we'll get. We haven't got anything against the foreman and as a matter of fact Remarck can probably get another job and won't want his old one back. What we want to make sure of is that there will be no more discrimination in the future against our people. The best way to make sure of that is to sign a union agreement with us and deal in a civilized manner. We have a majority in your shop, Mr. Thomson. We're willing to submit to an election, or to any arrangement you like, to prove that we have a majority."

Field Examiner: "Suppose we hold the matter of Pete's discharge in abeyance while you two confer on this broader question of representation and a union agreement. I don't want to bulldoze you, Mr. Thomson, but this case has dragged on too long. Are you willing to confer with the union right away while the charges in Pete's case are held up?"

Mr. Thomson: "That will be perfectly satisfactory to me, sir."

During the next four weeks the regional director wrote twice to the union asking about the results of the conferences with the company. On June 21, the union wrote the regional director, in part, as follows:

Please be advised that since the hearings in your office several conferences have taken place between the Sands Point Neckwear Company and the United Neckwear Workers which resulted in the signing of an agreement which recognizes the union as collective bargaining agent of the employees.

. . . The reason for Mr. Remarck's withdrawal is that he doesn't care to work there after the shop has been unionized. He feels that his presence there may jeopardize the pleasant relations established by the union and the firm, due to the argument which precipitated his discharge. I am also informed that Peter Remarck obtained a job in another trade and that whenever he is ready to return to the union he will get a job as a presser in the Neckwear Industry.

Enclosed in this letter was the following statement:

I, Pete Remarck, herewith agree to withdraw charges I brought against the Sands Point Neckwear Corporation at the Labor Relations Board for dischargal for union activities.

[*signed*]   PETE REMARCK.

This case is classified in the board's records as *adjusted*. That is, the case was not dismissed, nor entirely withdrawn, nor did it involve formal hearings, reports, decisions, and orders. It was settled by informal conferences in which both parties were willing to make concessions and in which there was no overt hostility. In this case, the union gained an advantage from the settlement. In the case which follows, the employer emerges with a slight advantage.

EARLY in April, 1938, Juan Santos of Hoboken, New Jersey, wrote to the New York Regional Office that he had started work for the Artificial Limbs Company on September 21, 1936, and that for a year thereafter his work had always been considered satisfactory. On November 13, 1937, however, he joined the C.I.O. and "became very active." On November 18 he was notified in writing that he was laid off until further notice. For the next five months he returned regularly every week to the plant to look for work. On April 6, 1938, Mr. Raisen (the employer) finally told him that he never would rehire him; that he had "betrayed the company . . . because there was a lot of dissension among the workers because of my union activities"; that he "need not come back"; and that he had "been discharged for no other reason but my membership and union activities in the C.I.O." Santos concluded his letter by requesting that he be reinstated with back pay.

To this letter the C.I.O. union appended a list of five other workers said to have been discharged on the same date and under the same circumstances. After the charges had been properly notarized, a conference was arranged which was attended by Mr. Raisen for the company, Mr. Sucri for the C.I.O., the six discharged workers, and a field examiner for the board.

The examiner's notes on the conference, in part, follow:

"Mr. Raisen a reasonable kindly man—says layoff due to slack work—kept them on longer than he should have —all are to be called back when work is available—except possibly Juan Santos—he has persisted so in bothering them at plant about job, and other workers report he's threatening to kill Raisen unless he gets his job—so he told him he'd not reëmploy him as he was too troublesome. Did not know of aforementioned union."

Then one by one the workers' cases were covered. In each instance the story was essentially the same. The workers expressed their belief that they had been fired for reasons related to union activity. Mr. Raisen explained that times were slack and that someone had to be laid off. The workers countered by supplying reasons why, if someone had to be

laid off, they were not the logical ones unless the cause of
their discharge was union activity. Mr. Raisen went over
each case in detail, presenting reasons for believing that
the seniority of this group of workers was less than that of
the remaining staff and explaining that they would be
taken back on the same basis.

As the conference wore on, it became apparent that the
complexities of the situation would make it impossible to
set up an objective standard for determining Mr. Raisen's
motives for the discharges. Consequently, Mr. Raisen's
manner and bearing under polite questioning became the
only clue. Since Mr. Raisen's manner was excellent, and
the union, having inherited the case from a foregoing union,
was not anxious to press the matter, an agreement was
reached. The company agreed to promise preferential reinstatement of five of the workers, but reserved judgment
in the case of Juan Santos.

On April 28, the field examiner received the following
letter from Mr. Raisen:

. . . Permit us to thank you for the kind and impartial attitude you took at our discussion at your office yesterday, and
we are pleased to comply with your request of preferential re-
employment of the workers in question.

In the case of Juan Santos, we cannot give you a definite
promise now, but will ask your indulgence until such time as
the others shall have been reëmployed.

We wish to assure you that we will treat his case with all the
fairness and impartiality it deserves.

Assuring you of our sincerest efforts to coöperate with you
in every respect, we remain, etc.

The field examiner then wrote the union:

Considering the facts surrounding this case and the uncertainty
of the merits in regard to Mr. Santos, we are considering this
matter *adjusted*.

As the board is empowered to effect the reinstatement only of employees who have been discharged as a result of union activity or sympathy, Mr. Santos' case simply fell back into the gray background of the millions of workers desperately seeking employment during the "recession."

In the first three years of the board's work, 55 per cent of its cases were settled by adjustment comparable to that effected in the two preceding cases.[5] These cases rarely are news and never make the headlines. The board is, in effect, providing the machinery by which thousands of the complicated personnel problems of industry may be settled in as dignified and just a manner as possible. In the course of this work, the board's agents have secured voluntary compliance with the law in thousands of cases, have averted scores of strikes, and settled many more—all without the use of the formal machinery provided by the National Labor Relations Act.

In total, 95 per cent of the actions brought under the act are settled without formal procedure: 16 per cent by dismissal, 24 per cent by withdrawal, and 55 per cent by adjustment. In the remaining 5 per cent of cases, resort is had to formal hearings, reports, decisions, and orders. A small number of these, such as the Remington Rand, Consolidated Edison, Ford, Republic Steel, Weirton Steel, Seamen's Union and Longshoremen's Union cases, have been the basis for forming a good deal of public opinion about the board's work. The 5 per cent of formal actions may be illustrated by the following case.[6]

On the basis of charges filed by the Furniture Workers' Union of Memphis, Tennessee, the regional director of the Atlanta, Georgia, office of the board issued a complaint on May 9, 1936, against the Memphis Furniture Company. The complaint alleged that the company was interfering

WE NEED A NEW OFFICER ON THAT BEAT

with the right of its employees to join the union by discharging active union members, spying on union meetings,
campaigning verbally against the union, and in other ways
preventing its workers from enjoying their rights under
the act.

The company replied, denying the entire complaint. The
board therefore ordered a formal hearing before a trial
examiner. This hearing was held on May 21, 22, 25, 26, and
27. The company, the union, and the board were represented by legal counsel. The company contended that the
act was unconstitutional, that the board did not have jurisdiction, and that the evidence was insufficient to support the
complaint. After five days of examination and cross-
examination by all of the attorneys, the trial examiner
closed the hearings and studied the evidence.

Somewhat later the trial examiner issued an intermediate
report confirming the board's complaint. To this report the
company presented written objections and exceptions. Over
a year later, on July 9, 1937, the company reargued the case
before the National Board at Washington. Finally, on July
15, 1937, the board issued its "Decision and Order." The
story told by this document follows:

The Furniture Workers' Union was chartered in Memphis in 1934 as an affiliate of the Brotherhood of Carpenters, which in turn is affiliated with the A. F. of L. The
union remained small and inactive until February, 1936,
when a membership drive was begun. Negroes were urged
to join, interest in the union rapidly increased, and tentative
overtures were made to the company for a collective bargaining agreement. Almost immediately the company management began an active campaign against the union. On
April 4, the company superintendent finished a conversation with a union member by saying, "I like you and be-

lieve you have reason. You have worked here a good while. I advise you not to have anything to do with the union—it would be best for you not to."

On April 6, the superintendent called in the recording secretary of the union and said that if there was any "labor trouble" the plant would shut down. On April 7, a foreman said to the union president, "Don't you think your job is worth more to you than that union? . . . It is interfering with your job. . . . I am sorry, but I thought you would be the last man to join the union." Within a few minutes after this conversation, three active union members were discharged. One of these men was asked by his foreman, "What in the name of God do you mean by getting mixed up with that union? . . . I hate to see my men get fired, but I'm afraid they will." Another was told by his foreman that he did not know the reason for his discharge. "Not dull business . . . your work is perfect . . . can't tell why. Have orders from the superintendent to lay you off."

That night, one of the discharged men, Barmer, and four other active union members met at the Labor Temple to discuss the situation. They decided to call up the superintendent and ask for a conference. One of their number telephoned this request, but met with a point-blank refusal. The following day, all four men who had met with Barmer were summarily discharged. They were all highly skilled men who had been with the company a great many years. They all had sufficient work on hand to keep them busy for many weeks ahead. All were union officers or active members.

During the same morning, Forester, the president of the union, was fired. Forester was a highly skilled cabinet repairman receiving $25.00 a week, the highest pay in the plant. He had worked steadily whenever the cabinet room was in operation. On one occasion he was the only man in his department to be kept at work. Twice in the previous eighteen months he had been offered higher pay by a rival concern, but each time the company had raised Forester's wages. A few minutes after his discharge, his foreman said to him, "If you pull out of the union, I will put you back to work. If you don't do it, I can't put you back. The union won't get you anything."

On the same day Mrs. Barmer was discharged. She was not a union member and had worked in the upholstery department for fourteen years. Her foreman said, "I have nothing to fire you for. As far as I know, your work is satisfactory. The reason you are being fired is because your husband is."

Later the same day R. R. Jordan, a brother of one of the discharged men, was questioned by the superintendent. "Where do you stand? . . . I advise you not to attend the union meeting tonight. If you do, why, I will know it. . . . I have no personal grudge against your brother. I like him and think he is a nice man, but he just got mired too deep and got caught like the rest." That night R. R. Jordan joined the union. Across the street from the union's meeting place, in an automobile parked without lights in a dark alley, was the company's timekeeper. Upon being accosted by a union member, the timekeeper said that he had been told to spy on the meeting, and that the president of the company had suggested that he try to attend the meeting itself.

On April 10, R. R. Jordan was discharged along with another active union member. On April 13, Alonzo Dabney, who made a speech on April 11 urging other Negroes to join the union, was discharged. Soon after, two other workers, both of whom had disregarded warnings not to join the union, were discharged. In all, thirteen employees, including most of the union's officers, were fired between April 7 and April 22.

In the meantime, on April 14, a committee from the union called upon the president of the company. President Janes said, "I have no intention of recognizing any union. I am firing whom I please and hiring whom I please. I have always done it and will continue to do it as long as I operate the business. And as for your being fired, you were not fired. You just quit. The minute you joined the union you were automatically fired."

Although the union then secured the attendance of the Commissioner of Conciliation of the United States Department of Labor at a conference on April 21, no further results were obtained by it. On April 24, the union submitted a tentative draft of a contract. President Janes absolutely refused to consider any agreement proposed by the union. The union then began to prepare for a strike, but decided instead to appeal to the board for the reinstatement of its members and the enforcement of its right to collective bargaining.

In the hearings before the board, the company presented no witnesses and no material of importance. It did not avail itself of the opportunity to contradict the witnesses of the union. It rested its case chiefly upon the alleged unconstitutionality of the act and the alleged lack of jurisdiction by the board. During the year which followed the hearings, the constitutionality of the act was upheld by the Supreme Court. The Court also handed down decisions which made perfectly clear the jurisdiction of the board over this case.

Consequently, the board finally ordered, on July 15, 1937:

Courtesy of H. I. Carlisle and the *New York Herald Tribune*

THE UMPIRE BEGINS TO GET WHAT HE HAD COMING

1. That the company cease and desist from discouraging membership in the union by discharge of or discrimination against union members, and that the company cease interfering with the right of its workers to self-organization.

2. That the company offer reëmployment to the discharged workers and pay them the wages that they would normally have made from the time of discharge to the time of the offer of reëmployment, minus any earnings which they might have enjoyed in the meantime.

3. That the company post notices in conspicuous places in its plant saying that it would cease and desist from its antiunion practices.

4. That the company notify the regional director within ten days of the steps which it had taken to comply with the board's order.

It is fortunate for the successful operation of the National Labor Relations Act that in less than 5 per cent of its cases does the board meet with such determined resistance to the principle of collective bargaining and such deliberate violation of the law of the land. If the percentage of recalcitrance were much increased, the act would soon become incapable of enforcement. It is a tribute to the good sense and law-abiding character of the overwhelming majority of American employers that obdurate refusal to accept the letter and spirit of the act has been no more widespread than is indicated by the records of the board.

This general acceptance of the National Labor Relations Act has come about in spite of the almost unanimous opposition of the nation's press, the hostility of influential columnists, the organized action of certain lawyers' groups, the public and private activities of a few senators and representatives, and the brutal physical resistance of important industrialists. If the National Labor Relations

Board is to continue to act as an agent for the orderly carrying out of the processes of collective bargaining, its success will depend upon continued acceptance and understanding of its work by the general public in spite of the purveyance of misinformation by uninformed or prejudiced individuals and organizations.

The following chapters are concerned with the historical background of the act; the way in which the board has dealt with such problems as antiunionism, collective bargaining, industrial disputes, interunion conflict, and the unfair practices of labor; and the manner in which the board is related to our system of courts, our civil liberties, and our democratic processes.

CHAPTER II

THE BACKGROUND

UNIONS are combinations of workers to improve their conditions, usually by raising their wages and shortening their hours of labor. Trusts are combinations of businessmen usually formed to raise their prices and control their output. Why should unions be regarded by the law as a less reprehensible form of combination than trusts? The answer is that, until recently, they have not been so regarded.

Until 1824 in England and 1842 in this country, unions were looked upon by the courts as conspiracies which were illegal regardless of their purposes and their methods. But in 1842 a Massachusetts court declared that combinations in restraint of trade were not in the abstract unlawful.[1] It all depended upon what they were after and how they tried to get it. This did not represent much of an improvement in the legal status of trade unions. It remained for the judges to decide whether the intent, the means, and the ends of unions were lawful.

There were subtle distinctions to be made. First, if a union's actions were intended to injure an employer, they were illegal. But if they were intended to help the workers, they were permissible. Is a demand for a wage increase an injury to an employer or a help to the workers? It was up to the judge.

Second, did unions operate in restraint of trade? Was an employer prevented from having free access to the labor market? Was the public prevented from having free access to the producer's goods? If so, then the union which thus acted in restraint of trade was behaving illegally. Who decided whether a picket line prevented the employer from having access to the labor market, or whether a union boycott prevented the public from having access to the producer's goods? Again, it was up to the judge.

Third, did the methods of the union, whether directed toward lawful ends or not, involve violence, force, fraud, coercion, threats, or intimidation? If so, the union could immediately be prevented from continuing its efforts toward perfectly legal ends. Who decided whether the use of the word "scab" was intimidation or effective English? Who determined whether a union's threat to strike was coercion or an exercise of the right not to work? Once again, it was up to the judge.

This was the common law with respect to trade unions throughout the nineteenth century and the first thirty years of the twentieth. It was up to the judge. The courts, whether state or federal, were empowered to give life or death to combinations of workers by deciding whether they might solicit members among unorganized groups, threaten to go on strike, go on strike, use their funds to support the strike, advertise the existence of the dispute, use a picket line, refuse to buy a producer's goods, or print a "We Don't Patronize" list in their own publications.

It is unnecessary in 1938 to defend in detail the proposition that judges are human beings whose decisions are profoundly influenced by their social and economic background. Within the last two years, the people of this country have received a liberal education in this respect by watching the Supreme Court completely reverse itself on fundamental issues of interpretation of an unchanged basic law.[2] If this is true of the highest court in the land, it is even more evident in the lower federal and state courts which are concerned with interpreting law most of which is un-written (except in the form of earlier decisions) and which deals with conflicts of social and economic power.

For more than a century and a quarter, a limited number of human beings occupying strategic positions in our society have held the power to determine whether or not the motives, behavior, and objectives of unions have conformed to their own conceptions of reason, justice, and social propriety. On the whole, the judicial conception of social propriety has been that of the employing and owning groups. This is neither new nor surprising. There is little in the law of trade unionism to guide the judges except their own social preconceptions. One need be neither a cynic nor a Marxist to observe that our judges go to school and college with our employers and owners, score in the nineties and low hundreds at the same country clubs, play diverse systems of bridge together, have mutual friends in the corporate and legal fraternity, witness the intermarriage of their sons and daughters, and in their declining years express common concern over the diminishing income from similar types of investment. It would be unreasonable, or at least naïve, to expect a judge to shed his past life each time he donned his judicial robes.[3]

Consequently, one would expect to discover, as indeed one does, that within the last thirty years judges have ruled:

1. That if a worker signs a "yellow-dog" contract not to join a union, organizers may be prohibited from approaching this worker with the intention of persuading him to join a union.[4]

2. That if a union's methods or purposes are illegal as, for example, in the case of a strike for a closed shop, all acts connected with the strike are illegal, including the

exercise of such civil liberties as making speeches and holding meetings.[5]

3. That if one man in a union commits an illegal act, all other union members are responsible even though they are unaware that the act is taking place, or vote against it.[6]

4. That it is illegal to strike in sympathy with other workers in the same industry, or to strike for the closed shop, or against working on nonunion-made materials, or against yellow-dog contracts, or against an employer's violation of an agreement.[7]

5. That grimaces, gestures, looks, epithets, and jeers by pickets, or posting more than one picket at each factory gate, are illegal.[8]

6. That "peaceful picketing" is as much a contradiction of terms as "chaste vulgarity," "peaceful mobbing," or "lawful lynching." [9]

7. That a union may not peacefully persuade its own members not to work upon nonunion-made materials.[10]

8. That union periodicals may not advertise the fact that good union men do not patronize certain firms.[11]

This was the common law, frequently reinforced by state law as interpreted by conservative courts throughout the period from 1842 to the coming of the New Deal. There were, of course, liberal courts which applied the same common and statute law in a completely different manner. But such courts were distinctly in the minority. Most trade-union leaders, whether conservative or radical, most students of labor, and the liberal section of the public regarded the judicial system of this country as having an obviously antiunion bias. These groups agreed that the courts gave to combinations of workers a legal status much inferior to that of combinations of employers.

The celebrated "rule of reason" applied by the United

States Supreme Court to cases arising under the antitrust act seemed to allow combinations of employers to do whatever they wanted to do and at the same time to forbid combinations of workers to do almost identical things. In many judicial jurisdictions trade unionism could advance only in flat defiance of judicially construed common and statute law. In the face of a widespread and deep-rooted urge toward collective action by workers, it is not surprising that this situation led to a profound contempt on the part of organized workers for "law" and "justice" as applied to trade unionism.

In addition to the common and state laws respecting trade unionism, federal law has had something to say about the legal status of organized labor. In 1890, the Sherman Antitrust Act was passed in response to the wide popular fear and hate of the huge business combinations which were then beginning to develop. With the exception of a short period under Theodore Roosevelt, the Sherman Act proved to be unenforceable against Big Business. Against combinations of workers, however, the Sherman Act was effective. Although the Sherman Act did little more than codify the existing common law against conspiracies in restraint of trade, it made easier the intervention of federal administrative and judicial agencies in trade-union affairs. In 1895, the Sherman Act was employed to assist in breaking the American Railway Union strike and in jailing Eugene V. Debs for contempt of a federal court.[12] In 1908, the Sherman Act was invoked against a successful union boycott and the union was destroyed by the award of damages of $234,000 to the company. In this case the Supreme Court held that even the most harmless acts used in promoting the boycott were illegal.[13] In 1911, in a case which involved a successful boycott by the A. F. of L. against an antiunion stove-manufacturing concern, the officers of the A. F. of L. were forbidden even to say or write anything in favor of the boycott.[14]

The outcry of organized labor against these decisions and renewed popular demand for more vigorous antitrust legislation led to the passage of the Clayton Act in 1914. The Clayton Act was designed to increase the stringency of antitrust action and to improve the legal status of organized labor. With respect to the latter, the act placed limits upon the use of the injunction in labor disputes in federal courts and set forth in statute form some of the more liberal court interpretations of the common-law doctrine of conspiracy.

Although the language of the act was vague, it seemed to say that federal courts must not prevent unions from using peaceful assembly and peacefully conducted strikes and boycotts in pursuit of their objectives. Furthermore, it seemed to say that even sympathy strikes by unions in the same industry were not in themselves illegal. The act was extravagantly greeted by union leaders as an epochal advance in the legal status of trade unionism.

Within a few years, however, it became obvious that the legal status of trade unionism was no better after the Clayton Act than it had been before. During the World War and the postwar period, the federal courts, upheld by the Supreme Court, effectively nullified both the sections of the act that were designed to prevent monopolistic restraints upon interstate commerce and the sections of the act that were intended to grant greater freedom to collective action by workers. Under the "rule of reason" the courts decided that business combinations were not in themselves bad. It depended upon what they did. The courts were able to find that the behavior of business combinations was almost invariably "reasonable." During the same period, the Supreme Court in four important cases made it plain that trade unions were usually unreasonable.

In 1921 the Court held that a strike by the Machinists' Union against a machinery-manufacturing company was intended to injure the employer rather than help the workers, and that the union's effort to persuade New York printing establishments not to use the company's products was a secondary boycott. Consequently both the union's ends and means were illegal.[15] In the same year, the Court held that the use of more than one picket at each factory gate constituted intimidation and was, therefore, illegal.[16] In a case which dragged on from 1914 to 1925, the Court established the principle that an unincorporated union may be sued as an entity.[17] In 1927, the Court forbade the Stone Cutters' Union to apply a union rule that members should not work on nonunion-cut material, thus outlawing even the peaceful primary boycott.[18] This decision completed the final nullification of the Clayton Act since it meant that any union policy could be regarded as illegal restraint of interstate commerce, whereas in the case of business combinations only "unreasonable" restraints (and very few of these) were considered illegal.

It may be said, therefore, that until about 1930 the common and federal law of conspiracy, as interpreted by conservative judges, accorded to trade unions a legal status far below that which was enjoyed by organized business and considerably below that which unionism enjoyed at the bar of public opinion.

Thus far, we have considered only the legal status of unions under statutory and common-law definitions of "conspiracy" and "restraint of trade." These doctrines might be applied against unions either by criminal proceedings at law or in equity proceedings to secure injunctions against union actions, or by civil suits for damages in either state or federal courts.

It must be remembered, however, that in addition unions and their members have always been liable to prosecution under state criminal law and local ordinances. Since the Civil War, but especially since the "red scare" days of the early nineteen-twenties, unions in many states have been subject to laws forbidding the "enticement" of workers away from their "labor contracts" with employers, and laws forbidding criminal syndicalism, criminal anarchy, sedition, and incitement to insurrection. Such laws may easily be, and have repeatedly been, applied against non-political, conservative unions by the simple expedient of calling the union members "anarchists," "syndicalists," "Bolsheviks," or "Communists." [19]

Under local ordinances, unions and their members may be jailed and severely fined for distributing union literature,[20] "disturbing the peace," "obstructing traffic," or "committing a nuisance" while conducting union rallies or picket lines, violation of health or zoning regulations, littering the streets, trespass, and so on. Furthermore, there are the ordinary state criminal laws against murder, kidnaping, assault and battery, threats and intimidation, mayhem, arson, and destruction of property which may be enforced against union members or leaders if their behavior takes any of these forms. Finally, by the use of state militia, special police, sheriffs, and deputy sheriffs as strikebreaking agencies, or by the assumption of a passive attitude toward the beating, kidnaping, and murdering of union members or the destruction of union property, the administrative officers of the state and local governments may, and frequently do, deny to union members any legal rights whatsoever.[21]

On the whole, however, these aspects of the legal status of trade unionism during the pre-New Deal period were probably no more of an obstacle to the advance of organized labor than the absence of any legal protection against the antiunion use of the economic power of employers. The larger the employing agency, the greater is its economic power over the life and activities of the individual worker. When the worker loses the ownership of his tools, and therefore his power of self-employment, and when competition among employers for workers in the labor market disappears in the face of a constant surplus of labor, the economic power of the individual worker over his employer also disappears. He cannot threaten to employ himself or to accept other offers of employment if he has neither the means nor the opportunity to carry out his threat. He is compelled, therefore, to accept such terms of employment as employers are moved to offer. The economic power of the employer, on the other hand, acting through corporate devices and employers' associations, approaches an absolute control over the economic life of the individual worker.

In the pre-New Deal period of the labor movement, there were few legal restrictions upon the right of the employer to use his economic power against unions. Government barely tolerated the existence of unions once they had been established, but offered no protection during the formative period. Employers could speak as freely as they wished inside and outside of their plants against unions in general and particular. They could use their own or their stockholders' funds in effective propaganda campaigns against unions. They could require workers to sign yellow-dog contracts that they would not join, assist, or express sympathy with unions while employed by the company. These contracts could be made the basis of injunctions against organizers' efforts to persuade workers to join a union.

The employer could join an association in which he agreed not to deal with unions and, through the courts, he could compel other employers to abide by their "open shop" agreements.[22] He could lock out his workers for union activities or for "any or no reason." [23] He could discriminate against workers in the conditions of their employment or discharge them for union sympathies without fear of reprisal from the law.[24] He could maintain a black list of "troublemakers" or a white list of "good citizens" with no more than the slimmest possibility that laws against this form of conspiracy would be enforced.[25]

The employer could hire professional strikebreakers and plant guards and was "permitted" to pay for sheriffs' deputies and city police service during strikes. He could employ spies to report on union plans, sow dissension in union ranks, encourage the commission of unlawful acts by unionists, and destroy the morale of union members and their families. He could create a fake union controlled by himself and recognize it to the exclusion of a genuine workers' union, thus sitting on both sides of the bargaining table at once.

All this the employer could do without encountering the warning finger of the law or, except in the most flagrant instances, suffering the frown of public opinion. Needless to say, employers did not universally resort to these measures. Not all workers, by any means, wanted to be organized. Millions of workers, through apathy, ignorance, loyalty to their employers, or the hope of individual advancement, preferred to go it alone. Secondly, many employers were willing to accept collective bargaining with their workers as being good business in the long run. Thirdly, as indicated above, the courts and the law were abundantly available to the employer who wished to devitalize union activity. But it is impossible to overlook the immense importance of the legally unrestrained use of the employer's economic power as a deterrent to collective action by workers.

The first change in this situation came in 1932 in the form of federal legislation. As a result of pressure from the A. F. of L. and from liberal sympathizers with labor's cause, the Norris-LaGuardia Act was passed by large majorities in both houses of Congress in 1932. About half of the act has to do with the *reasons* for which injunctions may be issued in labor disputes by the federal courts. The remainder of the act is concerned with limiting the *manner* in which federal court injunctions may be issued and enforced.

With respect to the grounds for issuing injunctions, the act holds that no United States court may prohibit workers singly or in combination from refusing to work, becoming members of a union regardless of a yellow-dog contract, paying strike benefits, publicizing the facts of a labor dispute in any manner not involving fraud and violence, assembling peaceably in connection with a labor dispute, or advising any other person to do any of these things. The act also declares that no federal court may hold any officer or member of a union responsible for unlawful acts of other officers or members except "upon clear proof of actual authorization, participation, or ratification of such act." Finally, in its definition of a "labor dispute" the act forbids federal courts to issue injunctions against sympathetic strikes, even though nationwide in scope, provided that the strike is directly or indirectly related to a single industry. Each of these declarations is aimed against specific court decisions previously mentioned.

In connection with the manner of issuing injunctions, a few words must be said about the nature of the injunctive process. Injunctions are issued by state or federal courts "sitting in equity" when civil suits for damages provide an inadequate remedy at law for threatened action. Injunctions are supposed to be issued only when irreparable damage is threatened, when the person appealing for the injunction comes into court with "clean hands," and when the threatened loss is greater than that which would be suffered by the defendant if the plea were granted. And the court must serve the injunction upon those persons against whom it is directed. Anyone who is not served with the injunction is not supposed to be bound by it. Finally, the injunction is enforced by the court through contempt proceedings and judgment is passed upon the defendant by the judge who issued the injunction. Fines or jail terms are at the judge's discretion. The issuing judge thus acts in the capacity of prosecutor and jury as well as judge.

As employed in the federal courts, and to a less extent in the state courts prior to 1932, the injunction became a powerful weapon against organized labor. Employers were frequently able to secure injunctions upon trivial pretexts without proving that there was an inadequate remedy through damage suits. The concept of "property" to which irreparable damage was done was greatly widened to include "good will" and the "right to do business." The principles of "clean hands" and "equal loss" received scant attention. The practice of issuing "blanket injunctions" covering "all persons whomsoever" was widely extended with the result that workers might find themselves in contempt of an injunction although they had received no notice of it. And, finally, injunctions were frequently issued which not only covered illegal acts but also prevented law-abiding unionists from performing perfectly legal acts such as the payment of strike benefits.

In the actual procedure of issuing injunctions, temporary restraining orders were granted to employers without hearing the union's side of the case. Although the judge had to hear both sides before a preliminary injunction could be issued, the delay was often sufficient for the employer's purposes. Hearings and appeals dragged on for years in important cases while the union's resources and power were exhausted. Finally, the method of enforcing injunctions through contempt proceedings was scarcely calculated to assure organized labor of the fullest measure of justice.

In many of these respects the Norris-LaGuardia Act offered unions an improvement in their legal status. Apart from the limits placed upon the subject matter for which injunctions might be issued, the following procedural requirements were enacted: Hearings in which only one party to the action is present may not result in the issuance of temporary restraining orders unless sworn testimony is presented sufficient to justify a preliminary injunction after a two-sided hearing. Restraining orders are to be valid for only five days. Witnesses must appear at the preliminary hearings as well as at the final trials. Money bonds may be required to enforce the doctrine of "equal loss." Unions may insist upon jury trial for contempt committed outside the immediate presence of the court. And unions may insist that the contempt trial take place before another judge if the contempt action results from a union's attack on the conduct of the original judge.

Most of these provisions of the act were already accepted as the minimum requirements of justice in liberal state courts. Some of the provisions had been included in the Clayton Act. Most of the federal courts and many of the state courts, however, had completely disregarded both the requirements of justice and the provisions of the Clayton Act. The indications are that the Norris-LaGuardia Act is enjoying much the same spottiness of observance with a gradual increase in the number of liberal spots.[26] In the meantime, twenty-one states have passed supplementary legislation either limiting the use of the injunction in labor disputes, or making the yellow-dog contract nonenforceable, or both.

Although the passage of the Norris-LaGuardia Act, supplemented by state legislation, undoubtedly marked a considerable advance in the legal status of organized labor, its limitations should be made perfectly clear. There are twenty-seven state court jurisdictions in which these laws do not apply. Most of these are southern or central states toward many of which industry is moving.[27] The "anti-injunction" laws do not touch upon the use of state criminal law and local ordinance against union practices. They do not prevent criminal proceedings under conspiracy or restraint-of-trade doctrines. They do not limit the antiunion use of the employer's economic power. And although their language is far more specific and inclusive than that of the Clayton Act, they still leave to the courts sufficiently wide powers of interpretation to nullify the intention of the legislatures if the courts desire.

While the legislatures were thus attempting to remove injunctive obstacles from the path of organized labor, public opinion had long since given verbal support to the idea that workers should be allowed to organize in order to equal the bargaining power of employers. This support, however, remained merely verbal as long as employers retained the unrestricted right to use their superior economic strength to crush unionism during its formative stages.

The intense suffering of millions of people during the depression fixed the attention of the nation on the anomaly of poverty amid plenty. The spectacle of slow starvation in the face of almost unlimited productive resources could be overlooked only by the socially blind. The belief gained wide currency that this anomaly was caused primarily by the immense and increasing inequality in the distribution of income. This inequality resulted in the piling up of superabundant means of production in the face of inadequate mass consuming power. It could be traced to restriction of output and the maintenance of semimonopoly prices by business combinations side by side with the holding down of the wage income of the great mass of consumers. Wages had a constant tendency to lag behind increasing productivity because workers did not have the organized power to drive them up. Prices did not fall in consonance with increasing productive power because organized business had the power to keep them from falling.

There were two possible ways out of this situation. Prices could be driven down by government regulation or persuasion backed by a renewed trust-busting campaign. Or wages could be driven up by minimum-wage and maximum-hour laws backed by increased governmental protection of the workers' right to organize. Government policy with respect to trust-busting and price regulation during the last six years has consistently reflected the confusion of public thought and the conflict of private interests on the issue.

Whether to break up business combinations and allow competition among smaller units to take care of prices, or whether to allow the persistence of large-scale semimonopolistic enterprises under government price regulation, or neither or both—this was the question. The past history of neither policy offered much comfort to the advocates of either program. It cannot be said that a clear-cut decision has as yet emerged. Meanwhile the proponents of government ownership as the solution of this problem bide their time.

With respect to wage regulation and governmental protection of the workers' right to organize, the policies of the New Deal have been far more clear. In the closing days of the Hoover administration and in the first special session of Congress under the Roosevelt administration, the Black Bill to regulate the hours of labor in interstate manufacture had an excellent chance of passing both houses of Congress. To the idea of regulating hours the regulation of wages was necessarily added in order to protect the weekly wages of workers. From this conception the National Industrial Recovery Act emerged by a process of accretion. The regulation of hours and wages necessitated the regulation of prices if the actual consuming power of workers was to be improved. It was then observed that any such complicated regulation of wages, hours, and prices would have to be sufficiently flexible to conform to the variety of conditions in different industries and localities. The idea of legislative regulation was therefore dropped in favor of administrative regulation through semi–self-governing code authorities. Finally, as a result of pressure from labor lobbyists and supporters, the now famous Section 7a was added. Section 7a gave formal governmental sanction to labor's right to collective bargaining through representatives of its own choosing and forbade employers to use their superior economic and social power to prevent the exercise of this right by workers.

The theory back of Section 7a was clear. Government could not police industry. Employers were organized and would unquestionably use their organized power, in spite of governmental warnings to the contrary, to continue traditional practices of undue restriction of production and raising of prices. Consumers, as such, could not be adequately organized or represented to protect their own interests. Labor, acting in a dual capacity as the largest body of consumers and as the receiver of wages, must be organized to protect the consumers from extravagant price increases and provide the workers with wage increases. But labor was not organized. Less than 10 per cent of American workers had had any continued experience in unions. One of the obstacles to the growth of organized labor was the antiunion economic power of employers. If labor was to be organized, this power had to be curbed. Section 7a was designed to call into existence a new deal to redress the balance of the old.

The effects of Section 7a were psychological rather than legal and judicial. As a declaration of governmental policy, its "guarantee" of the right to collective bargaining was a powerful stimulus to trade-union membership. Unionism ceased to be associated in the minds of thousands of workers with Moscow and became associated with the personality of President Roosevelt. The explicit prohibition of interference and coercion by employers in union affairs temporarily removed the fear of employer reprisals from the minds of other thousands of workers. By the same token, many employers accepted the spirit of this legislative declaration, altered their antiunion attitudes, and dropped their antiunion policies. The result was that hundreds of thousands of workers poured into unions, old and new, and the government's purpose promised to be achieved.

Very soon, however, the administration began to have the same experience with its efforts to equalize the economic power of workers and employers that legislatures had previously had with their efforts to equalize the legal position of the two groups. As employers' confidence and prosperity returned, those who retained their antiunion attitudes simply refused to comply with the intention of Congress. It was not difficult to abide by the letter of Section 7a, which was vaguely worded, and yet violate its intent. There was an important minority which did not trouble to concern itself with the letter. Verbal and written opposition to unions expressed inside and outside the shop, company-dominated unions, black lists, discharge of union members, and the use of professional strikebreakers, spies, and deputy sheriffs flourished on an unprecedented scale. The administration of Section 7a rapidly disintegrated in the face of this opposition. Organized labor soon felt the effects of this disintegration.[29]

The refusal of many powerful employers to abide by the spirit of Section 7a led to a wave of strikes by unions attempting to enforce their rights by their own strength. These strikes interfered with the recovery program of the N.R.A. Consequently, President Roosevelt, in August, 1933, appointed a National Labor Board to mediate these strikes and settle them if possible. The National Labor Board was composed of three labor members, three employer members, and Senator Wagner as chairman.

The difficulties of this board were immense. Its legal status (creation by an executive order of the President) was doubtful. It had to attempt a mixture of mediatory functions in settling strikes and judicial functions in enforcing Section 7a. Back of it lay a government and a people torn between a recovery and a reform program. Frequently this conflict was reflected in the problems before the board. Most important, however, was the fact that the board had no real powers of enforcement. After exhausting efforts to secure voluntary compliance, the board had no recourse except to turn its cases over to the compliance division of the N.R.A. for removal of Blue Eagles, or to the Department of Justice for court enforcement.

Neither of these agencies was equal to its task. The compliance division of the N.R.A. was powerfully influenced by employer sentiment and was unwilling to antagonize business interests. The Department of Justice was hamstrung, first, by the fact that it could not accept the evidence developed by the Labor Board. It had to prepare its own case anew. It had had no experience with this type of case and its sympathy with the board's position was not impressive. Second, there were grave doubts about the constitutionality of the National Industrial Recovery Act which gave the Labor Board its presumed authority. The administration in general and the Department of Justice in particular were unwilling to test the constitutionality of the act upon a labor issue. The result was that powerful employers were able to flout the orders of the board, destroy its prestige, and pave the way for disregard by lesser industrial figures.

Because of this situation, sentiment mounted in Congress in favor of a federal law which would remedy these defects. The Wagner Labor Disputes Bill of 1934 was designed to accomplish this purpose. Employer opposition and an administration divided within itself prevented the passage of this bill. In its place a compromise measure called Public Resolution No. 44 was adopted in June, 1934, in the face of a wave of strikes. In July, the President appointed a National Labor Relations Board of three impartial, expert members empowered to hold elections for workers' choice of bargaining representatives, investigate labor disputes, and hold hearings on charges of violations of Section 7a.

This board marked an advance over the National Labor Board in that it was created independent of the N.R.A., although its legal status depended upon the powers granted to the President in the Recovery Act. It was composed of full-time experts and could relegate its mediatory and voluntary compliance work to semiofficial panels of citizens connected with the regional offices while it devoted its full time to judicial work on cases of primary importance. But it still lacked power to compel compliance. In the crucial Houde Engineering Company case, for example, the employer successfully defied the board.[30]

In spite of this difficulty, the first N.L.R.B. was of considerable importance in protecting workers' rights to bargain collectively. It secured a notable amount of voluntary compliance with the intent of Section 7a. It began the process of building up a body of informed and experienced personnel. And it moved a long way toward clarifying and defining the issues involved in governmental protection of collective bargaining. Without this experience the National Labor Relations Act would not have taken its present definite form, nor could the new board have achieved the remarkable record which will be discussed in later pages.[31]

Nevertheless, from the point of view of protecting unions from the economic attack of a crucially important minority of belligerently antiunion employers, Public Resolution

Courtesy of Talburt and the *Washington Daily News*

WORTH LOOKING INTO!

No. 44 must be put down as a failure. The invalidation of the National Industrial Recovery Act, from which the board received its basic authority, put the final quietus on the board's efforts to accomplish its *raison d'être*.

One result of the Supreme Court's decision against the N.R.A. in May, 1935, was increased pressure from organized labor and its friends for the passage of the Wagner Labor Disputes Bill. This bill had already had extended hearings in February, March, and April and had passed the Senate. The Supreme Court decision precipitated its passage in the House. On June 27 the bill was approved by both houses and on July 5 was signed by President Roosevelt.

There are several aspects of the National Labor Relations Act which should be made clear. First, it was not an innovation. There lay back of it an extended experience with govermental attempts to protect the rights of workers to organize. This experience had been gained in the railroad industry under the National Mediation Board as well as under the National Labor Board, the first National Labor Relations Board, and the numerous satellite boards created during the N.R.A. period. The issues attending the passage of the N.L.R.A. were perfectly clear to interested parties. They were thoroughly aired during the debates on Section 7a and Public Resolution No. 44.

Second, the N.L.R.A. is concerned only with making collective bargaining possible in the face of the antiunion economic power of employers. It does not prevent employers from proceeding against unions in the courts by civil suits for damages, by instituting injunction actions under criminal-conspiracy and restraint-of-trade doctrines, by compelling the enforcement of ordinary state criminal law, or by applying local ordinances against unions and their activities. The act does not submit an employer to criminal prosecution, nor prescribe fines or imprisonment for violators, nor is it finally enforceable except through the circuit courts.

Third, the act is based upon the assumption that the principle of collective bargaining must be effectively established in our present form of industrial society in order to protect the individual worker, to insure the stability of our economic life, and, in the long run, to provide the most satisfactory industrial relationship for the individual employer.

Finally, the act is constitutionally grounded in a broad conception of "interstate commerce" and the obligation of Congress to remove the burdens on interstate commerce which result from industrial warfare. It was expected that constitutional justification for the act would be found in the ability of the board to minimize the stoppages resulting from strikes and interunion conflicts.

Each of these issues will be discussed in detail in the succeeding chapters.

CHAPTER III

ANTIUNIONISM

IT is frequently alleged by critics of the National Labor Relations Board that it is little more than an organizing agent for trade unionism. Put somewhat less bluntly, it is said that in administering the act the board is partial to unions and biased against the employer. Since the board thus far has an excellent record of support from the Supreme Court, the more responsible critics have altered the charge to read that the act itself is biased against employers and in favor of unions.

There is this much truth in the charge: In passing the act, Congress explicitly approved the principle of collective bargaining between workers and employers. It made this approval a part of national policy. It guaranteed to workers the right to bargain through representatives of their own choosing. In the light of experience it found, however, that a mere written guarantee was insufficient. A *right* to organize was meaningless if it could be upheld only by the sheer physical or economic strength of workers. A right must be administered and enforced under law and through the courts. The act, then, is partial to the principle of collective bargaining. The board is partial to the enforcement of the act. And the courts have thus far been partial to the partiality of both Congress and the board.

In a sense it is true that Congress, the board, and the courts are acting as trade-union organizers. One of the jobs of a union organizer is to defeat the employer's use of his economic and social power to crush trade unionism in its formative stages. To some extent Congress, the board, and the courts are relieving the union organizer of this task.

Congress did its part by writing Section 8 into the act. Section 8 states that it shall be considered an unfair labor practice for an employer: (1) "to interfere with, restrain or coerce employees in the exercise of the right" to collective bargaining; (2) "to dominate or interfere with the formation or administration of any labor organization or contribute financial or other support to it"; (3) "by discrimination in regard to hire or tenure of employment or any term or condition of employment to encourage or discourage membership in any labor organization"; (4) "to discriminate against an employee because he has filed charges under this Act"; (5) to refuse to bargain collectively with the representatives of his employees. Under the authority granted by Congress, the board has done its part by enforcing this section of the act. And the Supreme Court has done its part by upholding the policies and decisions of the board.

The board has had a full-time job in carrying out the intent of these provisions. Although it is true that the great majority of employers have accepted the letter and intent of the act and are induced to comply with its terms by the informal kind of proceeding described in an earlier chapter, the practice of antiunionism is deeply rooted in American industrial society. A powerful and influential minority of employers carry on this tradition. It is with this group that the board's formal decisions are concerned.

The board cannot compromise with the standard-bearers of antiunionism without inviting the collapse of the valuable conciliatory work carried on by its subordinate officials. The lessons of Section 7a and Public Resolution No. 44 are perfectly clear in this respect. One failure to enforce the act in an important case would quickly be followed by the flooding of the regional offices with complaints of infractions. The eyes of employers are fixed upon each successive decision of the board to a degree which is unprecedented in the history of federal administrative agencies. During this initial period of enforcement of the act, both the board and the antiunion employers stake a great deal on each decision. It is not surprising, therefore, that public and private discussion of the board's work has centered almost exclusively upon the cases in which the board has been faced with a powerful and intensely antiunion opponent.

Opposition to trade unionism has been very general in American industry since the earliest days of the labor movement. Although during the first half of the nineteenth century employers generally relied upon the common-law doctrine of conspiracy in their fight against unions, as early as 1798 they began to organize to oppose collective bargaining. After the Civil War the first national antiunion employers' associations appeared and during the 'eighties and 'nineties numerous employers' associations of the belligerent type carried on active and successful opposition to unionism in the printing and metal trades, on the railroads, and in the coal fields.

After 1901, the National Association of Manufacturers assumed the leadership of organized antiunionism and coordinated the efforts of scores of industrial, state, and district associations. Throughout the war, a lull in antilabor activities occurred, but in the "back-to-normalcy" postwar years, intensified work by the N.A.M. was supplemented by the United States Chamber of Commerce, the American Bankers' Association, and the National Metal Trades Association, supported by organizations in more than twenty states. During the depression, the antiunion programs of these associations declined in default of an active labor movement on which to operate. With the coming of the New Deal and its attendant spectacular increase in union membership, however, organized antiunionism was revived on a heroic scale and with increased subtlety.[1]

The officers of these associations, many of them with important vested interests in the perpetuation of their functions, and the leading industrialists who dominate them are the major opponents of the board and the courts in enforcing the workers' right to self-organization. Any inclination to underestimate the power and influence of this opposition should be dispelled by the success with which the policies and actions of the board have been misrepresented.

The nature of the board's problem in enforcing the right to collective bargaining in the face of this opposition may be indicated by a brief summary of the antiunion policies of the belligerent type of employers' association.

The basic activity of antiunion employers and their associations is propaganda. Throughout the last thirty years, publicity bureaus, subsidized speakers, pamphlets, press releases, and whispering campaigns have been maintained to spread the word that union leaders draw huge salaries, charge exorbitant dues, and squander the union's funds; that unions are rackets which extort tribute from the workers, the public, and the employers; that unions are anarchistic, syndicalistic, Bolshevistic, Communistic, Fascistic, and un-American; that unions are lawbreaking, subversive, irresponsible, terroristic, and violent. This exercise of social power has been very expensive, but may have been worth the money, for the time being, from an antiunion point of view. It has been carried on both inside and outside the shop and has recently been turned in full force but in slightly modified form against the board and the act. It presents the board with what is probably its greatest difficulty: the problem of free speech and press under the act.

The second important antiunion method has been the direct use of the economic power of employers and their associations. There are several forms: discrimination, discharge, yellow-dog contracts, black lists, lockouts, threats to move the plant to nonunion territory, and actually moving the plant.

The third category includes the more subtle policies such as company welfare work, espionage, company unions, and "independent" unions.

Finally, there have been and still are policies of antiunion violence in the form of beating, kidnaping, and murdering unionists, brutal smashing of picket lines and demonstrations, and using economic pressure to mobilize the community into citizens' committees, back-to-work movements, and vigilantism.[2]

In all of these ways antiunion employers have operated singly and in groups. Group action has taken the form of pooling funds for any of the above purposes, filling each others' orders in time of strikes, exchange of information, and the use of powerful economic compulsions against employers who refuse to assume an antiunion position.

These have been the major antiunion methods of the past and they now constitute the obstacles of the board and the courts in carrying out the national policy embodied in the act. It is of interest to note the manner in which the board has met these problems and the legal implements available against them.

On July 11, 1938, the editorial page of the *New York Times* carried an oblique attack on the board for an implied violation of civil liberties in the case of the Muskin Shoe Company. The facts of this case as established by board hearings were as follows: As soon as the United Shoe Workers (affiliated with the C.I.O.) began organizing in the Westminster, Maryland, plant of the Muskin Shoe Company, the management began an antiunion campaign. A union meeting was spied upon and foremen repeatedly questioned workers as to their sympathies. Plant officials warned workers "to keep out of this union business" and made uncomplimentary remarks about those who had joined the C.I.O. which, they said, was composed of murderers and gangsters. On July 29, 1937, the plant was closed down in the afternoon to allow workers to attend a "citizens' committee" meeting. At this meeting strongly antiunion sentiments were expressed and union organizers were labeled as Communists who had "come to stick their hands in the workers' pockets and take their money away."

On the following day, the company permitted the distribution throughout the plant during working hours of a pamphlet entitled *Communism's Iron Grip on the C.I.O.* This pamphlet, which has been widely disseminated by the Constitutional Educational League, Inc., consists almost entirely of a speech by Representative Hoffman of Michigan embellished with antiunion caricatures. The speech, delivered in the House of Representatives on June 1, 1937, was a tirade against the C.I.O. On the same day that this pamphlet was distributed, the employer discharged the president of the union and an active member.

In connection with the pamphlet the board said in its decision:

It is evident . . . that it was prepared as antiunion literature and any distribution thereof by an employer to his employees would have the necessary effect of intimidation within the meaning of the Act. . . . By permitting the distribution of the pamphlet on its time and property, the respondent indicated to its

Courtesy of Elderman and the *Washington Post.*

CAREFUL THERE, WHERE YOU'RE SHOOTING!

employees that it had adopted, as its own, the antiunion contents thereof, and that they should be guided accordingly.[3]

On July 7, 1938, the board ordered the reinstatement of the two discharged men with back pay from the time of dismissal and directed the company to cease its unfair practices. These unfair practices included the antiunion activities of the foremen and the distribution of antiunion literature on company time and property. The *New York Times* held this to be a violation of the rights of free speech and press, and reaffirmed this position on the following day after being fully informed of the facts of the case by the secretary of the board. "We see no reason to alter the opinion expressed in our editorial," said the *Times,* "that in this case, as in others, the Board has ruled in effect that the right of free speech must be sacrificed in order to promote the organization of trade unions." [4]

This case may be taken as a fair sample of others which raise the same issue. Let the background be briefly restated: Congress has made it a part of our national policy to promote collective bargaining. It held that antiunion intimidation was an effective obstacle to this policy. It therefore prohibited employers from intimidating workers in their decision to organize, not to organize, or as to how they would organize. It created a board to interpret the word "intimidation" and prevent its occurrence. The board decided that the distribution of antiunion literature on company time and property was intimidation. It ordered the employer to cease the practice. The employer may appeal, if he chooses, to the courts. The board's order may be enforced only through the courts. Is this a violation of the right of free speech and press?

The right of free speech and press is commonly interpreted to mean the right to say and print what you please subject to court action under law. One may speak obscenely, profanely, or libelously, but only subject to possible court action under various laws. One may print false financial statements, mislabel poisonous patent medicines, advertise fraudulently, write lewd books, draw obscene caricatures, or import foreign pornography, but only subject to the action of the authorities which are legally bound to interpret and enforce the laws dealing with these activities.

The rights of an individual or group to free speech and press are obviously limited by the rights of others. If society decides that pornography is bad for children, it says so in legal form and designates some agency to interpret and enforce the law. The judges may have some difficulty in deciding whether an object is pornographic or artistic, but they are compelled by the law to try to decide. No one seriously questions the judge's obligation and right to make a decision. If one does question this obligation and right, one must oppose the law against pornography and urge its repeal.

For more than a hundred years the courts have been empowered to enforce the doctrines of conspiracy and restraint of trade against unions. The law was as vague as the standards of art and pornography. The judge's background and the circumstances surrounding the case were, perforce, the criteria of decision. These laws have not been repealed. Under their terms judges continue to issue injunctions and make decisions which restrict the rights of speech and press of picketers, strikers, and boycotters. No one would question the judge's right to interfere *at some point* with the activity of strikers in using the spoken or written word. The *New York Times* has itself recently approved an injunction which forbade pickets by spoken or written word from boycotting advertisers in the *Brooklyn Daily Eagle* during the recent Guild strike against the *Eagle*.

Legal restrictions upon the speech and press of strikers have now been complemented by a federal act which guarantees to workers freedom from employer intimidation in the exercise of the right to collective bargaining. It is the duty of the board and the courts to interpret and apply this act in the light of the relevant circumstances of each case, even though this enforcement abridges the right of employers to distribute a pamphlet which says that John L. Lewis is a hireling of Joseph Stalin and that the name of Detroit is shortly to be changed to Lewisgrad. One may oppose this decision of the board, but not on the ground that it violates the right of free speech. Logically, one's opposition to the decision can rest only on an antipathy to the effective enforcement of the act.

If the board were to be restrained at every point where a decision cut across someone's absolute right to free speech, the enforcement of the act among antiunionists would immediately collapse. The board would be unable to prevent employers from bringing any form of written or verbal pressure to bear against workers' inclination to organize. In every antiunion situation speech and press play an important role. Some speech and some writing must be prevented if the act is to be enforced. It is the board's task to determine at what point it shall modify the right of speech and writing in favor of the right to collective bargaining. In each case it takes all the attendant circumstances into account and if the entire behavior of the employer adds up to a policy of intimidation, as in the Muskin case and scores of others, it orders the employer to

cease his policies including those carried out by voice and
the distribution of the written word.

Employers are still free to inspire and finance expensive
propaganda campaigns against unions in general and particular. Recent testimony before the La Follette Civil
Liberties Committee of the Senate shows that some employers generously avail themselves of this freedom. They
may also inspire and finance propaganda campaigns
against the board or condemn it as vigorously as the de-
cencies of speech permit. Of this freedom, also, employers
have abundantly partaken. The board is powerless to act
against these forms of speech and press unless in a particular situation taken in connection with other antiunion
practices they constitute intimidation of workers.

If the board decides that intimidation has taken place,
it orders the employer to cease those practices which constitute the antiunion situation. Henry Ford's declaration,
for example, that he would never recognize or deal with a
union of his employees, taken in connection with the physical assaults of his subordinates on union men, has been
judged by the board to constitute antiunion intimidation.
The Ford Company was therefore ordered to desist from
such antiunion declarations and physical brutality.[5]

If the attack on the board or its officers becomes so violent that it threatens the continuance of its proceedings
in a particular case, they may order the disbarment of the
offenders from the hearing or order the removal of the
hearings to a more judicial atmosphere. In the Weirton
Steel Company case, the arrogant and contemptuous manner of the company's chief counsel toward the board's trial
examiner eventually resulted in the disbarment of this
particular counsel from the proceedings. The organization
by the Weirton "hatchet squad" of an antiboard demon-

stration during which the trial examiner was hanged in effigy resulted in the removal of the proceedings to the near-by city of Pittsburgh. The company retained its freedom to spend its stockholders' money on placards denouncing the board, to hire groups of men appropriately stationed to shout "yellow" at the departing board officers, and to employ its own photographer in recording the event for the press and for posterity.[6]

It is safe to say that the act and the board do not constitute a new menace to liberty of speech and press in their accepted meaning. They are charting a new field in which the right to organize is being weighed against the right of the employer to do and say as he pleases in his employment policy. The rights of one individual or group cannot easily be expanded without limiting the rights of other individuals or groups. Labor's right to organization of its own choice has been guaranteed by the act. This necessarily involves limiting the right of employers to fight unionism. The board is compelled to weigh the two sets of rights against each other. Thus far, the courts have fully upheld the board's decisions with respect to the limits which it has set on the employer's right to free speech and press.[7]

The second category of antiunion policies is economic. Here, again, questions of relative rights are raised. Until 1933, the right of an employer to discharge, discriminate against, or lock out any or all of his employees for any reason was unquestioned. Until 1932, the employer could compel his workers to sign yellow-dog contracts and then use these contracts as the basis for injunctive action against organizers. He could blacklist workers throughout a whole industry without apprehension by the law. And he could threaten to move his plant or actually move it to another area for any reason he chose. The Norris-LaGuardia Act limited the validity of yellow-dog contracts; Section 7a, Public Resolution No. 44, and the N.L.R.A. marked successive modifications of employers' rights in the other particulars listed.

The act modifies these rights, however, only in one respect. The employer may not exercise them if his intention is primarily or solely to prevent his workers from joining a union of their own choosing. He may discriminate against, discharge, or lock out his workers; close down, dismantle, reorganize, or move his plant for any reason except antiunionism. The task of the board is to distinguish between an antiunion intention and any of the many other possible reasons for these acts.

In making this distinction, the board is faced with difficulties. Few employers frankly discharge or discriminate against workers for union activity. Long before the passage of the act, it was traditional in American industry that men were discharged for "being late," "impudence," "dropping tools," "failure to coöperate," and so on, rather than for union sympathies. Occasionally the board receives uncontradicted evidence in its hearings which simplifies its task: "Jack, if you want to know the reason why you are fired, the reason is the union." "Are you with the union or not? If you are with the union you cannot work here." [8] "Well, you know we don't allow no union workers on this platform." [9]

Usually, however, the employer insists that antiunionism has nothing to do with the case. The board then has to examine the entire situation. It takes into account such factors as the attitude of the employer toward unionism as expressed in other acts or statements, the length of service and experience of the workers in question, their efficiency ratings, the testimony of foremen or other workers, and

the treatment given to other workers of equal or less efficiency.[10] In making its findings, the board goes into
minute detail covering each worker affected by alleged discrimination or discharge and dismisses the charges in the
case of some employees while upholding them in the case
of others. The board's decisions in these cases provide an
extremely interesting record of industrial practices and
processes. The limits of space forbid the introduction of
more than one such case at this point.

On July 13, 1937, David Magzamen and Giuseppe
Rivoli were discharged by the Omaha Hat Corporation of
New York City. The employer asserted that the reason for
their discharge was that they were the worst finishers in
the plant; that they were neither good workers nor fast
workers, and that, in spite of their protests, they'd "got to
go." Magzamen and Rivoli charged that they had been
fired for union activity. The board investigated and after
formal hearings found the circumstances to be as follows:

The owner of the company had for five years before
July, 1937, successfully fought the unionization of his
workers. He had precipitated two strikes and broken them
with the aid of injunctions, thereby putting an end to the
workers' efforts to organize themselves. Soon after the
second strike, the employer organized the Omahaian Social
Club with the object of "fostering a spirit of fraternity
among the men." The membership dues and the expenses
of the attorney for this club were paid by the employer.
The employer and the attorney drew up an agreement for
the workers respecting pay rates and personnel policy. The
club dissolved, however, when the employer broke the
agreement by reducing wages and discharging a union
member.

Organizing activities were resumed at the plant in May,

1937. The names of members were kept secret because of fear of discharge. These fears proved well founded when Magzamen was discharged on June 15. The next day, however, he was taken back with the warning that he had "better stop talking." Finally, on July 13, he was again discharged after being bothered for a month by a hostile foreman. Magzamen went to the employer and asked, "What is the matter, Mr. Novgrod?" Novgrod showed Magzamen dozens of hats that he had finished during the previous week and said, "Well, I do not like them, that's all there is to it." Magzamen asked what the matter was with them and received no reply.

Rivoli was fired on the same day. He had quit twice during the previous six months because his pay was less than he could make elsewhere, but he had been urged each time to return. He was an expert finisher who had joined the union and been "squealed on." His foreman asked him who had given him the application blank. Rivoli countered, "Why you want to know those men?" The foreman replied, "Well, you know, Joe, I like to know. . . . Those men have to get fired." "Listen," said Rivoli, "I quit job, but you never know from my mouth who told me join union."

When Rivoli was fired he went to the employer, who told him, "I don't like your work," and pointed to a dozen of his hats. Rivoli objected and asked Novgrod to compare the hats that were supposed to be defective with a dozen made by anyone else. He asked, "What difference you find in this dozen and that dozen? And take two hats this way and mix them up. Show me the better hat over here now." Rivoli admitted that some of his hats were defective. He picked them out and explained that they were made of poor material, that they were bad when he first made them, that he turned them inside out to see if that would make them any better, but that they were just as bad and that he couldn't do anything about it as long as the material was inferior. Rivoli insisted to Novgrod, "Listen here, this not the reason you fire a man." But Novgrod said, "No, no, you got to go."

Although both Magzamen and Rivoli were supposed to have been fired for inefficiency, the board found that their pay compared very favorably with that of other expert finishers. Since they were both on piece rates and had to refinish defective hats without pay, their high wages were almost conclusive evidence of high efficiency. Magzamen had been employed for more than a year prior to his discharge and Rivoli had been hired and rehired three times at the company's insistence. It would appear, therefore, that the quality of their work could not have been much below par. Testimony showed that another employee who was found to be inefficient had been discharged two days after he was hired. The board therefore ordered that Magzamen and Rivoli be reinstated with back pay from the time of their discharge.[11]

Scores of similar cases of more or less complexity have faced the board during the last three years. In every case the discharge of union workers or discrimination against them has been accompanied by other actions which give a clear indication of the employer's intention. Even under these circumstances, however, the board has carefully distinguished between discharge for legitimate cause and discharge for union activity. It frequently dismisses the charges brought by some workers and upholds those of others even though the total position of the employer is obviously antiunion.[12]

It is to be expected that workers desperately seeking employment and unions pursuing shortsighted policies may try to use the board as a club to compel employers to provide work. The board must therefore protect itself by scrutinizing each case with care to distinguish the sheep from the goats among those applying for reinstatement. Much of this work is taken care of by the informal investigations of the regional offices. Dubious cases, however, are referred to the board.

An important part of the board's reinstatement work takes place in connection with industrial stoppages. If at the end of a shutdown, strike, or lockout the employer were free to refuse reinstatement to active union workers, there would be an open invitation to antiunion employers to use these stoppages as a means of breaking the union's strength. The board has therefore ruled that, regardless of the cause of the stoppage, the employer in rehiring must take back union as well as nonunion men without discrimination.[13] If the work available is inadequate, it must be shared in order of seniority. This means in effect that strikers continue to enjoy the status of employees if they apply for readmission, and the board proceeds to determine whether the refusal to rehire results from the fact that they are union members or from some other legitimate reason.

The reasons that an employer offers for refusal to rehire after a stoppage differ considerably from those given in the case of discharges. "Dropping tools" cannot be alleged if no tools have been in use. Another kind of reason is advanced and this provides the board with another set of problems. Some employers have offered to reinstate workers if they would abandon a strike. This offer having been refused, employers have held that they were not bound to reinstate union members. The board has held that an employer must not discriminate against strikers at the close of a strike merely because they have previously refused an offer to return to work. Otherwise an employer could offer completely unacceptable terms of reëmployment during a strike and then refuse to reinstate workers at the end of the strike. However, if at the end of the strike workers refuse to accept reëmployment because the wages are too low or for some reason other than an unfair labor practice, the employer cannot later be required to offer employment.[14]

The Mackay Radio and Telegraph Company blacklisted some of its workers during a strike and made it understood that they would not be reëmployed at the end of the strike. This caused the blacklisted workers to delay their applications for work until the company had filled their places. The company then contended that these workers had lost their privilege of reinstatement. The board ruled otherwise.[15]

Other antiunion employers have invented a number of other subterfuges to evade the prohibition of discrimination against union members. The board has had to deal with these under an amazing variety of conditions. It has had to distinguish between subterfuge and the honest use of the employer's unquestioned right to select or discipline his workers for reasons other than union activity. In so doing it has removed one of the most formidable obstacles to the right of collective bargaining and has at the same time limited only the antiunion use of the employer's economic power. In carrying out this obligation, the board has been uniformly upheld by the Supreme Court and with only occasional modifications by the circuit courts.

During the first three years of its operation the board and its offices handled 10,107 cases involving charges of unfair labor practices. Of these cases, 4,670, or 46.2 per cent, were charges of discriminatory discharge. In settling these charges, the board or its offices effected the reinstatement of 9,882 workers.[16] In most of these cases the reinstated workers were outstanding leaders of their groups. Their reinstatement therefore affected the attitude toward unionism of thousands of other workers. In the Jones and Laughlin case, for example, the reinstatement of ten workers by board order immediately affected the attitude of 27,000 fellow employees toward the Steel Workers' Organizing Committee.[17]

In spite of the evidence of antiunion activity on the part of thousands of employers, the board issued only 250 formal cease-and-desist orders during its first three years.[18] The remainder of the cases have been handled by the regional offices in the informal way described in Chapter I. This means that in spite of a great deal of remaining antiunion sentiment among superintendents, foremen, and other subordinate officials, an immense majority of American employers are willing to comply with the letter and intent of the act after the situation has been made clear to responsible employing officials.

As to the blacklisting of union members by employers throughout an industry, it goes almost without saying that the board has denounced this practice whenever it has been uncovered. It is difficult to imagine a practice more completely at variance with the intent of the act than the effective denial of a livelihood to a worker who has union sympathies. Long before the passage of the act, public opinion condemned this practice as being one of the cruelest forms of poor sportsmanship. Since it could be and was carried on very widely in complete secrecy, it was impossible to enforce the doctrine of criminal conspiracy against it. The board's powers of subpoena and its thorough investigation of each charge of unfair practice provide the first effective method of exposing these conspiracies to the public gaze. Exposure of the practice has been an important step toward its removal, but even more important is the board's power to order the reinstatement of workers who have demonstrably been blacklisted for union activity.

Yellow-dog contracts not only are outlawed by the Norris-LaGuardia Act and many supplementary state laws but are clearly contrary to the intent of the N.L.R.A. Antiunion employers who persist in their use have been compelled to become more subtle in the drafting of such contracts. In this move toward subtlety, the Brooklyn, New York, Chamber of Commerce under the guidance of L. L. Balleisen has taken the lead. So-called Balleisen contracts have been uncovered in several instances in the industrial East, but particularly in the vicinity of New York City. The Hopwood Retinning Company case furnishes an example of their use.[19]

The Hopwood Company threatened to move its plant from Brooklyn to New Jersey if its employees persisted in demanding collective bargaining. A strike was called but was quickly settled with gains to the men. Soon after, the union leaders were discharged. Organization work continued in spite of espionage by the company. Two weeks after the strike settlement, the company locked out all of its employees, closed down its plant, reorganized financially, and moved to New Jersey. The company offered reëmployment to its former workers only on condition that they sign a Balleisen contract. The contract stated in part:

. . . any Employee has a right to join any union of his own choosing, or to refrain from joining any union. Furthermore, no Employee . . . shall be obliged or required to join any union. The Employees shall not have the right to demand a closed shop or recognition by the Employer of any union, and the Employer has the absolute and unqualified right to hire or discharge any Employee for any reason or no reason and regardless of his or her affiliation or non-affiliation with any union.

In commenting upon this kind of contract the board said:

Despite the lipservice rendered by the terms of the contract to the right of any employee to join any union of his own choosing, the agreement deprives each employee subscriber of the fundamental rights inherent in union activity. . . . It would be hard to devise a more patently antiunion or "yellow-dog" contract, or one more discouraging to membership in a labor organization.[20]

Since the board condemns and invalidates these contracts as fast as they are exposed, they have not been of much comfort to the Brooklyn Chamber of Commerce or its industrial adviser. In spite of the reference to the closed shop (gratuitous in the case cited) and the reference to the right of workers to join unions, these contracts are so obviously illegal that it is difficult to understand why any employer would continue to accept and pay for advice that they be used. With each succeeding board order, the value of such advice becomes more dubious.

In connection with threats to move or the actual moving of plants from union to nonunion areas, the board has faced an intricate problem in the use of economic power to fight unionism. In many of the cases in which the board has been compelled to take formal action against unfair labor practices, this element has been present in the situation. Its commonest form has been the persistent circulation of rumors throughout the community that the company would move unless the workers repudiated unionism.

In small communities dominated by one or two industrial

establishments such as Ilion, New York,[21] or Athol, Massa-chusetts,[22] the circulation of such rumors has been a powerful force in mobilizing the sentiment of the entire community against organizing efforts. Under such pressure, communities which might otherwise have been apathetic or sympathetic toward unionism have been propelled into every degree of social and physical resistance to it.

In such cases, the board has ruled that the least that the company can do to comply with the act is either to deny the rumors vigorously and publicly, if they are false, or to confirm them if they are true and announce that the moving of the plant has nothing to do with unionism and that the community cannot, therefore, induce the employer to re-main in the locality by its antiunion behavior.[23] Either of these statements, clearly, would nullify this most effective of all antiunion uses of the employer's economic power.

In cases in which the movement of the plant has actually taken place from a union to a nonunion area, the board has to decide whether the motive for the migration was anti-unionism or to achieve perfectly legal commercial, techni-cal, and financial advantages. Here, again, the attendant behavior of the employer in other respects is of importance in arriving at a decision. In the case of the Black Shoe Company cited in Chapter I, there was no attendant anti-union behavior on the part of the employer and the charge that the company had moved to escape collective bargain-ing was therefore dismissed by the regional office.

In every case, however, in which formal action has been taken by the board, the moving of the plant has been merely the climax of a long series of determinedly antiunion moves on the part of the company. When the employer can disclose to the board no substantial gains from the move in the form of lower wages, taxes, rents, interest rates, power costs, and so on, the antiunion motive is laid bare. In the Omaha Hat Company and Hopwood Retinning Company cases discussed above, the move from New York to New Jersey was accompanied by a great variety of other antiunion actions and was not accompanied by any important commercial, technical, or financial gain. Antiunionism in violation of the act was clearly the motive for the move.[24] In other instances, however, both antiunionism and various reductions of cost are the motives. In such cases the attendant behavior and attitude of the employer become the bases for the board's decision.

If the board decides that the move was made to defeat collective bargaining, it offers the employer two alternatives. He is directed either to reinstate his former employees at the original place of business or to offer reëmployment to his former workers at his new place of business and pay the transportation costs of the workers and their families to the new locality.[25] Such a decision goes a long way toward the elimination of the "runaway shop."

This decision, however, does not prevent the migration of industry for other than antiunion reasons. Migration may be expected to continue as long as differentials in freight rates, wage rates, power costs, and so on continue. But it eliminates a powerful antiunion weapon especially in such mobile industries as textiles, garments, and hats, and may serve to deter Chambers of Commerce from exploiting the "contented" or "open-shop" labor of some communities at the expense of others.

As unionism spreads into the smaller towns and the more recently industrialized sections of the country, the necessity for such decisions will diminish. Even now they form an exceedingly small part of the board's formal orders. Without the decisions, however, the possibility of antiunion migration would invite a minority of employers to flout the act. As a result, the mayors and political machines of such areas as Jersey City and New Orleans would be encouraged in their policies of crushing unionism under the guise of "fighting Communism" in order to provide sanctuary for antiunion fugitives.

The third category of antiunion policies covers those of a more devious variety: espionage, company unionism, and "independent" unionism.

The investigations of both the La Follette Committee and the board have given extensive publicity to the widespread use of the spy system in industrial relations. For two generations, but especially in the last twenty years, antiunion employers have spent thousands of dollars on professional spies whose functions have been to ferret out union sympathizers and secure their discharge; insinuate themselves into unions and report union plans, promote discord, destroy morale, and encourage the unions to undertake unwise or illegal policies. Employers themselves have engaged in spy activities by assuming disguises or remaining in hidden positions and have induced their subordinates to do likewise. Spy agencies have also been employed to conduct whispering campaigns in industrial communities with the object of undermining the morale of union members by exerting pressure on their families and neighbors.

All these types of espionage have been condemned by the board as forms of intimidation or coercion of workers in their attempts to organize. Employers are ordered to cease and desist from espionage even though its use does not result in any further antiunion action. The board holds that the mere presence of spies undermines union morale. It might be added that as a corrosive of human and industrial relationships the spy system is hard to beat. The board, however, has not outlawed espionage for other industrial purposes such as the protection of trade secrets and the prevention of theft of materials, tools, and cash.[26]

In spite of the board's activities, the use of antiunion espionage remains general in American industry. It is supported by the employer's fear of the unknown and his natural human curiosity as to what is going on among his men, as well as by a program of discharge and destruction of the union. As the practice of collective dealing through mutually accredited representatives becomes more general, employers will dispense with expensive undercover operators. There will be several gains in this to the employer. He will save the initial cost of the spies. He will escape the results of their professional interest in fomenting discord and prolonging strife. He will find out what he wants to know by asking the union's agent. This information will be free because the workers' dues pay the agent's salary. Among employers in garments, coal mining, steel, and even automobiles, recognition of all this is dawning. But until the dawn spreads on the industrial skyline, rat-hole industrial relations will continue to prevail and the board will be compelled to exhume the rats.

Section 8 (2) of the N.L.R.A. forbids employers "to dominate or interfere with the formation or administration of any labor organization or contribute financial or other support to it." This is generally understood to mean that company unionism is outlawed. "Company unionism," however, is a vague phrase. It may mean that the membership of a union is restricted to the employees of one company and that it is neither subservient to an employer nor affiliated with other unions. Or it may mean a union so completely controlled by an employer that collective bargaining is a colloquy between one side of his mouth and the other.

Until the validation of the act by the Supreme Court in April, 1937, the great majority of company unions were of this last type. They were an escape from collective bargaining. They were formed, administered, financed, and dominated by the employer or his agents. They had no existence independent of the will of the employer and many of them were not unions at all but were "representation plans" perverted to communicate management's wishes to workers who were not consulted. Their sponsors recognized their illegality under the act by dismantling them in large numbers as soon as the act was upheld by the Supreme Court.[27]

Some company unions, however, survived. And from the potter's field of the deceased sprang a luxuriant foliage of "independent" unions. Until this time the word "independent" had been used to distinguish *bona fide* trade unions from company-dominated unions. Within two years the word has come to be associated with single-company unions controlled by employers in ways more subtle and devious than were their predecessors. The board has had to face the problem presented by the surviving company unions and the new crop of "independents." The problem is again that of distinguishing the sheep from the goats. Under the act, the goats are those that are dominated, interfered with, financed, or supported by the employer. The distinction is far sharper in the animal kingdom than in the board's domain.

The horns and the beard of the company-dominated union may frequently be seen in the prehistory of its formation, in the circumstances of its creation, in the absence of visible means of support by workers, in the surrounding behavior of the employers, in the evidence of indirect support by employer-dominated interests, and in the place and time of its meetings, if any.

In a recent study conducted by the board for its own information, it was found that of the "independents" from which replies were received, 93 per cent were formed after the passage of the act and 65 per cent appeared immediately after the validation of the act by the Supreme Court. Ninety-six per cent were confined to one company. Ninety per cent were formed in opposition to a union organizing campaign while others were formed in opposition to a strike in progress. Ninety-two per cent had some connection with a previous company union. Forty-five per cent received all their funds from workers, but only 33 per cent had voluntary membership, and only 21 per cent had no meetings on company time or property.[28] The results of this study bear out the experience of the board in individual cases indicating that a considerable per cent of the "independent" unions are under the remote or direct control of management. Consequently, between December, 1935, and February, 1938, the board ordered the disestablishment for collective bargaining purposes of thirty-one so-called independent unions.[29]

By no means all nonaffiliated unions, however, are disestablished by the board. After thorough investigation, the board frequently finds no evidence of employer control. Between October, 1935, and January, 1938, the board conducted 966 secret-ballot elections to determine workers' bargaining agents. In 212 of these elections, company unions appeared on the ballot. Of these 212 elections, the company unions won 103, or 48 per cent of those in which they participated, and 10.6 per cent of all elections.[30] In each of the instances in which the company union won it was certified by the board as the workers' bargaining agent. Obviously, therefore, neither the act nor the board outlaws company unions by name.[31]

In addition to the sanction given to some company unions by formal action of the board, the regional offices frequently dismiss complaints against company unions and allow them continued existence. In an open-shop industrial town in New England, the following sequence of events recently took place: During the N.R.A. period, a company union was established in one of the leading plants of the town. When the Supreme Court upheld the Wagner Act in April, 1937, this company union was transformed into an "independent." In January, 1938, the "independent" was used by the management to put over a 10 per cent wage cut. This was done so expertly that the union members cheered the management's announcement. Shortly afterward, however, leaders of the union agitated for affiliation with the national C.I.O. union in the industry. An organizer was sent for, members were recruited, and application was made for a charter.

During an organization meeting addressed by the national president of the union, a machinist in the plant heckled the president with a typewritten list of questions such as "Why aren't you incorporated?" and "Why are you controlled by Communists?" In a judiciously worded notice the management warned its employees against taking the C.I.O. plunge. Nevertheless, the independent union voted to join the C.I.O. national.

The next day the heckling machinist was observed moving through the plant talking with workers on company time. That night, without written announcement, a well-attended meeting of workers was convened for the purpose of forming Independent Union No. 2 in opposition to the C.I.O. From this meeting a local college professor who had previously addressed a C.I.O. meeting was ejected. A plant foreman narrowly escaped being elected president of the new union. The heckling machinist presided. Independent No. 2 was formally launched on a program of opposition to the C.I.O. and with no program respecting wages or working conditions.

For a short time both unions acted as grievance committees in the plant. The C.I.O. union charged the independent union with being dominated by the employer. A field examiner from the regional office of the board made an investigation but found insufficient evidence to issue a complaint. Shortly afterward, the management recognized Independent No. 2 as exclusive bargaining agent for its employees. The C.I.O. union, being immature and not sure of its majority, did not appeal for a board election, and Independent No. 2 remained the recognized union in the plant.[32]

In scores of other cases an investigation might result in an agreement with the company to disclaim any interest in the independent or opposition to the C.I.O. Or it might result in the compulsory disestablishment of the independent as collective bargaining agent. But this case, many others like it, and the record of formal certification of company unions by the board should indicate, however, that nonaffiliated unions are not outlawed by the act. Only if they can be shown to be company dominated is their dissolution ordered.

The final category of antiunion policies includes those which involve the mobilization of community forces against unionism. These forces have taken the form of citizens' committees, wholesale antiunion propaganda, back-to-work movements, vigilante terrorism, police or military violence, and judicial repression. The mobilization of these forces has now been reduced to a set pattern which, with the expenditure of a sufficient amount of money, may be applied to almost any community.

In the smaller industrial communities, however, or those overshadowed by industrial enterprises acting in common, this formula is particularly effective. First reduced to writing in connection with the Remington Rand strike of 1935–36,[33] the formula has been widely applied, but especially in the Midwest and industrial South. During 1937 and 1938 it appeared in Johnstown, Pennsylvania; Youngstown, Warren, and Canton, Ohio; Monroe, Michigan; Chicago, Illinois; Memphis, Tennessee; Mobile, Alabama; Dallas, Texas; Newton, Iowa; Jersey City, New Jersey; and New Orleans. The essential element in the pattern is the creation of an impression that the antiunion sentiments and actions are spontaneously generated in the middle-class public and are not inspired by employer interests. This sets it apart from the old-fashioned brand of antiunionism employing sheer economic strength or brute physical violence frankly inspired by antiunion interests.

In the use of organized "public opinion" as a strike or union-breaking weapon, the National Association of Manufacturers has publicly taken the lead. It published with approval its interpretation of the Mohawk Valley Formula, the strikebreaking technique of the Remington Rand strikes. It followed this with a bulletin entitled "Public Opinion Chief Factor in Ending Johnstown Steel Strike." [34] It then issued a pamphlet called *Industrial Strife and the "Third Party"* which enthusiastically described the manner in which public opinion had been enlisted to break strikes in 1937. Public opinion "has been expressed principally in two directions; a spirit of vigilantism in different areas of the country, . . . and, secondly, the formation of Citizens' Committees in communities afflicted with labor difficulties." The pamphlet then describes how the "aroused citizenry" of these communities "seething with vigilantism" brought about the formation of back-to-work movements sponsored by "independent" unions insisting upon protection of the "right to work." [35]

The ardor of the aroused citizenry also takes the form of toleration of repressive injunctions, police brutality, military strikebreaking, and the kidnaping, torture, and murder of union organizers. How aroused the citizenry become is suggested by their acquiescence in the appearance of such handbills and posters as the following:

COMMUNISM [36]

Will not be tolerated

KU
KLUX
KLAN

Rides
Again

Negro Longshoremen

Agitators are doing everything they can to get you in trouble.
The Klan is against Communism and Agitators
The Ku Klux Klan is watching. Be Careful
The Klan stands for Law and Order.

GO TO WORK

KU KLUX KLAN

P.O. BOX 742

WARNING [37]

Vigilantes are ready to take
care of any radical organizers.
Whistle code to be used as instructed.

ROPES ARE READY

If organizers do not accept these suggestions to leave town, they and their headquarters get the works at the hands of the aroused citizenry marching under the banner of law and order.

From the literature put out by the National Association of Manufacturers and allied groups, no one but an expert public-relations counsel could guess how expensive to company stockholders the arousing of public opinion actually is. The La Follette Civil Liberties Committee and the National Labor Relations Board, however, through the use of their subpoena powers have been able to provide persons interested in the nature of the free press and of free speech with data on this point.[38]

To support its "employee representation" plans through a series of metamorphoses which culminated in a back-to-work movement cost the Republic Steel Company $1,425,-696 between 1933 and 1937. Among contributions to "civic activities," the company paid $219,000 to the American Steel and Iron Institute, a leading antiunion employers' association. One activity of the American Steel and Iron Institute was the payment of $114,365 for an antiunion advertisement printed in 382 newspapers in connection with the 1937 steel strike.

Between 1933 and 1937 Republic, Youngstown Sheet and Tube, and the American Steel and Iron Institute paid out $248,654 for publicity work. Part of this publicity work consisted of employing a nationally read columnist and magazine writer whose articles appear as those of an expert to prepare booklets, lectures, and radio talks. Some of his talks were given before a series of "publicly sponsored" "civic progress meetings." The cost of his services was $28,599.

A number of "prosperity dwells where harmony prevails" advertisements were sponsored by the Youngstown Citizens and Civic Affairs Committee. These advertisements cost $8,279 and of this amount $5,280 was paid by the "Little Steel and Iron Institute." [39]

Intense pressure was brought to bear upon editors and managers of local papers in the steel area. Bankers, businessmen, and other prominent citizens were used in this connection. Speaking of an editorial writer, one Republic official wrote to another, "Even though the editor may not be thoroughly converted, I think he is converted against the Communistic C.I.O. He can be completely controlled by Victor and I feel can be christianized through the use of the right influence." [40] The "christianizing" of public opinion through the indirect pressure of bankers and advertisers, however, was not as expensive to the stockholders of the "Little Steel" companies as the direct purchase of advertising space, the employment of "impartial" lecturers, the bribing of mayors and police officials,[41] the purchase of tear gas and munitions which were turned over by the companies to properly aroused public officials,[42] and the payment of damages to men and women who were filled with buckshot by "unarmed" company guards.[43]

How thoroughly "christianized" a community must be to tolerate the savage antiunion policies of half a dozen powerful companies in this country can be appreciated only by reading the board's findings in such cases as those of Remington Rand, the Ford Motor Company, and Republic Steel.

The Mayor declared the emergency to be effective as of midnight, June 10. With that declaration "law and order" broke loose and Ilion became an armed camp, separated from the outside world. The number of special deputies was increased to 300, many businessmen serving in that capacity. The main road leading into the village was barricaded with a large chain. Squads of special deputies and the local police armed with shotguns— consisting of four to six deputies and one policeman in a squad— stood guard at the entrances to the village and patrolled the streets. Only persons with passes of the Association, those working at the Remington Arms plant and others satisfactory to the guards were permitted to enter the village. Arms had been secured that night at the Remington Arms plant and were carried by many of the special deputies and police. Others carried clubs. Private cars were used to serve as police cars. The headquarters of the Ilion unions, where the pickets gathered, and which were across the street from the plant, were padlocked by the Village Board on the basis of one complaint by an adjoining landowner. The Chief of Police, in answer to protests of union leaders, stated that "Lieutenant Governor Bray declared martial law on the request of Mayor Whitney of Ilion"—which was denied by Bray and was obviously false. When an investigator attached to New York State Department of Labor, who had been sent to Ilion to investigate the situation upon complaint of the unions, questioned the necessity for such measures, he was informed by the spokesmen for the Joint Valley Board that "as Mr. Rand had threatened to move the plant from Ilion, and it would be the ruination of all four villages, . . . it was absolutely necessary that the strikers were shown that they were in the wrong and have them return to work." [44]

. . . . .

Well, first near the northeast corner of the overpass [a union man] was attacked by four or five men who kicked him in the general region of his stomach and plugged him from the rear and were endeavoring to pull his coat over his head and then an increasing number of men fell upon him . . . a separate individual grabbed him by each foot and by each hand and his legs were spread apart and his body was twisted over towards the east, over to my left, and then other men proceeded to kick him in the crotch and groin, and left kidneys and around the head and also to gore him with their heels in the abdomen, or the general range of his solar plexus.

. . . [Another union man] had his fists crossed over his forearms and looking under out of his hands with a look of terror written upon his face, with his face blanched white around his upper lip and nose and mouth, with the exception of a trickle of blood coming from his nose. . . .

One girl near me was kicked in the stomach, and vomited at my feet, right at the end of the steps there and I finally shot an imploring glance at one of the mounted policemen, to whom I had previously spoken and he dashed over on horseback to the west side of the fence and in a rather pleading tone, sort of "For God's sake" tone in his voice, seemed to direct his remarks to this well-dressed gentleman in brown, and said, "You mustn't hurt those women: you mustn't hurt those women;" and I was attracted to the manner in which he spoke, because he seemed to speak as one not having authority in the situation and seemed to be pleading rather not to injure the women.[45]

.   .   .   .   .

I was under the table laying flat for ten minutes. . . . I heard a man from the outside say "God! They're not blanks; they're bullets." . . . Then when I heard that I crawled from the table and . . . I went into the kitchen. And there were five women and around seven or eight men. . . . We waited there for a little bit and we shut the windows all around us. . . . There was so much tear gas and the women were all choked up . . . a man said "I will go out and see what happened."

When he opened the door I saw a deputy sheriff shoot . . . the guy right in the leg. He said "God! I am hit." . . . And we

Courtesy of Fitzpatrick and the *St. Louis Post-Dispatch.*

THE MODERN JOSHUA: STAND STILL!

carried the man into the kitchen and laid him on . . . a low
ice box. . . . A woman went to get hot water to clean him. And
by the time she came, the kitchen was all full of blood. There
was blood all over the kitchen there coming from his leg.[46]

Against the policies embodied in the Mohawk Valley
Formula, the board has only limited sanctions. It can
order a company to cease and desist from intimidation and
coercion of its employees. It can order the disestablishment
of company-controlled unions and their alter ego back-to-
work phases. It can expose the part played by companies
in arousing communities to violent vigilante action. It can
order the reinstatement of discharged workers, with the
exception of those who have been convicted of offenses
greater than misdemeanors during the course of a strike.[47]

But the board cannot institute criminal proceedings
against the officers of companies who are directly or indirectly responsible for the assaults, murders, trespasses, and
thefts which are visited upon union members and property.[48] These matters remain within the control of authorities subject to the same pressures as those exerted upon
communities at large by antiunion companies.

And the board cannot enforce its orders except by recourse to the circuit courts. After the circuit courts have
reviewed the evidence and procedure of the board and upheld its orders, the companies may appeal to the Supreme
Court. When the Supreme Court upholds the circuit courts'
decisions, companies may still refuse to obey the circuit
courts' orders. If they do so, as in the Remington Rand
case, the successive board and court orders are enforceable
through contempt-of-court proceedings. Except for the
piling up of back wages to workers whose reinstatement has
been ordered, there are no financial or penal sanctions
applicable against violators of the act. Punishment for

contempt of the circuit court is at the discretion of circuit-court judges. The Remington Rand, Ford Motor Company, and Republic Steel cases are now in various stages of progress through this judicial gauntlet, with prolonged delays in view.

It should be indicated at the close of this chapter, as at the beginning, that it is a small minority of very powerful employers who are thus placing themselves in a position not merely of antiunionism, but of deliberate defiance of the legislative, executive, and judicial branches of the government. Were this not true, the administration of the act would long since have collapsed. The great majority of cases of alleged antiunionism which come before the board are settled by more or less amicable agreement in an informal way which is rapidly educating both employers and workers in the details of the behavior expected of them under a legal guarantee of the right to collective bargaining.

CHAPTER IV

COLLECTIVE BARGAINING

I T is easier to defend collective bargaining than to define it. The man on the street defends it because of a common sympathy with workers as underdogs. His defense, however, is likely to be easily disturbed by other stereotyped attitudes such as the union man as racketeer, as terrorist, or as subversive social element. He concludes that he favors collective bargaining "if properly regulated and conducted." He is therefore involved in a difficult definition of the "proper" regulation and conduct of collective bargaining. This definition is difficult not only because of the great number of technicalities involved, but also because accurate information about the issues and the methods employed in a particular situation is almost impossible of attainment through the public press.

The sociologist does not "defend" collective bargaining. He accepts it as a basic and inevitable form of social behavior. He sees people at all times and in all places acting in groups for group ends. He understands that the urge toward collective action among workers cannot be eliminated except by brute physical force or by removing the conditions from which the group objectives emerge. He knows that either of these courses involves rupture of the existing social fabric. If the sociologist could be induced to prescribe for the health of the body politic, he would urge that individuals be allowed freely to associate with each other in pursuit of common interests. He would recognize, however, that there are conflicts of interest among social groups that must be resolved if the well-being of the national group is to be preserved. He would expect the national group to assert its superior strength by defining the relative rights of the various economic and social groups within the national boundaries. Such a definition, again, is very complex. At this point the sociologist defers to the practical politician, the judge, and the administrator.

Increasingly the pressure of social forces compels economists to "take sides" consciously in questions of conflicting group interests. This is an advance because economists have always taken sides, but not always consciously. Having descended from the icy heights of authority to the lowlands of social conflict, they become more useful. They see what the lowlands are like at close range, which is a big advantage to anyone who wants to describe them accurately. And, having come down among men, their pronouncements have to be judged upon their own merits rather than by the degree of sepulchral resonance achieved in such phrases as "the law of supply and demand."

Few economists, therefore, in these days will risk a statement that fundamental economic law proves collective bargaining to be either futile or injurious to the interests of the worker, as well as to the employer and the consuming public. There are too many economists in the lowlands who would inquire who was paying for this statement from Olympus. There are also too many economists whose investigations do not reveal a highly competitive and frictionless economic world controlled by impersonal natural laws. They see instead a world in which group action toward common economic ends is a major force in determining the direction of economic change.

People with common economic interests become reluctant to compete with each other. They organize around the maintenance of the prices of their products and services.

They begin to talk in terms of "a reasonable price," "fair competition," "an honest day's pay." Some individuals refuse to come in, or break away from their groups and group codes. They see a temporary advantage in walking alone. If enough break away, the group disintegrates, "cutthroat competition" is reëstablished, the individualists or "scabs" engage in a struggle for survival. From this struggle a new group, perhaps in much modified form, emerges and reasserts its control over the price of the product or service.

Gentlemen's agreements or conventional prices break down under pressure of changed circumstances or the actions of the "cutthroats." From the resulting competition, trade associations, "Judge Gary's dinners," trusts, holding companies, mergers, communities of banking interest, territorial pools, and national spheres of interest emerge.

Workers compete against each other and destroy the conventional fair day's pay. Local craft unions are formed. Changed circumstances or "scabs" destroy these price controls. Crafts amalgamate. Amalgamated crafts federate. Industrial unions appear and consolidate on a federated basis. All of these economic groups are concerned with and influence the price of their products and services. Collective human control over prices is a fact which cannot be obscured by the pontifical message of economic "science."

Some price controls, however, are more nearly perfect than others. Combinations among workers are more difficult to effect than combinations among owners and managers. The common interests of workers are not as immediately apparent. They are more likely to be torn by racial, religious, linguistic, or sectional conflicts. There are more of them to be brought into line. Their economic resources, waiting power, and information are more limited than those of owners and managers. Opposition to workers' group action is buttressed by legal and judicial sanctions.

Consequently, many economists take sides among price-control groups and favor those of workers over those of owners. They are moved to take this position either by the condition of particular groups of workers as compared with that of owners and managers, or by the enormously unequal distribution of income between the great mass of workers and the small class of owners and managers.

Faced with the desperate privation of the fruit and vegetable pickers of California [1] as compared with the condition of the organized owners and managers of this industry, and informed as to the economic, legal, and judicial means whereby this disparity is preserved, some economists come out in favor of collective bargaining for these workers. Human sympathy and the facts of the situation prompt them to take this position. Other economists, surveying the almost fantastic inequality in the distribution of income, conclude that the far more nearly perfect price controls of the owning and managing groups as compared with those of workers are in large measure responsible for the inequality in income distribution. Few care to defend this inequality in public. Most condemn it as inequitable by any standard of justice. Many point to it as the basic cause of recurrent depression and the anomaly of poverty amid plenty. For reasons of national well-being, therefore, they encourage the development of collective action among workers to offset the effect of group action by owners and managers.

In passing the National Labor Relations Act, Congress accepted this point of view. In so doing, it apparently reflected mass opinion. The act declares it to be a part of the policy of the United States to minimize

the inequality of bargaining power between employees who do not possess full freedom of association . . . and employers who are organized in the corporate or other forms of ownership association . . . [which] tends to aggravate recurrent business depressions, by depressing wage rates and the purchasing power of wage earners in industry.[2]

Any economist, however, who favors collective bargaining by wage workers is hard put to it to define what he means by collective bargaining. There is great variety in the forms and methods of group action. Some of these may be considered good, others bad from the national point of view. There are questions as to what the collective entity is which is to engage in a particular bargain; who its representatives are to be; how and on what basis they are to be chosen; and of what the bargaining process actually consists.

Congressional draftsmen were faced with these questions when the act was drawn up and debated. Experience under Section 7a and Public Resolution No. 44 had emphasized the difficulty of dealing with them legislatively. Accordingly, the act remained silent with respect to the goodness or badness of trade-union policies. This was left to local ordinance, state law, and judicial interpretation of existing federal and common law. The selection of the appropriate bargaining unit, the certification of group representatives, and the practical definition of the bargaining process, however, were entrusted to the administrative action of the board.

Congress laid upon employers a duty to bargain collectively with the representatives of the majority of workers in any unit appropriate for bargaining purposes. In so doing it was specific about one point which had been the focus of bitter controversy under Public Resolution No. 44 and Section 7a. The act contains a requirement that the representatives of a group of workers shall be determined by a *majority* of the workers in the group. Congress thus followed the precedent set by most democratic political organizations and by corporations.

This provision, however, met with bitter hostility from organized antiunion groups. Antiunion industrialists had shown deep concern for the rights of workers' minority groups. They had insisted that only *proportional* representation met the requirements of justice, and they had successfully confused the majority rule provision with the closed shop. Under Public Resolution No. 44, the old N.L.R.B. had made decisions requiring employers to deal with the representatives of a majority of the workers in an appropriate unit.[3] Antiunion employers, especially in the automobile industry, made an issue of this and insisted that they be allowed to deal also with the representatives of as many minority groups as existed in the voting unit.

Bitter experience indicated to labor leaders and their Congressional sympathizers that the real motive behind this concern for the rights of minorities was usually a desire to play the minority groups against each other and against the majority group in the bargaining process, with the result that collective bargaining became a farce. In an automobile factory in 1934, for example, there might have been at the same time an A. F. of L. federal labor union with a 60 per cent majority, a company union with 20 per cent, the Mechanics Educational Society with 10 per cent, a 5 per cent fragment of Father Coughlin's followers, a 2 per cent fraction of Stalinists, a 1 per cent splinter each of Trotskyites and Lovestoneites, and a 1 per cent remainder of fifty individuals, each one representing himself.

Proportional representation under these conditions would have resulted in negotiations between the company, seven sets of group representatives, and fifty individuals speaking for themselves. Proportional representation produces competitive underbidding to an extent only slightly less than is true where there is no group action at all. It effectively nullifies collective bargaining behind a shower of crocodile tears for the rights of minorities. Congress eventually disregarded the shower and provided for majority rule.

Although the act specifically allows employers to make closed-shop agreements, majority rule should not be confused with the closed shop. Under a closed-shop contract, an employer agrees not to hire anyone who is not a member or who will not become a member, within a stated period, of the union with which the agreement is made. These contracts are permitted under the act as long as the union in question is not controlled by the employer and has a majority status. But whether they are agreed upon or not is no concern of the act or of the board.

On the other hand, the board is required to enforce majority rule. Under majority rule, the workers may or may not join the union which acts as their representative. If a majority of the workers vote for a union or designate it in some other way as their bargaining agent, it becomes the representative of all the workers in the voting unit regardless of membership or nonmembership in the union and regardless of whether they voted for it, against it, or not at all. This is an exact parallel to any political situation in which an elected Republican member of Congress, for example, becomes the representative of all the people in his district regardless of their party membership, and regardless of whether a particular individual voted for or against him, or not at all.

But beyond this requirement for majority rule, Congress left to the board the intricate task of defining collective bargaining. In scores of formal decisions the board has subsequently constructed this definition. It has provided the man on the street, the sociologist, and the economist with at least a partial description of the program to which many of them have lent their approval.

Legalized group action involves limiting the rights of other groups as well as defining those of the group in question. The board immediately runs into this fact in the process of certifying the bargaining agent of a group of workers. Three problems arise whenever the board tries to discover what agent has the allegiance of a majority of workers in the voting group. The first is the determination of the appropriate group of workers among whom to hold an election. The second is the time of the election. And the third is the meaning of the word "majority."

Section 9 (b) of the act says that "the board shall decide in each case whether . . . the unit appropriate for the purposes of collective bargaining shall be the employer unit, craft unit, plant unit, or subdivision thereof." Suppose that in a merchandising concern there are 1,000 production workers, 718 of whom would vote for a union, and 600 clerical workers, 400 of whom would vote against it. Should the election be held in the two groups separately or in the concern as a whole? If the election is held in the plant as a whole, the production workers will get the union they want, but the white-collar workers will be represented by a union they don't want. If the election is held in the separate units, the majority of each will be satisfied, but there will be dissatisfied minorities in each.

Suppose that among the production workers there is one department of 200 women, 150 of whom don't want a union. Should they be put in one unit and the 800 men in another? If this is not done, the election will compel the women to accept the union, willy-nilly. Suppose that among the 800 men there is a foreign-language group of 100, most of whom don't want a union. Should they be separated out and allowed to bargain for themselves? Suppose that within this foreign-language group there are twenty who don't believe that there is pie in the sky when we die and have joined the I.W.W. Should they be separated out and allowed to vote by themselves?

Suppose that within the remaining 700 production workers there is a group of 22 patternmakers who, if they had a chance, would vote for a union of their craft. Should they be allowed to elect their separate representatives? And finally, if there are 10 assorted workers in no recognizable category who don't want to be represented by union agents, why should they not be separated out and each one be considered an appropriate voting unit to cast a unanimous ballot for himself? It is apparent that Congress, having settled the majority-rule issue, reopened it and handed it back to the board in the form of selecting the appropriate voting unit.

If the plant as a whole is selected as the appropriate unit, the ballot would result as follows:

For the Union
668 male production workers
 50 female production workers
200 clerical workers
918 *Total*

Against the Union

- 400 clerical workers
- 150 female production workers
- 80 foreign-language workers
- 22 patternmakers
- 20 I.W.W.
- 10 other male production workers
- <u>682</u> *Total*

The union, having a majority of all the workers in the plant, would become the exclusive bargaining agent.

If, at the other extreme, it were decided to break up the plant into the greatest possible number of units, the result would be that the union would represent 668 production workers; the Patternmakers' League would represent 22 craft workers; the I.W.W. would represent 20 foreign-language workers, and the company would bargain individually with 600 clerical workers, 200 women, 80 foreign-language workers, and 10 other male production workers. In the first case, the minority rights of 682 workers would be disregarded. In the second, collective bargaining would become a farce and the intent of Congress would be flouted. Yet there is no clear line of demarcation between the two extremes. It is up to the board to lay down the line.

This problem becomes acute under three sets of circumstances: when there is a large minority of workers hostile to the union which would represent them if they were included in the appropriate unit; when the employer is hostile to unionism and would successfully evade collective bargaining if he could persuade the board to include in the appropriate unit a sufficient number of workers loyal to him and hostile to unionism; when two hostile unions are competing, one of which would become the exclusive bargaining agent if the whole plant were to be selected as the appropriate unit, but both of which would become agents for their respective units if the plant were subdivided into smaller constituencies.

All of these situations are constantly confronting the board. The size of the problem is increased still more by the board's power to extend the appropriate unit upward from the plant to the company, the holding company, regions of an industry, or the industry as a whole. The board's power to expand the appropriate unit upward is coextensive with the employers' use of associations as bargaining agents.[4] If, as in the case of Pacific longshore work, employers form local associations and then group these associations together for a common regional employment policy, the board has the power to rule that the entire Pacific longshore industry is the appropriate unit within which to determine the workers' bargaining agent. If employers' associations on the Pacific, the Atlantic, the Gulf, and the Great Lakes should band together, there is no legal reason to prevent the board from deciding that the entire industry should be the appropriate election unit. In fact, this is the logical outcome of the long-continued trend toward collective action among employers as well as among workers.

In the absence of any strict criterion of judgment as to what the appropriate unit should be, the board is compelled to rely upon common sense. The factors which compose common sense may be briefly listed as: the history of labor relations in the industry, or between a particular employer and his workers; the existing form of workers' self-organization; the eligibility requirements for membership in the union or unions involved; the nature of the several types of work which may be carried on in the units in question; the various skills employed; the form, amount, and method of payment of wages; the supervisory authority of some workers as compared with others; the permanence or impermanence of employment of the several groups; the functional coherence of the processes performed; geographical considerations—all these are criteria upon which the board bases its decisions.[5]

It is obvious, however, that in a particular situation many of these criteria may be in conflict with each other. The board is therefore compelled to weigh them against each other. Geographically separate processes in production may be functionally intimate. Salaried workers may receive lower pay than wage workers. Close historical ties may bind workers of disparate occupations. The board must decide among these conflicting factors. Only a faithful reading of its detailed decisions can suggest how painstakingly the board has weighed these conflicts.[6] Such mistakes as may have been made are immensely overborne by the consideration that often it is more important to come to a decision, even though relatively arbitrary, than to allow conflict to continue to disturb the process of production.

The second problem which the board has had to face has been the determination of the time at which an election or other form of certification shall take place. In any industry which suffers from fluctuations in employment, the outcome of an election may differ considerably, depending upon when it is held. Ordinarily, the board decides that the workers eligible to vote shall be those on the pay roll at the time at which an appeal for an election is made.[7] But if there are casual workers who come and go and whose vote may change the outcome of an election, or if an employer has succeeded in retaining a greater number of nonunion than union workers during a slack period, or if a company-influenced union appeals for an election during a strike while union workers are replaced by nonunion men—in all of these situations, and many others similar, the board must exercise its discretion. There can be no fixed rule except the application of the basic policy of the act—the establishment of stable collective-bargaining relationships between employers and the representatives of the majority of workers. No permanent injustice can be imposed upon large minorities of workers by the board's decisions, since a subsequent appeal for a new election is always possible. In the meantime the issue is settled.[8]

The third problem before the board in this connection is the definition of the word "majority." There are three possible meanings. Does it mean a majority of those working in the appropriate unit? Does it mean a majority of those voting in an election in which a majority of the workers in the appropriate unit cast ballots? Or does it mean simply a majority of those voting in an election?

The board began with the first interpretation and adhered to it for about a year. It refused to certify any union as an exclusive bargaining agent unless the union received a majority vote of all the workers in the unit. In the Chrysler Company case, for example, the Society of Designing Engineers received a majority of the votes cast, but only 125 out of 700 voted. The board therefore refused to certify.[9]

The experience gained in this first year, however, convinced the board that it would have to abandon this position in favor of the third interpretation: that a majority of those voting in an election is sufficient for certification. One of the reasons for adopting this interpretation may be illustrated by the case of the R.C.A. Manufacturing Company.[10]

A bitterly fought strike in the Camden, New Jersey, plant of R.C.A. was precipitated by a controversy over representation between the United Radio and Electrical Workers and the Employees' Committee Union. The former is a C.I.O. affiliate and the latter was a local company union. The United petitioned the board for certification and the strike was settled by an agreement between the company and the United. One of the terms of this agreement was that in an election to be held by the board, the winning union would have to have a majority of all those eligible to vote. The Employees' Committee agreed to be bound by this stipulation.

A few days before the beginning of the election, the Employees' Committee suddenly refused to take part in it. From that time until the closing of the polls, the committee put on a campaign to boycott the election. The campaign consisted of the distribution of circulars predicting violence, bloodshed, rioting, street fighting, general disorder, and perhaps loss of life if workers took part in the election. Threats to take pictures of workers who voted were circulated. A sound truck broadcast similar warnings in the vicinity of the plant. Under these circumstances, anyone appearing at the voting booth thereby identified himself as a C.I.O. adherent and the voting process ceased to be secret.

As a result of these tactics only 3,163 ballots were cast though there were 9,752 eligible workers. Of these 3,163 votes, 3,016 were cast for the United. The board certified the United as the exclusive bargaining agent for all the workers in the plant. In coming to this decision the board was influenced by two considerations. First, it is a universally recognized practice of political democracy that a majority of those voting in an election win it, even though only a minority of the total electorate appear at the polls. But, second, and more important, this case and many others similar made it obvious that to require either that a majority of the total electorate vote for a union or that a majority of the total electorate appear at the polls placed a heavy premium on exactly the kind of tactics used by the Employees' Committee in this case.

All of the attendant circumstances of the R.C.A. case indicated that the Employees' Committee represented a small minority of the workers. Yet its tactics of withdrawal and terrorism prevented the United from either receiving a majority vote of all those eligible, or attracting to the polls a majority of those eligible. The adoption of either of these requirements encouraged boycotting of elections by minority unions of all kinds, and terrorism either by minority unions or by antiunion employers. On the other hand, the adoption of a ruling that a majority of those voting is sufficient to win an election impels everyone to participate, whether pro- or antiunion, and destroys all incentive on the part of the employer to prevent workers from participating.

Since July 1, 1936, the board has adhered to this ruling.[11] Its success is attested by the fact that during 1937, 95.6 per cent of the workers eligible to vote in board elections actually cast their ballots. This compares with the 64.1 per cent of eligible workers who cast ballots in 1936.[12] Although other factors enter, it is unquestionable that the board's adoption of the accepted practical definition of the word "majority" has had a great deal to do with this spectacular increase in workers' exercise of the franchise.

The adoption of this policy by the board soon necessitated another change in its election rules. Until this time, if there were two unions voting against each other in an election, the board provided no space on the ballot for those who wanted to vote against both unions. This was not an injustice to the antiunion workers since they could defeat both unions simply by not voting. For example, if there were 1,000 workers eligible to vote, and Union A received 200 votes while Union B received 250, neither union would have received a majority of those eligible to vote. Unionism would therefore have been defeated by the majority of nonvoting workers. But as soon as the board adopted the ruling that a majority of those voting was sufficient to elect the exclusive bargaining agent, it became apparent that in such a case Union B would have been elected although 550 workers had received no opportunity to express their opposition to both unions.

Consequently, the board has since provided a space on the ballot for those who do not wish to be represented by either organization.[13] In the above illustration, the results of the ballot under the board's present ruling would be: Union A, 200 votes; Union B, 250 votes; neither union, 550 votes. The board would refuse to certify any union as exclusive bargaining agent, although either of the unions might be able to secure an agreement with the employer to bargain for its members only.

Soon after this ruling was adopted, a further difficulty became evident: A small minority of antiunion workers might prevent large pluralities of union voters from securing a majority of the votes cast. If 100 out of 1,000 voters cast their ballots against either union, while Union A received 475 votes and Union B received 425, neither union would have the necessary 501 votes for election. In the Fedders Manufacturing Company case 875 workers were eligible to vote. Of these, 814 actually voted. The Steel Workers' Organizing Committee received 400. A local company union received 369. Forty-one voted for neither organization and four votes were void. A majority preference had been expressed for none of the three possibilities. The board therefore adopted the policy of holding run-off elections in which workers are given an opportunity to vote

Courtesy of Elderman and the *Washington Po*

IT'S FULL OF TERMITES!

for or against the union receiving the highest number of votes, in this case the S.W.O.C.[14]

By a series of administrative rulings in which one decision has given rise to the necessity for another, the board is defining the details of industrial democracy in the familiar manner of the administrative and judicial process. The flexibility of this process in the face of unforeseeable circumstances constitutes its incontestable superiority over the rigidity of legislative definition. "Government by law rather than by men" is a half-truth. Laws have to be administered. No law can meticulously prescribe for every situation. Government by men under law is well illustrated by the manner in which the board has worked out the political aspects of collective bargaining.

The board's first election was held in October, 1935. Between that time and January, 1938, the board held 966 elections. The general acceptance of the board's interpretation of industrial democracy is indicated by the fact that in 80.4 per cent of these 966 elections, the balloting took place with the full consent of the parties concerned. In only 19.6 per cent of the cases was the board compelled to hold formal hearings and order elections in spite of the opposition of either the employers or the unions concerned.[15] From a reading of the daily papers one would conclude that few, if any, elections were held except over the dead bodies of the representatives of the employer, the A. F. of L., or the C.I.O. This impression has been created partly as a result of the newspaper axiom that peaceful doings make poor headlines and partly by the campaign waged by many publishers to discredit the board as a disturbing factor in industrial relations.

Of the total valid ballots cast in board elections in this period, 81.1 per cent were for trade unions, 13.6 per cent were for company unions, and 5.3 per cent were for no union.[16] Some of the less literate critics of the board have pointed to this as evidence of its pro-union bias. Since only 25 to 30 per cent of the gainfully employed workers in the country are trade-union members, the board must surely exercise a baleful influence, mesmeric or otherwise, to produce an 81.1 per cent pro-union vote. That the board is not a six-eyed Svengali is suggested, however, by two considerations. First, workers who vote for unions do not necessarily join and pay dues to them. Second, unions appeal for elections only when there has been a considerable period of organization and when they feel that they have a good chance of winning. The board's figures, therefore, reflect the pro-union sentiment only of those industries, companies, or plants in which a high degree of organization has been achieved. They do not pretend to reflect the nonunion or antiunion sentiment of those areas in which no union activity exists.

In connection with the rights of minority groups of workers, it is of interest to note that in the elections won by unions, the winning union received an average of 68.3 per cent of the valid votes cast.[17] By comparison with ordinary state and national elections or primaries, this is a large majority. In the overwhelming Democratic landslide of 1936, President Roosevelt received only about 63 per cent of the popular vote. The problem of minority representation in industrial politics is considerably less acute than in territorial democracy.

The board is empowered to use means other than elections to determine the proper bargaining agent of a group of workers. In many cases, comparison between the company's pay roll and union-membership cards, signed applications for membership, attested signatures on petitions, or the recipients of union strike relief is all that is necessary to establish the fact that a union has the allegiance of a majority of all the workers in the appropriate bargaining unit. In these ways the board is frequently able to save the time and money involved in formal elections.[18]

In the first three years of its operation the board based seventy-one certifications on membership cards, applications, or signatures as compared with more than a thousand certifications based on secret-ballot elections during the same period. Of the seventy-one certifications which were not based on elections, forty-one were granted in cases in which only one organization was involved, twenty-six where two organizations were concerned, and four where three unions were contesting for bargaining rights. Seventy per cent of the 50,000 workers eligible to express a preference in these cases designated the certified union as their bargaining agent.[19]

When the final result of either an election or another form of polling is the certification of the union or any other agent as the exclusive bargaining agent of the workers in question, it is then the duty of the employer to recognize that agent; that is, to express willingness to deal with it in matters affecting wages, hours, and other working conditions.

Even in so simple a matter as recognition, however, the board has repeatedly faced a problem of primary importance. It has frequently occurred that employers have recognized unions as the exclusive bargaining agent of their workers when there was great doubt as to whether the union was really supported by a majority. This has taken place not only when employers have recognized company unions in preference to affiliated organizations, but also when employers have recognized A. F. of L. affiliates in preference to competing C.I.O. unions or vice versa. When such recognition is accompanied by a closed-shop contract, the opposition, even though in a majority, may be compelled to join the union favored by the employer.

The present defensive position in which the A. F. of L. has placed itself, or has been placed, during the rapid rise of the C.I.O. has made A. F. of L. unions, rather than C.I.O., the usual participants in such collusive agreements. It is perfectly clear, however, that such recognition, whether of A. F. of L., C.I.O., independent, or company unions, and whether or not accompanied by closed-shop agreements, is illegal on two counts under the N.L.R.A. It violates the provision for majority rule and it violates the interdict against interference with or domination of a union by an employer. The fact that A. F. of L. affiliates have been caught enjoying the fruits of collusion with employers is part of the reason why the A. F. of L.'s present attack on the board is as bitter as that of the most antiunion employers in the country.[20]

One case may be cited which will illustrate the usual methods of collusive agreements between employers and any variety of union. In 1933 and 1934, the Consolidated Edison Company of New York, Inc.,[21] established employee-representation plans in all of its affiliated companies in the vicinity of New York City. The plans were completely financed by the company and were elaborately organized by officers and employees who performed their "union" duties on company time and property. These plans were used by the company on several occasions to inform its employees of company decisions affecting them. In July, 1936, for example, the company called a meeting of representatives to inform them that a pay cut was being restored and, in December, 1936, a meeting was called to announce that there would be no Christmas bonuses. At no time was the plan used for collective bargaining.

In opposition to this company-controlled representation plan, an Independent Brotherhood of Utility Employees was organized by some of the workers themselves. This brotherhood, having convinced itself that the representation plan was company controlled, attacked it as such. An article in its monthly, *Live Wire*, entitled "Turkeys or Layoffs for Thanksgiving," expressed its attitude toward the company union. Having become discouraged with its independent status, the brotherhood, in March, 1936, joined an A. F. of L. union, the I.B.E.W. Discontented, however, with the subordinate status accorded to industrial locals in the craft-controlled I.B.E.W., and disappointed with the lack of progress made during the first year of its affiliation, this local, in March, 1937, left the A. F. of L. and joined the C.I.O.-affiliated United Radio and Electrical Workers. The C.I.O. thus inherited the tradition of independent unionism among Consolidated Edison employees.

The United immediately began an active organizing campaign. The company met this by starting a movement to get workers' signatures on a petition to continue the representation plan. Before the company's program was well under way, however, the Supreme Court, on April 12, 1937, upheld the constitutionality of the N.L.R.A. The company abruptly abandoned its campaign for signatures and arranged conferences with the international president of the I.B.E.W. On April 20, a company official called a meeting of employee representatives and announced that he intended to recognize the I.B.E.W. Ignoring opposition and requests for delay, the company released for publication a statement that the I.B.E.W. had been recognized. Employee representatives learned of this agreement from the afternoon papers on leaving the conference with the company official. The A. F. of L. affiliate thus inherited the tradition of company-controlled unionism among Consolidated Edison employees.

Shortly afterward, the acquiescent officers of the company union became the officers of the seven new locals of the I.B.E.W. These officers, paid by the company and retaining for several weeks the perquisites of representation-plan officials, carried on the active work of soliciting membership on company time and property. They were assisted in this by foremen and supervisors, and by A. F. of L. organizers who were allowed access to company premises while C.I.O. organizers were denied admission. Signs were posted on the offices of some company foremen saying, "Pay A. F. of L. dues here." Under these arrangements, the I.B.E.W. locals rapidly gained in "membership." Few company-controlled unions have been born with greater company solicitude. Relations between the company and the national union were later solemnized by the announcement that six of the seven I.B.E.W. locals had as members a majority of the workers in their constituencies and that the company formally recognized all seven locals as the bargaining agencies for their members and informally recognized them as *exclusive* agents for their respective groups.

The board's action in this case was in effect to declare that the seven offspring of this affair could not thus be legitimatized. It directed the company to cease encouraging the I.B.E.W. in all the ways described and to desist from discouraging the C.I.O. union by espionage, discrimination, and discharge. It ordered the reinstatement of six discharged C.I.O. members. It set aside the contracts between the company and the seven locals not only as exclusive bargaining agents but also as agents for their members only, since these members had been obtained through the interference and domination of the company.

On December 5, 1938, the Supreme Court affirmed the board's right to jurisdiction over this case, upheld the board's order reinstating the six C.I.O. members, and held that the contracts could not and should not be interpreted as conferring *exclusive* bargaining power upon the I.B.E.W. The Court, however, reversed the board's order requiring the invalidation of the contracts as applying to union members only. It held that the board had presented insufficient evidence that the union members were unwilling to accept the I.B.E.W. as their bargaining agent. The Court implied that the mere fact of coercion was not enough to justify a conclusion that the union members would have voted against the I.B.E.W. if an election had been held as a part of the board's investigation. Justices Black and Reed sharply dissented from this view. They agreed with the board that the contracts were the logical culmination of the coercion and should be set aside.

By an even more careful preparation of its cases than is apparent in the mass of evidence accumulated in this instance the board may be able to avoid similar decisions in the future. If not, collusive arrangements will be encouraged.

Cases of collusion between employers and unions come to the attention of the board in three ways. Sometimes unions appeal to the board against unfair labor practices by an employer who is accused of dominating a union with which he has signed a contract. In these cases the validity of the contract is only indirectly raised. The chief issue is the unfair practice involved in dominating the union. In thirty-eight cases the board has disestablished the company-dominated union as the bargaining agent, and in twenty-seven of these cases the contract between the employer and the union has been specifically annulled. The plaintiff against the company-dominated union was an A. F. of L. affiliate in fourteen cases, a C.I.O. affiliate in nineteen cases, an independent national union in four cases, and in one case both the A. F. of L. and the C.I.O. joined in opposing a company-dominated union.[22] The A. F. of L. has thus given strong support to the principle that unions encouraged or dominated by the employer should not be entitled to the execution of contracts.

The matter is frequently raised, however, in a second way. In eleven cases the validity of the contract itself has been the central issue. In these cases, the employer has been charged with signing a contract with a union which did not have a majority status and thus committing an unfair practice by encouraging one union at the expense of another. In ten of these eleven cases, the contract included a closed-shop agreement. The eleventh was the Consolidated Edison case discussed above. All of the unions involved in these collusive agreements with employers were A. F. of L. affiliates. In ten cases a C.I.O. affiliate was the complaining union and in one it was the Brotherhood of Railway Trainmen. In all cases the board set aside the contract collusively established and ordered the employer to cease encouraging A. F. of L. affiliates at the expense of other unions.[23]

These decisions of the board have received wide publicity because of the bitter protests against them voiced by A. F. of L. spokesmen. The principle against which the A. F. of L. protests is exactly that which it upholds when its own affiliates are the complainants and company unions are the "victims." The only difference is that the issue is raised in a slightly different manner. In the company-union cases, the existence of a collusive contract was generally only one of the ways in which an employer favored the company union over others. In the A. F. of L. cases, the collusive contract was the central issue although there were usually other methods by which the employer favored his chosen union. This emphasis on the contract issue in the eleven A. F. of L. cases has enabled the A. F. of L. to direct its fire against the board for "violating the sanctity of contract" without attracting attention toward the cases in which it appeals to the board to disestablish company unions and, incidentally, to violate the sanctity of company-union contracts.

It would be strange, however, if employers were universally so afraid of the C.I.O. that collusive contracts between C.I.O. affiliates and employers were never signed. There is at least one instance in which the board has set aside a C.I.O. contract on this ground. This instance occurred in the third category under which collusive agreements come to the attention of the board. Unions frequently appeal, not against the employer, but in effect against another union which may have a contract with the employer but which the complaining union asserts is not the proper bargaining agent. Here again the contract is not the central issue. The central issue is, "Which union is the proper bargaining agent?" The board investigates and, either with or without an election, decides whether either or neither union has a majority status. If the union with the contract turns out to be without a majority, its contract is either annulled or turned over to the complaining union for execution. In at least one instance, evidence of collusion between the employer and a C.I.O. union has appeared. In others no question of collusion was raised even indirectly, but

C.I.O. contracts have been set aside or transferred to A. F. of L. unions because the former no longer had a majority.

In the Mine B. Coal Company case,[24] for example, there was strong evidence that the company had favored the United Mine Workers of the C.I.O. over the Progressive Mine Workers of the A. F. of L. The board held that the closed-shop and checkoff contract between the company and the U.M.W. was not a bar to an election since there was little evidence that the U.M.W. had a majority at the time of the signing of the contract. An election was ordered and the Progressive Mine Workers won by 404 to 25. In other cases the board has held that the existence of a contract between a C.I.O. affiliate and an employer was not a bar to investigation of the question of proper representation when complaints have been brought by A. F. of L. affiliates.[25]

That there have been many more instances in which C.I.O. affiliates have been complainants against A. F. of L. affiliates than vice versa by no means indicates that the board is partial to the C.I.O. First of all, it is up to the union to bring the complaint. If A. F. of L. unions do not complain to the board that C.I.O. unions do not properly represent the workers, they cannot then be heard to complain that the board does not settle such cases in their favor. Second, it is to be expected that during this period of rapid C.I.O. growth, part of which is at the expense of the A. F. of L., many more contracts will be transferred from A. F. of L. to C.I.O. unions than the other way around. If it were the A. F. of L. which was receiving wholesale defections from C.I.O. ranks, it is doubtful whether the A. F. of L. would protest vigorously against being awarded the execution of contracts originally signed with C.I.O. unions which no longer represented the workers concerned.

Third, most C.I.O. affiliates make a practice of organizing the workers first and then asking for a contract with the employer. In many cases which have come to the board's attention, A. F. of L. unions have secured the contract with the employer first and then have signed up the workers. The first policy is much less likely to result in collusive arrangements than the second.

It must be concluded that as far as the principle of setting aside collusive contracts is concerned, or of suspending contracts while investigation of the majority status of a union is undertaken, the A. F. of L. has no case whatever against the board. Under either the unfair-practice or representation sections of the act, the board can do no less than inquire into the situation. If preliminary investigation suggests that an employer and a union have cooperated in compelling workers to join one union rather than another, or if there is evidence that a union no longer is the freely chosen agent of a group of workers, the board is bound to proceed further with its hearings even if the result is the annulment of a contract or the transfer of its execution to another union. Under the terms of the act, there can be no question about the validity of the principle embodied in these policies of the board. There may, of course, be occasions in which the board is wrong as to the facts rather than the principle of a particular case. It is interesting to note, however, that in the Consolidated Edison case, about which the A. F. of L. has raised its greatest protest, the A. F. of L. objects to the principle rather than the board's evidence, while the Supreme Court modified the board order on the ground that there was insufficient evidence to support it.[26]

By defining the appropriate unit for collective bargaining, by setting the time for election of representatives, by conducting the election or other form of polling workers' preferences, by successive interpretations of the word "majority," by formal certification of the duly selected representatives, by excluding collusive agreements from the field of permitted forms of union recognition—in all these respects the board has set up a working interpretation of the word "collective." But what is "bargaining"?

In some respects it is almost as difficult to compel people by legislation to bargain sincerely as it is to compel people by legislation to laugh heartily. Both bargaining and laughing involve prior attitudes which are difficult to induce even by the best Congressional draftsmanship. Collective bargaining in industry cannot amount to much unless the employer is willing to divest himself of the attitude that "these are my men and I know what's best for them" or "these are my terms, you can take them or leave them." These attitudes, survivors of the old master-servant relationship, are deeply imbedded in our industrial folkways. The most sincere, law-abiding, well-wishing, and idealistic employers who have "done the most for their workers" often have the greatest difficulty in adjusting themselves to a position of legal bargaining equality.

The act's requirement that employers bargain collectively has brought into sharp silhouette the fact that, except where unionism has long existed, there has been no bargaining at all between workers and employers in American industry. Employers who are able to conduct skilful, prolonged, and amicable bargains in the purchase of raw materials, in the selling of their products, and in the financial aspects of their affairs are bewildered by the necessity for actually bargaining with workers. This bewilderment is supplemented by a prevailing belief that union representatives are shady characters at best and that the workers they represent are ungrateful and overbearing. The arrival of a union representative frequently startles an employer into hostile acts which he later regrets but is unable to mend. His attitude is that of an uneasy cat surveying the approach of a dog superior in size but inferior in breeding.

Under these circumstances, the board's fundamental task is that of educating both employers and workers' representatives in the ways of effective collective bargaining. The great bulk of this educational work is carried on in the regional offices. This work is paving the way for the gradual acceptance of genuine collective relationships in industry. The fulfilment of this obligation requires all the patience and tact necessary in primary education. The board experiences difficulty in securing personnel sufficiently trained in this exacting kind of work. Its staff is in somewhat the same boat as employers and workers. They also learn. As they learn, their experience becomes available to the succeeding groups of employers' and workers' representatives who file, brief cases in hand, through the offices of the board.

But not all the work of defining the bargaining process can be carried on informally in the regional offices. In some cases antiunion attitudes are so deeply entrenched that they are not susceptible to the educational process. Compulsion, through the issuance of formal orders, becomes necessary. These formal orders are both important and dangerous. Important, because they become precedents for future action; and dangerous, because mistakes are costly in terms of public acceptance of the board's work.

In making these formal decisions the board relies upon analogies to other forms of bargaining and upon reference to the accepted practice long since worked out in the fields where collective bargaining has for years provided stable industrial relationships. The board has thus developed a set of both affirmative and negative principles.[27]

The basic affirmative requirements of bargaining are that both parties approach each other in good faith, with open minds, willingness to come to a decision, and power to commit their clients at least on the basis of subsequent ratification. The responsible bargaining agents should meet each other personally. There should be interchange of ideas, "communication of facts peculiarly within the knowledge of either party, personal persuasion, and the opportunity to modify demands in accordance with the total situation thus revealed at the conference." [28] Ordinarily there should be proposals and counterproposals, and negotiations should continue as long as there is any possibility that an agreement may be reached without resort to force. If an agreement is finally reached, it should usually be reduced to writing.

Negatively, the board has ruled that a mere statement that "these are my terms, take them or leave them" does not constitute bargaining, nor do "discussions designed to clarify employer policy" but not including "negotiation looking toward the adoption of a binding agreement between employer and employees." [29] The fact that workers are on strike does not release the employer from obligation to bargain with their representatives since strikers, under the terms of the act, remain employees as long as the strike is current, and since one of the objectives of the act is to shorten or eliminate strikes through the maintenance of the bargaining process. Bad faith may consist of hamstringing the union with needlessly long-drawn-out and profitless negotiations, refusing to submit counterproposals to those made by the workers, attempting to secure a settlement with persons other than those designated by the workers as their agents, deliberately misrepresenting the issues involved, giving false reasons for refusing to continue negotiations, and refusing to resume negotiations after new factors have been introduced into the situation.

In applying both these affirmative and negative rules, the board takes into account the employer's actual economic condition and the previous status of personnel relations as well as the letter and intent of the act. If the board concludes that an employer is refusing to bargain collectively with the proper agents of his employees, it cannot punish him for this refusal. It orders him to cease and desist from this and the other unfair labor practices which almost invariably accompany a refusal to bargain. Affirmatively, this means that the employer must begin to bargain in good faith. If he refuses, the board's order can be enforced only by appeal to the circuit court for appropriate action. Since bargaining is not likely to amount to much in the conflict situation produced by court orders, the purposes of the act are clearly to be best achieved by emphasis upon education and conciliation. Thus, although the board performs judicial functions, much of its most valuable work is a by-product of its major purpose.

Most of the bargaining rules listed above would be generally accepted by ordinary people as indispensable to the kind of bargaining in which they engage almost every day. One rule, however, may require some justification. Although in ordinary business life a refusal to "put that in writing" is generally regarded as clear evidence of bad faith, some industrialists have been willing to spend millions of dollars of their stockholders' money, to pervert the integrity of the public officials, editors, and ministers of their communities, and to sacrifice the lives of a score of their workers in asserting that written agreements are legally unnecessary and socially undesirable.[30]

One thing should be made perfectly clear at this point. The act does not require that collective bargaining conclude in an agreement. If bargaining in good faith as defined in board decisions does not result in an agreement, employers are released from further obligation under the act until there appears to be something to be gained by resuming negotiations. This cannot be overemphasized. To require that an agreement be reached would ultimately compel the board itself to lay down the terms of the agreement whenever the parties concerned could not reach an understanding. This would substitute compulsory arbitration for economic strength as the determinant of the terms of employment. It would outlaw strikes and deny to employers the use of their economic power. The board does not and cannot engage in arbitration, and the act specifically affirms the right of workers to resort to strike action. The act and the board are designed only to induce workers and employers to exhaust the possibilities of peaceful negotiation before resorting to the weapons of industrial war. The board has ruled that *if* an agreement is reached, it should be reduced to writing.[31]

The ostensible cause of the Little Steel strike of 1937 was the refusal of a "united front" of several steel companies to sign written agreements with representatives of the Steel Workers' Organizing Committee. Company spokesmen asserted that this refusal was necessary because the S.W.O.C. was controlled by Communists, was irresponsible, and was seeking to establish the closed shop throughout the steel industry. None of these charges had or has any significant basis in fact. Far less evidence of

Communist influence, let alone domination, is apparent in the S.W.O.C. than in the maritime and automobile unions in which "Communist" influence has been magnified out of all proportion to reality. This charge marked the trail of the familiar red herring with a somewhat more offensive odor than usual. The S.W.O.C., in spite of its immaturity and the difficult conditions of its operation, has a record of responsible observance of over four hundred signed contracts. Major officials of the U. S. Steel Company have repeatedly and publicly attested the satisfactory character of their contractual relations with the union. This record is extraordinary even among mature unions. Far from being dedicated to the imposition of the closed shop, the S.W.O.C. has in general been content with majority rule, and under the many signed contracts which it executes with U. S. Steel subsidiaries it deals for its members only, although in many instances, by taking advantage of the majority rule provision of the act, it might become exclusive bargaining agent.

The fact that these accusations were not true is irrelevant, however, except in so far as they indicated the bitter hostility of these steel companies to collective bargaining of any kind except that in which they controlled both sides of the bargaining table. As used by the steel companies, the words "Communist," "irresponsible," and "closed shop" meant: "Any union which is not company controlled is *ipso facto* Communist"; "any union sufficiently independent to influence the terms and enforcement of an agreement is irresponsible"; "any shop in which a union has any strength is a closed shop." Nevertheless, in the Inland Steel Company case, the S.W.O.C. appealed to the board on the written-agreement issue and the board was provided with a test case.

After an exhaustive survey of the facts of this case and of the nature of collective agreements in general, the board concluded, nearly a year later, that if an oral agreement is reached, a refusal to reduce it to writing is an unfair labor practice. The board emphasized, however, that there is no compulsion upon an employer to reach an agreement and that if neither party desires it, an oral agreement need not be reduced to writing.[32]

In coming to this conclusion, the board was influenced by analogy to general business practice and by reference to the history of collective bargaining. From these references the following considerations emerge: Most businessmen do not feel that a business transaction has been completed until it has been reduced to writing. The more complex the agreement, the more obvious the need for a record. A refusal to write out the agreement and sign it is usually an evidence of bad faith. The more complex the agreement, the more obvious the bad faith if a signed contract is refused. Collective agreements are extraordinarily complex affairs. Wherever collective bargaining has been established on a satisfactory basis, written agreements have been universally adopted as indispensable to peaceful and productive relations. The signing of an agreement has the symbolic effect of burying the hatchet, smoking the pipe of peace, or photographing the public handshake. It announces that factory smoke will soon replace nausea gas as an atmospheric impurity and that production is the order of the day. To refuse to sign is a declaration of war.

The overwhelming common sense of these observations is supported by considering the nature of typical collective agreements. In pure craft agreements the document recording them may not be over a page or two in length. But in many of the amalgamated-craft or industrial agreements

Courtesy of Elderman and the *Washington*

MAKING IT LEGAL

which are more complex, the document may run from twenty to fifty pages. It usually contains a preamble declaring mutual good will and defining terms. The mere definition of terms may occupy many pages.

The body of the agreement painstakingly enumerates the different occupations and the conditions under which they are to be carried on. This enumeration of occupations, trades, services, piecework or daywork, fixed payments or bonuses, periods and forms of payments, speeds of work, overtime, holidays, vacations, rest periods, meal hours, apprenticeship and journeyman regulations, job rights, degrees of seniority, job-rotation arrangements, hiring and layoff procedure, sanitation and safety provisions—all these may require many more pages.

In the concluding sections of the agreement provision for interpretation, enforcement, change, and renewal of the contract, interdicts against strikes or lockouts, and the prescription of penalties or adjustments for infractions require still further space. To expect this material to be committed to memory is an absurdity. To insist upon it is to invite the immediate or ultimate collapse of collective relationships. An employer who announces a refusal to sign a written agreement under these conditions is in fact announcing a refusal to bargain collectively. This is only slightly less true when the trade agreements are simpler in form and depend upon day-to-day negotiations for precise content.

In the men's and women's clothing, hosiery, glass, pottery, railroad, and printing industries in which extensive experience with collective bargaining has been had, the board's insistence upon the written form of agreement is accepted as a commonplace. When the scope of collective bargaining is broadened to cover whole sections of an industry, written and signed agreements commend themselves to any person who is mentally normal and not opposed to collective bargaining in fact as well as in name.[33]

Collective action is deeply rooted in normal social behavior and current economic necessity. In general principle it is so widely accepted by the man on the street, the sociologist, the economist, the legislator, the judge, and the businessman that even its bitterest enemies do not care to oppose it in public. In testifying before the La Follette Committee, Tom Girdler, leader of the country's antiunion forces, said: "The most vicious and untruthful charge against the company is that we do not accept the principle of collective bargaining. We not only accept it but we practice it and have for years. Republic will deal with representatives chosen by any group of its employees." [34] Everybody, then, agrees on the principle of collective bargaining. But what is it?

As soon as the promotion of collective bargaining becomes a part of national policy, the definition of collective bargaining ceases to be academic. There must be a definition to fit every case. No law can lay down such a definition. An administrative and quasijudicial board must do it. In fulfilling its definitive role, the National Labor Relations Board has begun to give content to the principle of collective bargaining.

The details of this chapter need not be summarized at this point. It may be suggested, however, that any company which invests hundreds of thousands of dollars in controlling its own representation plan, spends thousands of dollars on antiunion espionage and publicity, engages in wholesale discharge of union leaders and sympathizers, expensively and persistently misrepresents the nature and objectives of the union soliciting a bargaining relationship, repeatedly issues contradictory statements as to whether an agreement has been reached with this union, and finally refuses to sign an agreement admittedly reached—such a company is not engaging in collective bargaining in good faith with the freely chosen representatives of a majority of employees in an appropriate industrial unit.

This negative conclusion marks an advance in public policy. Fortunately, it need not stand by itself. In thousands of unpublicized cases, the representatives of employers and workers who pour through the offices of the board are receiving a practical education in the nature of collective bargaining which is perhaps the most valuable contribution of the act to industrial relations.

CHAPTER V

INDUSTRIAL PEACE

THE constitutionality of the National Labor Relations Act rests in the intent of Congress to remove from interstate commerce the restrictions placed upon it by industrial conflict. In a series of recent decisions the Supreme Court has broadened its interpretation of commerce to include manufacturing and other local activities which have a direct bearing on interstate commerce. Within this area of industry the N.L.R.B. is now empowered to operate.

The people in one state are powerless to protect themselves against economic injury originating elsewhere. They cannot plan or legislate outside their own jurisdiction. Yet their economic interdependence ties their destinies to those of people beyond their boundaries. Simultaneous action by all the states is not to be expected, since each state appears to win a competitive advantage by failing to adopt regulatory legislation. If the losses which attend industrial conflict are to be reduced, the federal government must assume the initiative. This was the view adopted by Congress when it passed the act in June, 1935, and by the Supreme Court when it upheld the act in April, 1937.

It was hoped that the act might reduce the extent and severity of strikes in a number of ways. First, since a large per cent of strikes result from workers' efforts to secure recognition of their unions and to prevent discrimination against their members, it was hoped that a legislative guarantee of the right to recognition and freedom from discrimination would make strikes for these reasons unnecessary. Second, since strikes frequently result from the accumulation of grievances which might be amicably settled if dignified means for their disposal were at hand, it was hoped that, by encouraging the development of collective bargaining, the machinery for adjustment would become generally available. Third, since many strikes result from the desperation of workers in substandard shops or industries, it was hoped that the development of nationwide unions would standardize the conditions of workers throughout industries and the nation as a whole. Finally, since industrial unrest in general is created by the obvious contradiction of poverty amid plenty, it was hoped that at least one source of this contradiction might be removed by the development of greater equality of bargaining power between workers and management.

Newspaper readers will recognize that these great expectations were not realized. The number of strikes increased from 2,014 in 1935 to 2,172 in 1936, and 4,740 in 1937. In terms of man-days of work lost there was a slight decrease from 15,456,337 to 13,901,956 between 1935 and 1936. But in 1937 the figure rose to 28,424,857.[1] These figures have been seized upon by critics of the act as proof of the incapacity of the board and the necessity for repeal or revision of the act. Senator Burke of Nebraska, for example, in nationwide broadcasts and public addresses has repeatedly inferred that a major cause of the depression has been the administration of the act. "Cure the defects in the Act and its administration, and a long step will have been taken toward ending the depression."[2] Others have contented themselves with asserting that the board has stimulated industrial unrest. The Governor of Oregon recently declared:

We have seen the original democracy of the labor unions shoved aside by these petty lords who have established their own rule of revolutionary dictatorship. We have seen the economic development of our State "hamstrung" by this campaign of striking. . . . This has been made possible by ill-conceived legislation in the form of the Wagner Act. The evils of this act have been augmented and magnified a thousandfold by faulty and insincere administration on the part of the National Labor Relations Board.[3]

Many liberal supporters of the board have held their breath and hoped for better days. And, finally, some observers have wondered whether these figures prove anything except (a) the difficulty of proving anything in the social sciences, and (b) that Rome was not built in a day.

Suppose it is agreed that the validation of the act by the Supreme Court in April, 1937, was the cause of the mounting wave of strikes during the ensuing summer. Then, by the same kind of reasoning, the fact that the man-days lost through strikes in the first six months of 1938 was 76.9 per cent less than in the corresponding months of 1937 must have been due to the successful operation of the act! [4] This kind of reasoning may be suitable to editorial pages and political hustings, but it sheds little light on anything except the vested interests of those who indulge in it. Not only does the complexity of social forces forbid this kind of reasoning, but it also explains why a strikeless utopia cannot be created overnight.

When the causes of strikes are analyzed, it is found that a large percentage results from issues related to union organization. From 1920 to 1926, when the labor movement was relatively dormant, this percentage ranged from 17 to 20. From 1927 to 1929, as organizational activity increased somewhat, the figure went up from 36 to a high of 41. During the depression, it declined to a low of 19 but thereafter increased to 32 per cent in 1933, 46 per cent in 1934, 47 per cent in 1935, 50 per cent in 1936, and 56 per cent in 1937.[5]

It is with these strikes for union organization that the activities and powers of the board are most closely associated. If they could be eliminated, while other things remained equal, the number of strikes could be reduced by more than half. For a number of reasons, however, it will be a long time before they can be eliminated.

First of all, "other things" notoriously do not "remain equal." While the N.L.R.A. did guarantee to workers the legal right of recognition of their bargaining representatives, two "other things" happened. The first was an extraordinary increase in organizational activity by existing and developing unions. The second was an equally intense opposition to unionism by powerful and well-organized antiunion forces. The new board was put in the unenviable position of having to attempt to handle by remote control the impact between an irresistible force and an immovable body.

The passage of the N.L.R.A. and its subsequent validation by the Supreme Court had a psychological effect on American workers which was even more profound than that of Section 7a. It gave added prestige and security to organized labor. It lessened the fear of antiunionism. It brought hundreds of thousands of men and women into newly created unions. It stimulated conflicts over personalities, policies, and philosophy within the labor movement. It precipitated new methods, dramatic personal conflicts, and the flinging down of the gage of battle to organized antiunionism. The labor movement, which had previously been a relatively quiet stream overflowing occasionally into the adjacent meadows, became a roaring torrent heaving at the boulders of traditional opposition and threatening the dikes of social stability. The board was given a tin pail and a trowel and told to go to work.

There were those who denied to the board the use of its tin pail. Shortly after the board began operations, the lawyers' committee of the American Liberty League issued a 127-page brief in which it was "proved" that the act was unconstitutional and that employers need pay no attention to it. Lawyers engaged by powerful employers' associations gave the same counsel. Hundreds of employers in all states of the union acted upon this advice.[6] They either completely disregarded the act or became somewhat more subtle in their antiunion methods. Since there was no precedent in American practice for disregarding Congress and waiting upon the Supreme Court, the board proceeded with its attempt to enforce the act.

This attempt was all but nullified in important cases, however, by a swarm of injunction suits. Although the board held that it had been granted prior jurisdiction in cases arising under the act, ninety-seven injunction suits were initiated in federal district courts. The board was forced to turn its attention from administrative work to litigation. For two years it fought these injunctions and eventually won them all, but in the meantime its work suffered and workers became restive under the delay.[7] There was every indication that the act might turn out to be another Section 7a.

Union leaders were compelled to turn to strikes as a means of securing recognition when they found their ranks being decimated by this legal war of attrition. In the Brown Shoe Company case, for example, before the board could enforce its decision it had to go through thirty-four separate legal steps which took it from a federal district court to the United States Supreme Court and occupied a period of thirteen months. The Bethlehem Shipbuilding Corporation case involved twenty-seven separate legal steps occupying twenty-two months.[8] Few unions can go through such extended periods of inactivity and hold their members in line while waiting for the courts to confirm what the law has given.

Wherever antiunionism was deeply entrenched, therefore, the act was practically inoperative from the autumn of 1935 to the spring of 1937. The immediate effect of the act was to stimulate a resurgent labor movement which found its legal channels blocked by legalistic obstacles. It therefore resorted to the traditional methods of strike action.

The case of the United States Stamping Company and Enamel Workers' Union No. 18,630 illustrates this situation.[9] The union was established in 1933. By June, 1935, it had secured authorization from 282 of the 411 workers in the production and maintenance department of the plant to act as bargaining agent for them. It requested the company to enter bargaining negotiations, but the company refused. In August, the union appealed to the board and was certified as bargaining agent. The company continued to refuse negotiations until finally, in November, the union called a strike. On November 29, 1935, the strike was ended by an agreement of the company to abide by the results of an election to be held by the board. After a hearing early in January, 1936, the board ordered that an election be held on January 20. The election resulted in a clear majority for the union.

In spite of its agreement, the company protested: (1) that the act was unconstitutional; (2) that the election was invalid because the clerical and other nonproduction workers were not allowed to vote; (3) that the "ballot was a fraud on its face and was not held [*sic*] in accordance with the election laws of the state of West Virginia"; (4) that "the said election has all the earmarks of an election conducted under the management of Adolph Hitler rather than under the American system"; (5) that the election was "an unconstitutional attempt to have the United States Stamping Company recognize the 'American Federation of Labor,' which it will not do."

Before receiving formal certification from the board, union representatives were told by an agent of the employer:

The law isn't determined yet. If the N.L.R.A. is determined to be the law of this country, it will not require any act on the part of the United States Stamping Company to agree with it. . . . [The act] is not a law until some court passes on it. . . . We are not going to be pushed into anything. We understand our rights—but when you talk about having an election and a fair election, the way I see the election it was a Hitlerized affair—planned just like Hitler.

On the following day, February 11, 1936, the board certified the union as exclusive bargaining agent.

On six occasions during the following eight months, the union attempted to negotiate an agreement. The company temporized, introduced spurious issues, and finally refused absolutely to deal with the union as the workers' agent. Accordingly, on October 9, 1936, a strike vote was taken and after the company had refused to negotiate further, 240 out of the 394 workers on the pay roll at that time went out on strike and stayed out until the board was again called into the situation on April 23, 1937. In the meantime, the employer had defeated the strikers with an injunction and with strikebreakers. Nearly two years after it had originally requested negotiations with the company, the union thus found itself further than ever from its goal in spite of repeated intervention by the board.

Hearings on the new complaint took place during May, 1937. The trial examiner found evidence of antiunion espionage and discriminatory discharge in addition to the refusal to bargain collectively. Subsequent proceedings dragged on through June, July, August, and September. Finally, the board itself received and reviewed the case and eventually, on February 10, 1938, ordered the employer to cease his antiunion practices, reinstate the discharged strikers, and bargain collectively with the Enamel Workers' Union.

This was the third time in three years that the board had ordered the employer to bargain with the union. This order is enforceable only by appeal to the circuit courts, with the subsequent possibility of appeal to the Supreme Court, and the final possibility of contempt proceedings back in the circuit courts. This case is not unusual. None of the thirty-four legal steps involved in the Brown Shoe Company case were present because in the above recital the case had not yet entered the courts. It is not surprising that unions resort to strikes under these circumstances. Nor is it surprising that neither the act nor the board has been able to eliminate strikes springing from these causes.

After the Supreme Court's decisions upholding the act, many of the legalistic obstacles were removed. The act suddenly became operative in the many areas in which employers were more impressed by the Supreme Court than by Congress. In the Jones and Laughlin Steel Company case, for example, one of the members of the original "united front" against unionism in the steel industry agreed early in May, 1937, to submit to a board election. This brought to an immediate end a short strike which had been called to effect union recognition and the reinstatement of discharged union leaders. In the election, the Steel Workers' Organizing Committee won by a two-to-one vote and signed a contract covering 27,000 workers. Shortly afterward Pittsburgh Steel and Crucible Steel followed suit and signed agreements with the S.W.O.C.[10]

Whereas in the eighteen months before the Supreme Court's decisions the board had been able to hold only 76 elections, in the following twelve months there were 1,142! [11] The figures on strikes handled by the board give similar evidence of the effect of the Supreme Court's decisions upon the ability of the board to carry out its mandate from Congress. In the first twenty months of its operation before June 1, 1937, the board was able to bring to a close only 423 strikes. In the following eleven months 724 strikes were settled—nearly twice as many in slightly more than half the time. In the first twenty months of its operation the board was able to prevent the calling of 236 strikes. In the succeeding eleven months, this figure was increased by 309. In the first twenty months, the board reinstated 77,370 workers after strikes or lockouts and 2,575 workers after discriminatory discharge. In the succeeding eleven months, these figures were increased by 105,284 and 6,886 respectively.[12]

The record of the board during its first three years was 1,293 strikes settled out of 1,724 handled—an average of 76 per cent success. During the same period the board averted the calling of 593 strikes.[13] It is useless to speculate upon what might have happened in these 593 cases if the board had not been in existence. Perhaps they would have been called but for the intervention of the board. But perhaps there would have been no unions to call them if the act empowering the board had not been passed. These figures are worth quoting, however, on every occasion that the board is accused of creating industrial strife. There is less question that the activities of the board are at least part cause of the observable decrease in the duration of strikes that are actually called.

One example of the work of the board in averting threatened strikes may be recalled to mind. In the Memphis Furniture Company case, cited in Chapter I,[14] the company actively resisted workers' efforts to organize and refused to bargain collectively with the Furniture Workers' Union. Antiunion statements, espionage, and discharges were the company's weapons. Point-blank refusal to bargain with the union after repeated requests was finally met by a union strike vote and the laying of plans for a walkout. Through the informal intervention of a board official, however, the union was persuaded to lay its case before the regional office of the board. As an eventual result of the board's intervention, the company was ordered to cease its antiunion policies, reinstate the discharged workers, and bargain with the Furniture Workers' Union.

In contrast with this relatively peaceful acceptance of the Supreme Court's decisions were the actions of those who had little more regard for the Supreme Court than for Congress. The remainder of the Little Steel united front, employers in the New York shipyards, the New Jersey and Pennsylvania silk mills, in Maine shoe factories, and in Ohio rubber companies refused to accept the verdict of the highest court in the land and precipitated strikes by refusing recognition to petitioning unions. These five strikes alone covered 30 per cent of the workers involved in organizational strikes during the months in which they occurred.[15] Had recognition been granted in conformance with the act, these strikes might have been avoided or shortened as easily as they were in the cases of the three steel companies which broke away from the antiunion united front.

That strikes in these instances and in many others similar but less important were not avoided cannot be blamed upon the act or the board. A new social policy affecting the employer's traditional "rights" as profoundly as the act does must be expected to result in determined resistance on the part of some employers for a considerable time to come.

Nor can it be expected that union leaders will quickly surrender the methods of the past. The act entitles unions to exclusive recognition only when they cover the majority of workers in an appropriate unit. The strike is a method of securing recognition not only from employers but from other workers. Unions sometimes call strikes as a means of securing a majority status. Until they have a majority, there is little point in appealing to the board for an election. They therefore strike first and appeal to the board afterward. The dramatic situation produced by a strike jostles the habits of workers, realigns personal and institutional loyalties, and sometimes results in the formation of a union which could not have been established by a sober appeal to wage and hours issues.

If a low-power electromagnet is held under a paper of iron filings, the filings adjust themselves in the polarized pattern familiar to every schoolboy. If the paper is turned slowly at right angles to the magnet, the filings may remain in their former position. If, now, the paper is gently tapped, the filings scramble toward a new polarization. In an industrial situation, the tapping of the paper is pro-

Courtesy of Elderman and the *Washington Post*

WE CAN SETTLE IT OUT OF COURT, JUDGE!

vided by a strike. The alternative to tapping the paper is to step up the current in the magnet until it overcomes the friction of the filings on the paper. In some instances, to increase the appeal of unionism in a partly organized group of workers is a slow process. An organizing strike provides a quick alternative.

In this kind of situation the act is gradually accomplishing two things. It provides certainty of recognition once the majority has been won and the employer legally compelled to comply. At the same time, it weakens the public support of a union if a strike is called before an appeal to the board for certification is made. It is reasonable to suppose that both of these factors will reduce the number of "organizing" strikes. In the meantime the board must wait for both employers and labor leaders to adjust themselves to the spirit of a new social policy. It is doubtful whether additional legislation can do much to speed up the adjustment.

When it is said that over 50 per cent of current strikes are directed toward establishing or maintaining the existence of unions, the matter is considerably oversimplified. Standard statistical practice breaks down "union organization" strikes into six subgroups: recognition; recognition and wages; recognition, wages, and hours; closed shop; discrimination; other reasons. It will be seen that the board has direct control over only two of these issues— recognition and discrimination.

Strikes against discrimination should be unnecessary under the act. Workers have merely to appeal to the board for reinstatement and the board proceeds as quickly as possible to make the minutely detailed investigation of the merits of the case which has already been described. If a union has a majority of workers, it has only to appeal to the board for certification in order to secure recognition. These two issues are directly under the board's control and, as employers and labor leaders adjust themselves to the act, strikes for these reasons should be eliminated.

But the board cannot prevent strikes for the closed shop since this institution is specifically permitted under the act. (The wisdom of this provision will be discussed in Chapter VII.) Since the remaining three groups involve a complexity of strike causes, the board is only partially responsible for their settlement. When strikes involve wages, hours, or other conditions in addition to recognition, the board is able to deal only with the issue of recognition. Even if it is able, as it very frequently is, by intervention to settle the matter of recognition, it may not be able to settle the mixed remaining issues. The strike is simply transferred from the mixed-issue column of strike statistics to the wages or hours column and the board is powerless to proceed further.

In the month of February, 1938, which was fairly typical as to distribution of strike causes, 50.7 per cent of the strikes beginning during the month came under the head of "union organization." Under this heading were the following subgroups: [16]

Issues	Per cent of Total Strikes
Recognition	4.7
Recognition and wages	13.3
Recognition, wages, and hours	17.3
Closed shop	10.0
Discrimination	2.7
Other	2.7
Total	50.7

It may be seen that during this month the board had direct influence over only 7.4 per cent of the total number of strikes (recognition and discrimination). It had a partial influence over 33.3 per cent (the mixed-issue group). And it had a remote but entirely informal influence upon 10 per cent (the closed-shop group). It is not surprising, therefore, that the board was unable to bring all the industrial lions and lambs into communion.

In fact, when the board's social setting of a resurgent labor movement, legalistic obstacles, contumacious employers, impatient union leaders, and limited sphere of operations is considered, it is apparent that the board has been both hailed and condemned with too much vigor. It cannot, by taking thought, add much to its legal stature, create industrial peace, cause and cure depressions, or make a utopia of the country overnight. Within the limits indicated, however, the effectiveness of the board in diminishing the impact of organizational strikes may be expected gradually to increase.

With respect to other causes of industrial conflict, the board's operations can take effect only over a much longer period of time. Many industrial conflicts, particularly those of short duration and high frequency which may not appear in strike statistics, result from the absence of means of dignified communication between workers and management. Other strikes are for improvements in wages, hours, and other working conditions. In February, 1938, taken again as a typical month, wage and hours issues accounted for 30 per cent of the strikes and other working conditions for 14.6 per cent.[17] These issues come into the board's province only in so far as the existence of the act and the board may gradually encourage the adoption of collective bargaining as a means of settling them. Informally, the board may mediate directly in matters of this type. But formal government action is reserved for the conciliation agencies of the United States Labor Department and state Labor Commissioners. An immense amount of unpublicized conciliation, mediation, and voluntary arbitration is carried on by these agencies. In February, 1938, 40.9 per cent of the strikes during the month were assisted toward a settlement by governmental agencies of various kinds.[18]

The carrying out of these services is not, however, the primary reason for the board's existence. It is not supposed, formally, to be concerned with the terms of an agreement in the way that mediatory agencies are. Its work is supplementary to but distinct from that of the federal and state labor departments. It is an independent agency whose threefold task is to prevent antiunion policies by employers, certify the proper collective bargaining agencies of workers when and where they come into existence, and enforce upon the employer the duty to carry on the bargaining process with workers' representatives. The carrying out of this task can have only a remote and long-run effect upon industrial peace in so far as it stimulates the adoption of collective bargaining as a means toward peace.

Since the war, American employers have become increasingly conscious of the need for some form of organized communication between themselves and their employees to take the place of the direct personal relationship familiar in small-scale industry. They have recognized that industry may increase enormously in scale without destroying the grasp of management upon problems of production, sales, and finance, but that personnel relations quickly become incapable of comprehension unless an organized form of communication is substituted for the direct personal relationship.

The piling up of a hierarchy of supervisors, foremen,

and superintendents cannot provide this communication between workers and responsible management for at least two reasons. First, the men in direct charge of production are usually selected for technical proficiency. They are not necessarily trained in or adept at personnel relations. Second, they speak for management, not for the workers. Their task is to get out production, not to air grievances. They are likely to think of production in mechanical and financial rather than human terms. Having overlooked, neglected, or suppressed the human requirements in production, they are astonished, grieved, or angered when the human relationships explode and production costs soar as a result of conscious or unconscious sabotage, high labor turnover, walkouts, sitdowns, stay-ins, boycotts, and riots.[19]

Having recognized this problem in the early 'twenties, even the most advanced and socially conscious American managers were unwilling or unable to turn to outside, independent unionism for an answer to the problem. There were several reasons for this. Fundamentally, management feared the potential strength of unionism if granted a coöperative status in industry. It was more afraid of the effect upon industrial control, wages, and hours than it was concerned over its personnel relationships. Having created a conflict situation between itself and unionism, it judged unionism in terms of the conflicts which its antiunionism engendered. Few industrial leaders had the statesmanship to see beyond this impasse. Fear led to hate. Hate led to conflict. Conflict renewed fear.

A second reason for the reluctance of management to deal with unions was the prevalence of paternalism in American industry. Our religious and pioneering forefathers handed us a mixed tradition of exploitation and moral obligation. In industry, this can lead to wage cuts and paternalism. "I treat my workers firmly but well. It doesn't do to spoil them. At Christmas time I am generous." This frame of mind is incompatible with outside unionism.

The third reason was that even the most enlightened management could not muster much enthusiasm for the kind of unionism they saw about them. In the basic industries there were no unions worth mentioning except in coal, clothing, and on the railroads. Elsewhere there were craft unions which were inapplicable to mass-production industries without creating a much worse personnel situation than existed in the absence of any unionism. Many union leaders were totally incompetent to deal with modern industrial conditions. They held their jobs through a combination of the compassion or disinterest of their followers and their own corpulent inertia. Some unions were racketized from within or without. Others were corrupted by political or employing interests. Such union-management coöperation as existed was likely, with several important exceptions, to be based upon collusion between union leaders and employers at the expense of the workers, the public, or both. It was not an encouraging picture to an employer who wanted decent and satisfactory relations with employees who had become nameless, impersonal productive units in a vast machine.[20]

For all or any of these reasons, employers turned toward a great variety of employee-representation or company-union plans. For a time, these seemed the answer to all problems. They need not be feared, because they could be controlled. Taken with their frills, such as employee-stock-ownership, profit-sharing, bonus, and welfare plans, they provided an immense field in which to exercise paternalistic inclinations. Springing pure and full grown from the brow of the employer, they had none of the shortcomings of youth or the accretions of senility.

Company unions, however, were frequently unsatisfactory both to workers and to management. Being controlled by management, they were little more capable of formulating and expressing accumulated employee grievances than was their antecedent supervisory hierarchy. Consequently, they often blew up in grievance strikes. Workers resented or saw through paternalism. The children grew up, looked the father in the eye, and departed to a far country. When they returned, it was in lock-step mass picket formation with an "outside" organizer in the lead. Company unions were pure but impotent. Workers wanted less purity and more power.

Company unions were local. They could not eliminate the sweatshop plants and industries by standardizing working conditions on a national basis. Company unions could not compete with organized management in controlling the division of industrial income. They could not drive up wages or shorten hours in consonance with the increased productivity of industry. This contributed to excessive profits, reinvestment, and speculation on the one hand, and inadequate purchasing power on the other.

Industrial management responded to this situation in different ways. Some employers declared open war, laid in munitions and tear gas, electrified their fences, and hired an army of thugs. Others became more subtle, adopted the modern theory of undeclared war, created puppet states in the form of "independent" unions, and filled the enemy territory with spies who provided "incidents" to justify the employer in "restoring law and order" through submissive citizens and public officials.

Still others, faced with a choice between the "racketeering" A. F. of L. and the "Communistic" C.I.O., accepted collusive agreements with the former. And finally, many employers, more responsive to changing times and opinion than others, surveyed the industrial scene in terms of the developments of the preceding decade.

They remained convinced of the necessity for organized personnel relations as a means of dealing with the multitude of human adjustments necessary to efficiency in modern industry. They were anxious to have sweatshops abolished in order to stabilize competition. They were willing to pay high wages, if their competitors followed suit, both because of human sympathy with workers' privations and because they realized that mass production requires mass consumption if depressions and technological unemployment are to be avoided.

They recognized that paternalism and company unionism could not accomplish these ends. They saw a new labor movement springing into existence in the 'thirties which was more vigorous, more adapted to modern industry, and more ably led than the labor movement of the previous decade. They saw public opinion crystallizing in legislation to meet these new conditions. They accepted the National Labor Relations Act, the board, the C.I.O., and the new and vigorous elements in A. F. of L. and unaffiliated unions.

This acceptance has borne fruit. After the passage of the act and before its validation by the Supreme Court, peaceful collective agreements were reached between various unions and the following companies or industries: United States Steel, covering 222,300 workers; General Electric, 61,700 workers; Westinghouse Electric, 41,500; Packard Motors, 16,600; Allis Chalmers, 12,700; and in anthracite coal, 110,000. This was in addition to 1,000,000 workers covered by collective agreements on the railroads under the National Mediation Board and Railway Labor Act.[21]

After the validation of the act on April 12, 1937, and before the end of the year, the following collective agreements, among others, were concluded: among brewery workers, 408 contracts; by the Amalgamated Clothing Workers, a contract covering 135,000 tailors providing for a 12½ per cent wage increase amounting to $30,000,-000 annually; by the United Radio and Electrical Workers, 510 contracts (this figure goes back of April 12 and therefore includes the General Electric and Westinghouse Electric agreements); Printing Pressmen, 210 contracts; Typographical Union, 141 contracts; United Rubber Workers, 18 contracts; in the shoe industry, about 150 contracts granting a 15 per cent wage increase and covering 52,000 workers; Steel Workers' Organizing Committee, 431 agreements covering 525,000 workers (including 55 contracts signed before April 12, among which were included most of the U. S. Steel subsidiaries); Textile Workers' Organizing Committee, 1,000 agreements, 244,116 workers; and transport workers' agreements covering almost all of the 75,000 transport workers in New York City.[22]

With a few exceptions, these agreements were concluded without prolonged or serious stoppages. They provide the basis for a satisfactory disposal of the personnel problems of industry and a civilized method of dividing its income. The agreements and their administrators on both sides are imperfect, but the participants are willing to agree that there is no short cut to industrial perfection and that negotiation and constant intercommunication on an equal basis offer the real hope of the future.

The most ardent supporter of the board and its work would scarcely assert (unless overheated by contemporary antiboard propaganda) that the board is exclusively responsible for these accomplishments in industrial peace. These and thousands of other unheralded agreements, like the very existence of the board itself, are the common products of decades of evolutionary development in industrial relations. Collective agreements are no more the product of the board than industrial disputes. Or, rather, agreements and disputes are to the same degree the product of the board. The board provides the foundations upon which collective agreements may be laid. But it also provides a legal and symbolic stimulus to the organizing activity which, in its preliminary stages, is frequently attended by industrial war.

The board may, and does, encourage the development of collective bargaining. But it cannot compel it. In the face of contumacious employers and immature unions, it cannot prevent the industrial conflict to which its existence is a stimulus. Nothing short of the absolute authority of a totalitarian state can suppress the visible evidences of industrial conflict. Even then the conflict itself cannot be eliminated.

The existence of the board represents an effort to retain the flexible and evolutionary processes of democracy and to escape the rigidities of totalitarianism. It expresses the distaste of the American people for compulsory arbitration which removes industrial conflict from the economic to the political sphere. It leaves to workers and management the control over their own destinies. It provides a framework within which this control may be worked out if the parties to industry prove sufficiently responsible and intelligent. The board has become the focal point of such an evolutionary advance. It is a product of the past, but a positive influence upon the future. In the long run, such influence as it has is wholly in the direction of industrial peace.

CHAPTER VI

INTERUNION CONFLICT

WHEN it was first said that half the working class could be hired to fight the other half, it was no joke. Often there is no necessity to hire the fighting done. There are real and apparent differences of economic interest, psychological attitudes, philosophies, and powers among workers which compare in intensity with conflicts between employers and workers.

Differences in skill are one source of conflict among workers. In a men's clothing establishment, for example, the pressers can make a good suit look like a poor one, or a bad suit look like a good one. Skilled pressers are relatively scarce. It is important to the employer to treat them well. His interests and those of the pressers are closely allied. He can secure other semiskilled or unskilled workers with comparative ease. He may be willing, therefore, to rob the wages of the unskilled to pay the wages of the pressers, if this is necessary to keep the pressers content. An issue is created between the two groups of workers which may become more acute than the issue between the employer and the workers. The same kind of conflict may exist between conductors and maintenance-of-way men on the railroads; between toolmakers and assemblers in an automobile plant; between patternmakers and floor sweepers in a steel mill; or between loomfixers and weavers in a textile concern.

Social traditions create psychological attitudes which result in trouble among workers. White collars are socially superior to overalls. It is useless to point out that the blue serge of the clerk may carry home less money than the blue jeans of the machinist. The clerk or the teacher or the stenographer feels and acts different from and usually superior to the machinist, the janitor, and the production worker. It is frequently of no avail to call all wage workers to stand together in a common front against the employer. When a crisis comes, psychological attitudes assert themselves with such force that economic interests are subordinated. Some groups of wage workers side with the employer against fellow workers whose clothes, accent, and manners are different.

Race, religion, nationality, and provincial attitudes cut straight across or smear the economic class lines drawn by the wage-profit relationship. "Catholics Unite" or "Come on, Irish" may be more powerful slogans than "Workers of the World, Unite" or "An injury to one is the concern of all."

Organizational traditions develop philosophies, loyalties, and personal powers which make as good a basis for conflicts in some situations as the exploitation of an employer or the aggressiveness of workers in others. A struggle between Progressive Miners and United Miners in Illinois, or between Longshoremen and Teamsters on the Pacific coast, or between United Textile Workers and Wobblies in Paterson has all the aspects, if not the equipment, of class war in Ludlow, San Francisco, and Gastonia. The internal struggles of the United Mine Workers or the United Automobile Workers are as vigorous as they are persistent.

Carpenters *vs*. Sheet Metal Workers, Stone Cutters *vs*. Granite Cutters, Flint Glass Workers *vs*. Glass Bottle Blowers, Butcher Workmen *vs*. Retail Clerks, Seamen *vs*. Marine Engineers, Electrical Workers *vs*. Radio Workers, United Garment Workers *vs*. Amalgamated Clothing Workers, and Ladies' Garment Workers *vs*. United Rubber Workers represent some of the possible forms and degrees of conflict among organized groups of workers.

Unemployment, insecurity, poverty, desperation, degeneracy is a causal sequence familiar enough in these and other times. At various points in the sequence, group action among workers breaks down. The struggle for existence becomes a struggle by each worker against the other. The garments of collective action are shed. The skin, the claws, and the fangs of primitive competition are exposed. The beseeching eyes of the wife, the pallid face of the child, the last piece of furniture in the stove, the last shred of respectability gone—under these conditions, competition becomes a reality. The union card goes in the basket. The head of the house slinks past the picket line. "Labor riots" are headlined. One group of hungry men falls upon another. One group protects its jobs. The other seeks them. Nobody wins, but the fight is as real as the fight between workers and employers.

Desperation leads to degeneracy. Sometimes one generation is sufficient. Sometimes it is the children of the unemployed who become the unemployable. Gangsters, racketeers, thugs, nobles, finks, stool pigeons, and spies—the hands of these are set against organized society in general and fellow wage workers in particular. It is no use classifying these workers as "slum proletariat." Dismissing them as such does not destroy the fact that they work for wages, that they can be hired to fight other workers, that they provide the labor force of espionage and strikebreaking concerns, that they staff the "service" bureaus of important automobile plants, and that they form the shock troops of political movements whose objective is to crush the organizations of fellow workers.

Conflict among workers is real. Any social policy directed toward peace in industry which overlooked this fact would be inadequate to its task. The National Labor Relations Act is primarily concerned with clashes between workers and employers. The act and the circumstances of the time, however, have thrust the board into the center of organized intralabor conflict. This was partially, but only partially, foreseen by the draftsmen of the act. It provides the board with difficulties as great as any that it faces in connection with organized antiunionism.

The board is not concerned with settling conflicts between professional spies, strikebreakers, thugs, gangsters, and "service men" on the one hand, and union men on the other, except to the extent that it prevents employers from hiring industrial degenerates as weapons against unionism. It cannot eliminate the conditions from which degeneracy emerges except to the extent that in the very long run collective bargaining taken with other social developments may diminish the prevalence of industrial degeneracy.

Nor can the board prevent the employer from hiring workers to replace those out on strike unless the strike is caused by or results in "unfair labor practices." If an employer recognizes a union, bargains in good faith with it, is unable to come to terms, is visited with a strike, continues to bargain upon request during the strike, commits no unfair acts during its progress, successfully replaces the strikers with new workers and resumes operations, neither the act nor the board has anything against him. The employer has won on a show of economic strength. The unionized workers have lost their jobs. Hate and bitterness may persist between the two groups of workers as long as memories are fresh. The board's hat contains no rabbits for such a situation.

The board is forced into intralabor conflict, however, whenever a question arises concerning the proper bargaining representatives of a group of workers. The board receives guidance from two fundamental precepts in the act: *self-organization* by workers and *majority rule* of workers. The board finds confusion in industrial life when it seeks to determine the *appropriate unit* within which self-organization and majority rule are to apply. In interpreting these three principles, the board must face every variety of interunion conflict.

The oldest type of interunion conflict is that between two craft unions fighting for the right to perform certain tasks which fall between the two crafts. This type has been superseded in importance by conflicts between industrial unions and craft unions. The craft union asserts its right to a separate existence within the industrial unit, while the industrial union claims exclusive power over the whole industrial unit. Finally, there have appeared conflicts between two or more industrial unions each asserting jurisdiction over a whole industry or over debatable sections of two industries not clearly classifiable in either.

Innumerable examples of each of these kinds of jurisdictional conflict have occurred throughout the life of the labor movement. The standard example of craft conflict is that between the Carpenters and Sheet Metal Workers. These unions have fought for nearly a generation over the right to install metal trim and the right to the membership of workers performing this task. For about thirty years the Brewers, a semi-industrial union, has fought various craft unions, especially the Teamsters and Coopers, who attempted to assert control over the workers in these crafts while the Brewers asserted exclusive control over the whole industry. A similar conflict went on for years in coal mining between the United Mine Workers, a purely industrial union, and such craft unions as the Machinists, Blacksmiths, Stationary Firemen and Engineers.

Conflicts between industrial unions have repeatedly occurred in the past between organizations duplicating each other in industry but kept separate because of differences in basic philosophy, policies, and personal ambitions. Socialist industrial unions fought A. F. of L. unions in the 'nineties and nineteen-tens. I.W.W. industrial unions fought A. F. of L. industrial unions in the 'tens and 'teens. Communist unions repeated this pattern in the 'twenties. C.I.O. and A. F. of L. industrial unions fight in the 'thirties. Independent national industrial unions such as the Progressive Mine Workers and the Amalgamated Clothing Workers in the 'twenties and early 'thirties fought A. F. of L. industrial unions over policies and personalities. Industrial unions within the same federation may contest control over debatable ground between two industries. Where, for example, does the woodworking industry stop and the furniture industry begin?

Jurisdictional fights, therefore, are not a new phenomenon. Nor are they peculiar to organized labor. They appear whenever there are differences of interests among associations of people. They are familiar in the history of employers' associations, the church, states' rights, and international relations. It is always difficult, sometimes impossible, to remove the sources of conflict. The only blanket solution to the problem is the setting up of a superior power to pass upon the questions involved and impose a settlement by which the contestants are compelled to abide. Such an imposed settlement is unlikely to succeed, however, unless it is attended by an effort to remove as completely as possible the sources of conflict. This takes time, conciliation, compromise, discipline, and responsibility among all the participants.

Industrial unionism has gone a long way toward settling open craft fights. It does not, however, remove conflicting interests *within* an industrial union. It sets up a superior power in the form of local, regional, or national officers to compose the differences among various classes of members, with the result that workers deal with employers in a solid unit. The conflicts go on in union meetings, in union homes, on convention floors, and in convention lobbies, but not on the job, the picket line, or in bargaining with the employer.

Industrial unionism cannot settle conflicts between autonomous craft and industrial unions. Only a higher authority, such as the A. F. of L. executive council or annual convention, can accomplish this. Lack of sufficient power and a recognition that "these things take time" have prevented A. F. of L. officers from successfully imposing settlements upon contesting affiliates. Frequently the Federation officers have had to choose between allowing a fight to continue or destroying the Federation by attempting to impose a settlement upon a recalcitrant union.[1] In this respect its decisions have often resembled those of the League of Nations. Recently, however, the pressure of events has increased the power of the executive council to settle wars within its own territories, especially among the weaker unions.

Nor does the mere existence of the C.I.O. eliminate conflicts among the unions which compose it. Thus far, outside pressures have prevented inside conflicts from becoming acute. The strenuousness of its external battles has overshadowed such collisions as that between the Ladies' Garment Workers and the United Rubber Workers over the membership of workers in the lastex undergarment industry. In the absence of formal constitutional machinery at the top of the C.I.O., personal relations among the leaders were sufficient during the first three years of its life to dispose of this and other similar issues. But the only ultimate guarantee of avoiding internal warfare is the establishment of a powerful central body by whose decisions affiliates may be compelled to abide. Such a central body was one of the significant consequences of the recent C.I.O. constitutional convention.

There exists no agency whatever in the labor movement sufficiently powerful to compose the spectacular differences between C.I.O. and A. F. of L. affiliates. These differences are intense for a number of reasons. First, they represent the familiar fight, in many instances, between modified craft unions and industrial unions. Second, they are embittered by contrasting philosophies, policies, personalities, and struggles for power. Third, they have been intensified by the inclination of employers in some cases to give preferment to A. F. of L. unions over those of the C.I.O. Interunion war thus tends to take on a tinge of class war. Finally, the C.I.O. has inherited from the A. F. of L. many of the most embittered disputes in existence long before the formation of the C.I.O.

This is the setting in which the board finds itself when it considers interunion conflict and its effects on industrial peace. This situation is clearly not of its own making or choosing. Nor can it avoid facing it in at least some of its aspects. The board is charged with the task of promoting

self-organization among workers. The board might conclude that self-organization includes the right of workers
to fight out their battles unimpeded by government. But
the board is also charged with the task of promoting industrial peace. Interunion rivalries destroy industrial peace
as effectively though not as extensively as class war. What
to do?

Two general classes of jurisdictional problems are presented to the board. The first is that involving unions which
are all affiliated with the same parent organization, such
as the A. F. of L. or the C.I.O. The second is that in which
the contesting organizations have different affiliations or
none at all. This group includes company or independent
unions against either A. F. of L. or C.I.O. unions, and
A. F. of L. unions against C.I.O. unions.

The board's answer to the first class of problems is
"hands off." When a fight breaks out between two unions
in the A. F. of L., and one union asks the board to intervene, the board replies that it is up to the Federation to
settle the matter. Presumably, if and when open interunion conflicts break out in the C.I.O., the board's answer
will be the same to that organization. The board's reasoning in this class of cases is illustrated by an example in
the aluminum industry and a series of cases in the tobacco
industry.

In 1934 and 1935 a number of industrial locals were
formed by the A. F. of L. in the aluminum industry.[2]
These locals were directly affiliated with the A. F. of L.
and belonged to no national union. As in the case of other
"federal labor unions," the dues of these organizations
were paid directly to the A. F. of L. executive council, and
they received services in return directly from the executive
council.

In 1934, a National Council of Aluminum Workers was formed from aluminum unions in different parts of the country to deal for these locals in matters of common interest. In 1935, the Alcoa, Tennessee, local withdrew from the National Council. The A. F. of L. insisted that the Alcoa local abide by an agreement which had been drawn up between the Aluminum Company of America and the National Council. The Alcoa local refused and appealed to the board to determine whether the National Council or the Alcoa officers spoke for the Alcoa workers

The board refused to intervene. It held that a real case of representation was not involved. There was no question that the Alcoa union spoke for the Alcoa *workers*. The real question, said the board, was whether the Alcoa officers or the National Council spoke for the Alcoa *union*. It held that this matter was up to the members of the A. F. of L. to fight out for themselves. The board thus interpreted the principle of self-organization to mean that this issue, "involving solely . . . the internal affairs of the American Federation of Labor and its chartered bodies, can best be decided by the parties themselves."

This was probably a sensible answer. It was not, however, the only possible answer. The board has the power to determine the unit which is appropriate for collective bargaining. It could have decided to hold an election covering all the workers in the National Council since the great majority of these were employed by the Aluminum Company of America. If it had done so, the election would have been won by the National Council and the Alcoa local would have been compelled to accept the verdict or secede from the A. F. of L. Conversely, the board might have held an election within the Alcoa plant alone. The Alcoa local union officers would have won, would have signed a separate agreement, and remained outside the National Council. Such a proceeding would have been bitterly resented by the A. F. of L. as "governmental dictatorship," and this resentment would probably have been echoed in the public press.

Since there was in existence an organized labor authority which was at least nominally superior to the contestants, the board decided that the principle of democratic self-organization was best to be served by allowing the workers to fight it out for themselves.

In the tobacco-industry cases, the issue was even more forcefully presented. In the Axton-Fisher Tobacco Company,[3] for example, the Tobacco Workers' International Union and the International Association of Machinists, both A. F. of L. affiliates, were competing for the right to represent the machinists' helpers in the company's plants. The Tobacco Workers appealed to the board for an election in which the production workers and the machinists' helpers would be one unit and the machinists the other. The Machinists contended that the machinists and their helpers should be one unit and the production workers the other. If the election had been held on the first basis, the Tobacco Workers would have absorbed the machinists' helpers, while on the second basis the Machinists would have won them.

The board refused to hold any election at all. It cited the Aluminum Company case as a precedent and repeated the language of that decision:

It is preferable that the Board should not interfere with the internal affairs of labor organizations. Self-organization of employees implies a policy of self-management. . . . In its permanent operation the act envisages cohesive organizations, well-constructed and intelligently guided. Such organizations will not develop if they are led to look elsewhere for the solution to such problems.

The problem faced by the board is similar to that faced by parents. The fond father has, at the extremes, two policies which he may pursue. He may take the newborn baby and toss him into the nearest snowdrift saying, "There, my friend, if you've got the real stuff in you you'll adapt yourself to your environment and make your way in the world. If you haven't any real independence and ingenuity, we're better off without you." Or the parent may keep the child in diapers until he is twenty-one. Depending upon the circumstances, the parent develops his child-rearing policy somewhere between these two extremes.

The board refuses to be foster parent to labor organizations which have the possibility of home care. In these cases it stresses self-organization and does not use its powers to determine an appropriate unit and hold an election in it. When the board is faced with a fight between two unions which do not have a common parent organization, however, it is forced to act.

There is usually little difficulty in determining the appropriate unit when the opposing unions are industrial in character. The chief question to decide is whether either union has a majority of the workers in the unit. This can quickly be settled by a secret ballot. In such cases the board immediately grants the request of either union for an investigation. If the board finds that neither of the unions is dominated by the employer and that a real question of representation exists, it polls the workers' preferences and certifies the winner.

Such elections have occurred between industrial locals

of the A. F. of L. and the C.I.O.; between either A. F. of
L. or C.I.O. unions and company or local independent
unions; between standard national independent unions
and any of the other three groups; and, in several instances, among three or more unions. Of the first 966 elections held by the board, 80.4 per cent were held without
protest by any of the parties concerned.[4] This number included not only industrial *vs.* industrial union elections,
but also the craft *vs.* industrial elections. In the pure industrial elections very little opposition by workers has
been experienced by the board. The certification of the
winner has usually brought to an end what might otherwise have been a prolonged and perhaps bloody interunion
fight. The losing union has almost invariably been willing
to abide by the result of the ballot. The work of the board
in this connection has saved workers, employers, and
consumers a considerable part of the cost of interunion
conflict.

Even when the unions involved are industrial in structure, however, the matter is not always simple. The question may arise in industrial elections whether the appropriate unit is the single plant, the company, or all the companies in a region. Although reference has already been
made to the case of the Pacific coast longshoremen, it will
bear repetition since it is the cause of profound dissatis-
faction among A. F. of L. adherents.[5]

Shipping and longshore work on the Pacific coast have
been in turmoil and in the public eye since 1933. In the
1933–36 period, the cause of the disturbance was the
effort of the revived labor movement to reëstablish itself
against one of the most determined antiunion groups of
employers in the country. In this effort, under new and
militant leadership, organized labor was remarkably suc-

cessful. Between 1936 and 1938, however, turmoil resulted chiefly from hostility between competing labor organizations.

Under the guidance of Harry Bridges, a new union, the Longshoremen and Warehousemen, was formed from the remains of an A. F. of L. affiliate and from the thousands of new recruits who poured in from the waterfronts all along the coast. Against this new movement were pitted the forces of Dave Beck's A. F. of L. Teamsters, other remnants of the old Longshoremen's Association, and various other A. F. of L. organizations.

This contest was deepened by a number of factors: (1) the entrance of the new Longshoremen's and Warehousemen's union to the C.I.O., the appointment of Harry Bridges as Western regional director of the C.I.O., and the fusing of maritime and inland unions under the C.I.O. banner against the consolidating A. F. of L. unions; (2) the "practical" politics of Pacific coast city machines in which labor forces often became involved in opposing camps; (3) the contrasting philosophies of union leaders divided among Republican, "nonpartisan," Socialist, and Communist faiths which resulted, for one thing, in lining up the Socialist-influenced Sailors' Union of the Pacific with the A. F. of L. instead of with the C.I.O.; (4) internal political and personal struggles in the C.I.O. unions; (5) the tendency of employers to play one group of workers against the other.

Into this embittered situation the board was thrust by an appeal from the C.I.O. longshoremen for certification as the bargaining agent for the entire Pacific coast longshore industry. This action was protested by employers and the A. F. of L. The nub of the situation was this. Of the 12,860 longshoremen on the Pacific coast, the C.I.O.

union had the membership of 9,557, or 74.3 per cent. It had a majority in each of the Pacific ports except four in Washington—Tacoma, Anacortes, Olympia, and Port Angeles. In these four ports, the A. F. of L. union was executing a contract with employers which had been signed before the splitting off of the C.I.O. locals. In all the other Pacific ports, the C.I.O. union was carrying out the same contract. The question was whether, in negotiations for a renewal of the contract, the C.I.O. union should deal for the entire coast, or whether each union should deal for the ports in which it had a majority.

The board found two outstanding facts bearing on the answer to this question. The first was that all the employers were bargaining together through the Waterfront Employers' Association of the Pacific. Both during the 1936 strike and in the subsequent period of peaceful collective dealing, representatives from each side spoke for the entire Pacific coast. The second fact was that collective bargaining on a local basis had been a failure. Bitter experience had proved this to both parties in the industry. The employers had found that their closely integrated interests compelled them to get together, and they had done so. The whole revival of the Pacific coast labor movement was based on the necessity for coastwise solidarity among longshoremen. This solidarity had been achieved and had led to relatively successful relations with an equally solid front of employers.

The united front of the longshore workers had been broken by an issue which was extraneous to successful collective bargaining. The political and personal rivalries between C.I.O. and A. F. of L. adherents had little bearing upon the economic issues of the employer-employee relationship. Yet they threatened the orderly handling of these economic issues. The board decided, in effect, that the relatively noneconomic interests of a 25 per cent minority of longshoremen were overshadowed by the economic interests of all the workers in the industry. It ordered employers to deal with the C.I.O. union for the Pacific coast as a single unit.

The A. F. of L. has denounced this decision on every occasion affording a suitable publicity medium. It regards the board's order as an annihilation of minority rights and an indication of pro-C.I.O. bias. It has announced its intention to fight such decisions by introducing amendments to the act which will make a repetition of them impossible.[6] It remains to be seen whether in the long run the basis for stable industrial relations on the Pacific coast has been laid. If so, this may be taken as justification for the board's decision. It is possible that the disaffection of the A. F. of L. unions will provide an opportunity for a renewal of the class war which characterized the 1933–36 period. If this occurs, some will place the responsibility at the feet of the board. Others will lay it upon the doorstep of A. F. of L. leadership.

In spite of occasional issues of this kind between industrial unions of different affiliations, the board's most frequent difficulties arise in connection with conflict between a craft union of one affiliation and an industrial union of another. The board must decide whether to hold an election with all of the production and maintenance workers as a single unit or to divide the plant up with the production workers as one unit and as many crafts as are identifiable in other units. In the first case, the craft workers' desires would frequently be swamped by the votes of the more numerous production workers. In the second case, the election may result in such a confusion of bargaining units as to destroy the workers' bargaining power.

During the first year of its operation the board was not disturbed by conflicts between A. F. of L. and C.I.O. unions. In 1936–37, however, these conflicts became acute. When they came before the board for settlement, it tended somewhat to favor the whole plant as the election unit. Since craft unions were almost sure to be swamped in these elections, this policy was denounced by the A. F. of L. Shortly before the 1937 A. F. of L. convention, the board adopted a modified policy which tended to allow craft unions a separate place on the ballot. This policy was denounced by the C.I.O. During the A. F. of L. convention, the C.I.O. was holding a conference in Atlantic City. At both meetings the board was condemned. The A. F. of L. damned the board for its early policy, and the C.I.O. for its later rulings. The public was treated to headlines coupling the A. F. of L. and the C.I.O. in common antipathy toward the board. This appeared to make antiboard sentiment almost unanimous.

The modified policy which invoked the indignation of the C.I.O. and failed to assuage the wrath of the A. F. of L. involved the following procedure: When the board is presented with conflicting appeals from craft and industrial unions, it first investigates the facts in the case. It attempts to discover whether the facts indicate clearly that one form of election or the other should be adopted outright. Sometimes it finds incontestable evidence that the claims of the craft union should be disregarded.[7] It may be, for example, that the craft union has only recently appeared on the scene; that it has no members; that no clear line of occupational, geographical, traditional, or financial

Courtesy of Elderman and the *Washington Post*.

HIS DECISIONS ARE QUESTIONED

separation can be discovered between the workers claimed
by the craft union and the rest of the workers in the plant.
In such a case, the board orders the election with the
whole plant as a unit. In other cases, however, the board
may find that the industrial union has no clear claims on
the craft workers; that the craft union has long been established and has a large majority of the eligible workers
as members; that clear lines of skill, method of payment,
and tradition separate them from the rest of the workers;
that the industrial union has failed to interest them and
that the industrial union's membership regulations ordinarily exclude the workers in question. Under these conditions, the board would order the holding of two separate
elections.[8] In one the craft workers would be given an
opportunity to vote for or against the craft union. In the
other, the production workers would ballot for or against
the industrial union.

It occasionally happens, however, that the evidence for
and against either policy is exactly balanced.[9] In these
cases the board has decided that the workers themselves
should determine the form of the bargaining unit. A vote
is taken in which the craft workers have three choices.
They may vote for the craft union, for the industrial
union, or for neither. The production workers, in another
election, have two choices—either for or against the industrial union. This form of election thus determines the
appropriate unit and the bargaining agent at the same
time. If the craft workers vote for the craft union and
the production workers for the industrial union, there are
two bargaining units, each with its own agent. If, however, both the craft workers and the production workers
vote for the industrial union, there is one bargaining unit
with one agent.

On the surface, this policy of the board in the debatable cases appears to allow to workers the absolute maximum of freedom to determine the form in which they shall be organized. What could be less dictatorial than giving the craft workers their choice among a craft union, an industrial union, or no union at all? What could be more democratic than allowing the production workers, ineligible to membership in the craft union, a choice between the industrial union or no union at all?

Actually, the decision of the board to allow the workers to select the appropriate unit is an evasion of the issue which favors the craft unions. The issue is: Shall a majority of the workers in a plant have a right to impose bargaining solidarity on all the workers in the plant, or shall craft workers, usually a distinct minority, have the right to make this decision? The board's policy in debatable cases puts it up to the minority to decide. The only time a craft union can lose is when a majority of the craft workers do not want the craft union. If a majority of the workers in a small but perhaps strategically located craft want separate representation and a separate contract, they can nullify the wishes of an overwhelming majority for plant-wide solidarity. This is a distinct departure from the principle of industrial unionism.

It is difficult to see how the A. F. of L. can find fault with the board in this connection. Although the C.I.O. has ceased its attack on the board in recognition of the board's great contribution to the cause of labor in general, the A. F. of L., on the contrary, has bitterly renewed its attack and proposes amendments to the act which will compel the board to go even further in the direction of craft unionism.

The A. F. of L. now favors the Railway Labor Act as

Courtesy of H. I. Carlisle and the *New York Herald Tribune*

SOMEBODY STOLE MY GAL

a model for amendments to the N.L.R.A.[10] Under the Railway Labor Act the National Mediation Board is obliged to hold elections and certify the winners within appropriate *classes* or *crafts* of workers. It has no authority to go beyond these units. For this policy on the railroads there is some defense. First, occupational distinctions on the railroads are sufficiently great to make craft demarcations possible in spite of occasional conflict over borderline cases. Second, the historical development of railroad unionism has been along craft lines. Third, the separate crafts act with such unity through joint boards that an approach to industrial solidarity is achieved. United workers dealing with united managers make possible one of the most successful examples of collective bargaining in the history of industrial relations.

For a policy of uniform imposition of craft unionism upon American industry in general there is no defense whatever, except the vested interests of a few craft officials. In the basic or mass-production industries there are frequently no occupational distinctions, no union traditions, and no union solidarity. To impose craft organization by government action upon workers in these industries would stultify collective bargaining from both the employer's and the worker's points of view. No more effective strait jacket could be devised except an outright interdict against trade unionism. From such a strait jacket the rank and file of the A. F. of L., with its directly affiliated industrial locals, its industrial departments of craft unions, and its national industrial unions, would suffer as much as the C.I.O.

Aesop told a fable about a dog trotting across a bridge with a big piece of meat in his mouth. When the dog reached the middle of the bridge, he saw what he thought was another dog with another piece of meat in his mouth. Being covetous, the dog on the bridge snapped viciously at his reflection in the water. Upon opening his mouth, his own meat fell into the stream. Aesop did not say whether the dog, having mistaken shadow for substance, then sat down upon his tail and howled. The presumption is that he did.

In the West Allis plant of the Allis Chalmers Company three A. F. of L. unions began organizing in 1933.[11] The Electrical Workers were successful in their efforts until 1935, but after that they began to lose ground. The Molders did not enroll more than 150 out of 1,000 eligible workers and the Machinists never created an effective organization. A directly affiliated industrial local of the A. F. of L. was started in the fall of 1935, but it made little progress against the competing efforts of the craft unions. Accordingly, in the late summer of 1936, the industrial local made efforts to expand its jurisdiction to cover workers claimed by the craft unions. This move was blocked by local and national A. F. of L. officials.

The industrial local, therefore, left the A. F. of L. in March, 1937, and joined the United Automobile Workers of the C.I.O. Within two months, the new C.I.O. local enlisted 7,000 of the 10,000 workers in the plant. Having received a contract from the company to bargain for its own members, the union appealed to the board for certification as exclusive bargaining agent.

The A. F. of L. intervened. Its counsel asserted that the plant should be divided up into eleven or more craft units! Upon considering this claim, the board found that six of the crafts concerned did not have enough interest to appear at the hearings. At least three others did not present evidence of membership sufficient to warrant further investigation. Two others, the Electricians and the Firemen and Oilers, were given a separate place on the ballot. The workers in these crafts were allowed to choose between the A. F. of L. unions and the C.I.O. union, while all the other production and maintenance workers were given a choice for or against the C.I.O.

Board member Edwin S. Smith dissented from this decision. He pointed out that the whole development in the plant had been overwhelmingly in the direction of industrial unionism; that the device of holding elections in the craft units was an abandonment of the judicial function of the board; that the "pseudodemocratic" poll permitted a small minority to control a decision of intense importance to a great majority; and that this decision threatened the future of collective bargaining at the plant. Without necessarily concurring in this dissent, it may be observed that the board showed great concern for the interests of A. F. of L. minorities at the expense of C.I.O. majorities.

In the Combustion Engineering Company decision the majority of the board went even further.[12] Without dissent from any party, the board first set aside the foundry workers as an appropriate unit to be represented by the Molders' Union. It then set off two other units among machinists and boilermakers in which the workers were to choose between the Machinists' and Boilermakers' Unions on the one hand, and the Steel Workers' Organizing Committee on the other. This decision was made in spite of the fact that the Machinists and Boilermakers had attempted to organize, between them, all of the workers in the plant outside the foundry. Having failed in this attempt, the unions fell back upon their craft strongholds and asserted the right to represent them, although the Steel Workers' Organizing Committee had been organizing upon an industrial basis and all the collective bargaining which had taken place was plant-wide in scope.

Board member Edwin S. Smith again dissented on the general ground that this was a "Heads, I win; tails, you lose" proposition not designed to promote satisfactory collective bargaining in this type of industry. Board member Donald W. Smith concurred in the decision with slight reservations.

With these decisions the A. F. of L. is not content. President William Green has condemned Edwin S. Smith as "impossible." [13] The executive council of the A. F. of L., in urging that the N.L.R.A. be amended to conform to the Railway Labor Act, is proposing, for example, that in the West Allis plant the board be compelled to divide up the plant into eleven appropriate units. The history of organizing efforts in this plant between 1933 and 1937 strongly suggests that if there were eleven unions there would be no members and no collective bargaining. Aesop wrote about another dog which, being unable to eat hay, nevertheless drove away the cattle which found nourishment in this fodder.

Ironically, the present election policy of the board is almost exactly that which was adopted by the A. F. of L. in 1934 before the C.I.O. split.[14] The issue was the same then as now. In automobiles, steel, rubber, glass, cement, aluminum, and other basic and mass-production industries, some workers or unions wanted industrial organizations covering all the production and maintenance workers in a plant. Other workers or unions wanted separate organizations for each of the occupational groups in these industries. The decision of the convention was a compromise. The production workers in these industries were told that they might have their big industrial unions covering the majority of workers in a plant. But, it was added, whenever it was possible to discover one or more groups of workers with separate skills, traditions, desires, and so on, these workers should be separated out and allowed to join their appropriate craft union. This decision, reaffirmed in the 1935 convention on the eve of the C.I.O. exodus, failed to work.

It is difficult to say how much of this failure was due to lack of good faith on both sides. It is unquestionable, however, that it could not have worked in the absence of any means of interpretation and enforcement. The parties concerned were simply left to fight it out for themselves. Speculation as to whether the C.I.O. split might have been avoided if there had been machinery for the application of the agreement is useless. It is noteworthy, however, that the machinery for effecting the A. F. of L.'s own 1934 program does now exist in the form of the National Labor Relations Board.

The extent of the board's contribution to interunion peace may be judged by the fact that of the first 966 elections held by the board, 563, or 58 per cent, involved two unions or more. The distribution of these conflicts among different union groups is shown by the table below.[15]

The peaceful settlement of the tangled conflict of claims presented in this table represents an accomplishment of great significance to industrial peace. Although the framers of the act did not foresee this situation, it is interesting to think about what might have happened to interunion relations if the services of the board had not been available as a means of amicable adjustment.

Perhaps the most significant item in this table is the fact that in the first 208 election contests involving both the A. F. of L. and the C.I.O., the A. F. of L. won only

Elections *	No.	Won by: A.F.L.	Opponent	Per Cent of Victories A.F.L.
A.F.L. *vs.* C.I.O.:	208	48	160	23
Ind. U.:	7	4	3	57
Co. U.:	71	43	28	60
A.F.L.:	6	6		
All Unions:	292	101	191	35

	No.	C.I.O.	Opponent	C.I.O.
C.I.O. *vs.* A.F.L.:	208	160	48	77
Ind. U.:	4	3	1	75
Co. U.:	117	64	53	55
Mixed:	3	2	1	67
All Unions:	332	229	103	69

	No.	Co. U.	Opponent	Co. U.
Co. U. *vs.* A.F.L.:	71	28	43	40
C.I.O.:	117	53	64	45
Ind. U.:	5	4	1	80
Co. U.:	2	2		
Mixed:	3	1	2	33
All Unions:	198	88	110	44

	No.	Ind. U.	Opponent	Ind. U.
Ind. U. *vs.* A.F.L.:	7	3	4	43
C.I.O.:	4	1	3	25
Co. U.:	5	1	4	20
All Unions:	16	5	11	31

23 per cent. This fact has been made the basis for much of the bitterness of the A. F. of L. toward the board. Such bitterness is, in some respects, comparable to an attack on the use of voting machines because they record the victory of the party with the largest number of votes. In the great majority of cases, the board is as powerless to affect the outcome of an election as an honestly operated ballot box or voting machine.

* "Ind. U." stands for "independent national unions"; "Co. U." stands for "company unions" or "local independent unions."

Courtesy of Elderman and the *Washington*

YOU GAVE HIM THE MOST ICING!

But in a small minority of cases the selection of the appropriate unit does affect the outcome of the election. It is of importance to know exactly what proportion of elections is affected by the nature of the voting unit. As noted above, there were 208 A. F. of L. *vs.* C.I.O. elections before January 1, 1938. Between January 1 and September 1, 1938, there were approximately 200 more of these elections.[16] By the fall of 1938, therefore, there had been 408. In these 408 elections the question of the appropriate unit was raised 130 times. In 60 of these 130 instances, it was the employer who raised the issue while the unions concerned were in complete agreement. In 22 other cases, minor matters of inclusion or exclusion of very small groups which could not have determined the outcome of the elections were the points at issue between the unions. These questions were settled without difficulty. There remained 48 cases in which the determination of the appropriate unit was of vital importance to the outcome of the election. These cases included craft *vs.* industrial, single plant *vs.* several plants, and local *vs.* regional issues. Of these 48 cases, 24 were clearly settled in favor of the A. F. of L.; 19 were clearly settled in favor of the C.I.O.; and five cases were compromised, but with the A. F. of L. receiving a slight advantage in four instances.[17]

It is therefore impossible to conclude that the board's policies explain the relative success of the C.I.O. in board elections. If an arithmetic test be applied, the board has leaned slightly, if at all, toward the A. F. of L. The relatively rapid advance of the C.I.O. must be explained in terms other than the partisanship of the ballot box.

The powers of the board give it the flexibility necessary to apply diverse policies under the variety of conditions which face it in American industry. Its prestige among union leaders is sufficient to bring about compliance with its decisions in the great majority of cases. There are indications that this relatively happy state of affairs may be brought to an end by legislative changes and by the refusal of losing unions to abide by board decisions.

Amendment of the N.L.R.A. to make it conform to the Railway Labor Act would destroy collective bargaining outright in some industries, would harass the employer with complex negotiations in others, and would multiply the points of jurisdictional conflict in the industries in which unionism survived. None of these developments can be considered a conspicuous advance toward industrial peace.

Refusal to abide by board decisions may take the form of strikes and picket lines conducted by the losing union against employers dealing with the winning union. Jurisdictional strikes now vary between 4 and 8.8 per cent of all strikes.[18] Any significant increase in this percentage is likely to lead to demands that board awards be made legally binding upon the losing union.

This could be done in at least two ways: first, by denying to unions the privileges of the act in proceedings against employers unless they conformed to board decisions in interunion affairs. Such a policy would be unfortunate since its chief impact would be upon workers who need all the protection they can get. The unions which are most likely to resist board decisions are those in which the rank and file have the least control over their officers. Workers needing protection against antiunion discrimination may be denied this protection from the act by the policies of officers over whom they may have little control. Although in the long run workers would get out of unions which were denied the benefits of the act, in the transition period they might undergo needless privation as a result of the shortsightedness of their officers.

Second, losing unions might be induced to abide by board decisions if the Norris-LaGuardia Act were amended specifically to permit federal courts to enjoin any strike against a board decision. Such injunctions could be made sufficiently sweeping to paralyze union activity in any strike of this nature. This also would be unfortunate. Injunction law has not succeeded in the past in inducing industrial peace. The Norris-LaGuardia Act marked a recognition of this fact. The N.L.R.A. went further by substituting administrative handling of human relations in industry for judicial repression. The advantage of the administrative process lies in its flexibility, in the expertness of administrators in their specialized fields, and in the general concept of removing the cause of trouble rather than suppressing the results. The leaders of organized labor will be shortsighted indeed if, by refusal to accept the board's decisions in interunion conflicts, they provoke legislative reaction.

Thus far, the interests of employers in interunion fights have been considered only indirectly. Although the fundamental philosophy of the act is that it is the workers' affair, and theirs alone, to decide whether they want one union or another, or none at all, the employer and the consumer are clearly interested in producing goods. If interunion conflicts interrupt production, the employer is entitled to ask whether he may not appeal to the board to put an end to the conflict. The act does not now provide formally for appeal by employers to the board for relief from union behavior. Should not the employer at least be allowed to request the board to hold an election and find out which union he is supposed to deal with?

It is probable that too much fuss is being made about this proposal by both its proponents and its opponents. Opponents say, first, that employers would use this power of appeal as an antiunion weapon by calling for an election before either union was well started in its organizing work. The psychological effect of defeat for both unions early in their careers would inhibit further organizing efforts. If only one union were present, an additional incentive would be provided to the employer to start an "independent" union in order to make possible an appeal for an election. Second, it is asserted that allowing employers to appeal would swamp the board with work which would prevent it from carrying on its more fundamental activities. Third, it is asserted that employers are really not badly off since they can almost always arrange informally for an election and can always force the board to intervene by refusing to deal with either union until the board has certified one as the workers' bargaining agent.

Against these contentions it may be said, first, that the board can prevent employers' appeals from becoming antiunion weapons by investigating each case to discover whether it is really an instance of serious interunion conflict or whether antiunionism is the motive. Second, the New York State Labor Relations Board permits employers to appeal for elections and has by no means been swamped with work. During its first year it received 46 petitions from employers as compared with 918 from workers or their representatives.[19] Third, if it is true in fact that employers can arrange or compel the board to intervene in interunion conflicts, it might as well be true in form.

The indications are that the matter has become a symbolic battle flag of pro- and antiboard forces. Anyone winning the flag would not win much. But anyone losing it would appear to have suffered a serious defeat. The issue is likely to become even more dramatic and less real if a formal amendment calling for this change in the act is introduced in the 1939 session of Congress.[20] The histrionics could be avoided and the essential results achieved if the board were itself to adopt a regulation permitting employer appeals. Section 9 (c) of the act now reads:

Whenever a question affecting commerce arises concerning the representation of employees, the Board may investigate such controversy and certify to the parties, in writing, the name or names of the representatives that have been designated or selected. In any such investigation, the Board shall provide for an appropriate hearing upon due notice . . . and may take a secret ballot of employees or utilize any other suitable method to ascertain such representatives.

There is nothing in this section to prevent the board from adopting a regulation permitting appeals for elections by employers.

The importance of interunion conflict as a disturbing factor in industrial relations should not be exaggerated. The fact that such conflicts average only about 6 per cent of the total number of strikes is a fair index of their relative unimportance. They should not, however, be overlooked. They have always been a thorn in the side of labor as well as of employers and the public.

By placing responsibility upon the A. F. of L. and the C.I.O. for the solution of internal difficulties and by adopting a flexible and realistic policy of settlement where no other means exists, the National Labor Relations Board is making an important contribution to industrial peace. Unions which temporarily suffer from board decisions will do well to refrain from lending support to legislative reaction.

Courtesy of Henry and the *CIO News*.

TO SPITE HIS FACE

CHAPTER VII

THE UNFAIR PRACTICES OF LABOR

THE Wagner Act is one sided. There is not a word in it about the unfair practices of labor organizations. It is directed against the employer exclusively. It is a biased and partisan piece of legislation. As such it encourages intimidation of workers, racketeering, gangsterism, irresponsibility and violence by union leaders and members. The act must be amended to outlaw these unfair practices of labor." [1]

Charges of this nature have been the daily fare of newspaper readers since the passage of the N.L.R.A. and, more particularly, since its validation by the Supreme Court in April, 1937. It is perfectly true that the act contains no references to the unfair practices of labor and that important sections of it are concerned with preventing employers from denying to workers the right to collective bargaining. Does it therefore follow that the act is one-sided and should be amended to bring it in balance?

Until the coming of the New Deal, there were no laws to prevent employers from using their economic power to defeat collective bargaining. The antiunion use of economic power was not only legal; it was a property right enforceable in the courts. There were no effective laws against black lists, white lists, yellow-dog contracts, espionage, propaganda, and professional strikebreaking. There were no laws against company-dominated unions or the use of economic power to mobilize communities into antiunion citizens' committees and back-to-work movements. There were laws against beating, kidnaping, and murdering, but in many antiunion communities these laws were not enforceable when the victims were union sympathizers.

It was apparent that neither local ordinance nor state law could fill this legal vacuum, since industries indiscriminately crossed local and state lines. If the obstacles to collective bargaining were to be removed by legal action, no agency short of the federal government could accomplish the task. The National Labor Relations Act was the result of this situation.[2] By interpretation, the act can be turned against all of the forms of antiunionism which were previously uninhibited by law. Did this create a one-sided legal condition in which labor was left free to do as it pleased?

A list of the unfair practices which are commonly attributed to labor organizations would include intimidation and coercion of workers by organizers, violence toward nonunion workers, mass picketing, stay-in strikes and boycotts; jurisdictional strikes, sympathetic strikes, strikes for the closed shop and strikes in violation of a contract; irresponsibility, racketeering, corruption, monopolistic practices, and autocracy. These practices cannot be bundled together under one blanket. They involve a variety of problems. They may be grouped in three general classes: (1) assaults on personal and property rights; (2) the legality of certain kinds of strikes; (3) the internal shortcomings of unionism.

Group action of any sort involves pressure by the group against the individual. Whether it is a college fraternity "rushing" prospective members, a trade association persuading a reluctant producer to abide by a cost-plus agreement, a state requiring its drivers to stay on the right side of the road, or a group of small boys removing the Eton collar of a city slicker, varying degrees of compulsion are used by the group to assure the conformity of individuals. This is no less true of labor organizations. The leaders or organizers of a union are those who usually exert the pressure against reluctant individuals.

Pressure against individual workers assumes a whole spectrum of forms ranging from verbal persuasion to physical violence. Somewhere in this spectrum the allowable forms of pressure pass over into forms forbidden by the well-being of society, the labor movement, and of the individuals who compose it. It is an unhealthy society which fosters groups whose existence depends upon violent compulsions. In the long run, the labor movement cannot prosper if it feeds upon violence. The interests of the individual worker clearly demand protection from violent forms of compulsion.

The point at which society should interfere in the use of group pressure against individuals varies with the circumstances. This is exactly the situation at present. Various interpretations of common law and a variety of state laws and local ordinances are applicable against the anti-social practices of labor organizations and their leaders. Moral intimidation or physical violence, all forms of picketing, all forms of trespass or damage to property, and all forms of boycott are completely covered by some kind of law, and have been covered for the last hundred years. State laws against assault, kidnaping, murder, violence in any form and threats of violence; common law against conspiracy and restraint of trade; local ordinances against obstructing sidewalks, loitering, vagrancy, disturbing the peace, blocking traffic, and a variety of other misdemeanors—all these may be applied against union members in police courts, state courts, or federal courts.

The passage of the N.L.R.A. did not repeal these laws. They remain enforceable and in many communities are enforced with excessive severity.[3] Does anyone want a federal administrative agency to assume jurisdiction over these matters? In answering this question, the contrast should be indicated between the manner in which an anti-union employer is treated under the act and the way in which many a picket is now handled by the police.

The N.L.R.A. involves no criminal procedure. If an employer is charged with an unfair practice such as discharging union members, the board investigates the charge, issues a complaint, holds hearings before a trial examiner, issues a trial examiner's report, studies this report, makes a decision, and orders the employer to comply. If the employer appeals from the board's order to a circuit court, and from the circuit court to the Supreme Court, and then continues his refusal to comply with the order, it is up to the circuit court to begin contempt proceedings against him. Only at this point may compliance be compelled. In the meantime, there is no jail, no fine, and no criminal record for the employer.

If, on the other hand, an employer or "loyal" workers complain to the police about the behavior of a group of union members, what happens? In a few communities the answer is "nothing." The police or the local magistrates may decide that the "loyal" workers are really professional strikebreakers trying to start trouble, or that the union workers are in fact perfectly orderly, or that if they are disorderly it is not the union's fault, or that the employer is wrong anyway and few workers support him, or that it is too close to election time to do anything about it.

In many other communities, however, the Black Maria swoops down upon the union members, the leaders are seized and shoved into the patrol wagon, the arrested men are literally thrown into the jug, excessive bail is set, the prisoners are "mugged" and thus commence a criminal record which will be used against them the next time the raid is repeated, heavy fines or jail terms are meted out, and justice dusts off its hands.

Suppose that, instead of this procedure, anyone suffering from actual or threatened injury to person or property in connection with a labor dispute were compelled to appeal to the board for relief. After charges against the offending persons had been made, the board would investigate. Soon the accused workers would receive polite but formal notes asking them to appear at the regional office on a certain date in company with the persons aggrieved. There would ensue a friendly and informal conversation in which the field examiner would attempt to mend the broken fabric of human relations. If the accused were hard boiled and nothing came of this conference, notice of a formal hearing would be given.

Counsel for the accused workers, the board, and the injured parties would appear. The accused workers would be politely addressed as "the respondents." A thorough investigation of the entire background of the situation would take place in the course of the hearing. A trial examiner's intermediate report would be issued and the respondents given a chance to desist from their tactics.

If the respondents were still adamant, the trial examiner's report would go to Washington. There it would be studied by the board and about six months after the original charge was made (provided that the board was pretty well up with its work), the respondents might be ordered to desist from their tactics—mass picketing, for example. But if the union thought that a vital issue was at stake, it might appeal for relief from the board's order to the circuit court. If it lost again, it might manage to discover a constitutional issue among the few remaining untested by employer appeals. If the Supreme Court upheld the circuit court, the respondents would be legally beaten, but might still be unbowed. They might keep on picketing, or boycotting, or intimidating. The circuit court would begin contempt proceedings against them. Finally, each of the workers found in contempt might be sentenced to three months in jail and for the first time the police would get their hands on the offenders. But for the board, they could have served a year in jail and been out by this time.

With respect to stay-in strikes the case is essentially similar. In spite of the fact that a stay-in strike is likely to result in less violence than a walkout of equal size, it offends state or common law against trespass and federal or common law against restraint of trade. Stay-in strikes are therefore enjoinable in both state and federal courts subject to the slight limitations imposed by the Norris-LaGuardia Act and its satellites in some states. Any employer aggrieved by a stay-in strike can go immediately to a state or federal court for an injunction. Rarely will he be required to establish "clean hands" or prove "equal loss."

If there is any delay or difficulty in securing the injunction from a federal court, the state courts are more immediately available. If the strikers defy the injunction, it is a matter of hours or days before clubs, tear gas, nausea gas, machine guns, and storming towers in the hands of local police and deputies or state militia can be put in action against the trespassers. Only when the eviction would involve a minor civil war or when state or local officials decide that mass violence would not essentially improve the situation, as in the case of the General Motors strike, is there a delay of more than a week or ten days in accomplishing repossession of the plant. Scores of stay-in strikes have been quelled in this manner in the last two years.

Contrast this with the situation which would exist if the N.L.R.B. were entrusted with the task of dealing with stay-inners. Before the board could order the eviction of the strikers it would have to investigate. This is a persistent habit of the board's staff formed in dealing with employers under the act as it now stands. The investigation might show that the strike was caused by the refusal of the employer to bargain with the accredited representatives of the workers. Just as the board now refuses to order the reinstatement of workers until it is proved that their discharge is a violation of the act, the board would refuse to order the eviction of the strikers until it found that a violation of the law by the employer was not the cause of the strike.

Even if the board did find that the strike was not the result of an unfair practice by the employer, but was caused by his inability to meet the union's terms after bargaining in good faith with it, the board could not itself enforce its eviction order. If the workers refused to pay any attention to the order of a circuit court, they would then be in contempt. The only difference between this and the present situation would be that the strikers would be in contempt of a circuit court instead of a state or district court, and that this procedure would take six months or more, instead of the present week or ten days.

Good friends of organized labor might find much of value in current proposals to give the board jurisdiction over alleged intimidation and coercion of workers, violence or threats of violence, boycotts, mass picketing,

stay-in strikes, and damage to employers' property occurring in connection with labor disputes. The results of
the board's methods of dealing with these issues might be
much superior in the long run to the summary "justice"
characteristic of much state and local control. The training, patience, and knowledge of federal administrators, the
uniformity of principle which the scope of their jurisdiction makes possible, and the substitution of a scientific
for a punitive point of view are all attractive aspects of
the board's work as compared with that of local authorities.

It is difficult to believe, however, that this is what the
proponents of change in the act are really after. The granting of jurisdiction to the board over these unfair practices
of labor would involve a rapid growth of federal power
at the expense of local and state rights. Such an extension
of federal power would multiply the administrative staff
and the funds necessary for the board's work. Ironically,
it is those who are most bitter about the extension of
federal power in the present version of the act who are
most vocal in their demands that it be further extended.
It would appear, therefore, that such proposals to expand
the board's jurisdiction are either ill-founded political shib-
boleths or mere attacks on the board, made in bad faith
since there is no desire that the proposals be adopted.

The present policies of the board do have some bearing
upon the unfair practices of labor listed in the first group.
Although intimidation of nonunion workers by union organizers is exaggerated out of all relation to reality, it
does unquestionably take place. The election policies of
the board are planned to eliminate intimidation either by
employers or organizers as completely as the machinery of

democracy is ever able to accomplish freedom from compulsion.

Balloting takes place in a closed booth. The ballots are clear and simple. There is no possibility of tampering with them either before or after they are given to the voter. Watchers for the employer, the unions involved, and the board are invariably invited to scrutinize each voter's claim to the franchise. Contested ballots are carefully investigated.[4]

When the board certifies a union without an election, it assures itself that there has been no intimidation by union leaders in securing the membership cards or signatures upon which the certification is based. If there is any doubt about freedom from intimidation, the board holds an election.[5]

The process of choosing a union, which was sometimes carried on in the preboard era with fists, brass knuckles, bats, stones, and guns under the docks and in the back alleys, now takes place with increasing frequency in the solitude of a voting booth. There, a worker is alone with a ballot, a pencil, and his inclinations.

The second relation of the board to the unfair practices of labor is negative. The question is often raised whether the board should order an employer to reinstate workers who have engaged in illegal practices. The board's final position in this matter is as follows: If workers have been convicted of criminal offenses such as aggravated assault, wilful destruction of property, kidnaping, murder, and so on during the course of a labor dispute, the board does not order their reinstatement along with other striking workers entitled to their jobs.

If, however, workers have been convicted of misdemeanors which ordinarily occur during labor disputes, the board does not find this a bar to their reinstatement or an obstacle to ordering the employer to bargain with the union of which they are members. The reasoning in these cases is that if the strike was caused by unfair practices on the part of the employer, he shares responsibility for the acts committed by workers in connection with the strike. The employer should therefore be ordered to reinstate those whose misdemeanors resulted from the strike.[6] It should be noted that the board's order of reinstatement, in these cases, does not free the workers from prosecution by local and state authorities.

The second group of alleged unfair practices of labor includes a variety of strikes whose objectives are considered to be antisocial. Strikes for jurisdiction over members or jobs, strikes in sympathy with other workers, strikes for the closed shop, and strikes in defiance of an existing contract are those which are commonly included in this category.

From a utopian point of view, all strikes are senseless. There is no more point to settling questions of precise economic adjustment by resort to strikes and lockouts than there was to settling matters of justice through trial by ordeal. Modern industrial conflicts represent only a slight advance over medieval methods of settling human differences. Tear gas and propaganda have been substituted for fire and water.

But we do not live in a utopia in which wage incomes are meticulously balanced against the prices of finished goods, profits carefully determined in relation to the need for capital, and working hours painstakingly adjusted to productivity. We are not likely to move into a planned utopia overnight. We have moved out of a society (if we

Courtesy of Talburt and the *Washington Daily N*

SLIGHTLY WARPED!

ever occupied it) in which economic balance was maintained by the operation of free competition. We cannot go back to it without surrendering modern methods of production and accepting a society in which far less than our present population and living standards could be maintained.[7]

Collective bargaining and peaceful arbitration of wage, hour, and profit relations are a step in the direction of planning for economic balance. The greater the area of industry whose problems are focused in a single bargaining relationship, the closer the approach to real economic planning. In the American railroad industry, for example, the development of collective bargaining has reached a point at which the sporadic small-scale strikes of the past have been almost entirely eliminated by the machinery of arbitration. The threat of a large-scale strike with all of railroad labor and management lined up on opposite sides carries with it such immense dangers to all of the parties concerned with railroading that the principals are compelled to face the situation in terms of long-range planning for the industry. Sheer economic force has to give way to an attempt, at least, to plan the future of railroading because the problem is presented to the participants upon an industry-wide basis. But the development of such economic planning is still in its early infancy in most of the rest of American industry. Strikes represent one of the growing pains of collective bargaining. How much will be gained by prohibiting certain kinds of growing pains?

The N.L.R.A. does not prohibit any kind of strike. In fact it says, "Nothing in this Act shall be construed so as to interfere with or impede or diminish in any way the right to strike." [8] Should the act be amended to prohibit strikes over jurisdiction, strikes in sympathy with other workers, strikes for the closed shop, and strikes in defiance of an existing contract?

The answer to this question lies in considering the social value of the objectives listed. Jurisdictional strikes have already been discussed. In summary of this discussion it may be repeated here that, first, jurisdictional conflicts within a single federation such as the A. F. of L. ought probably to be left to the workers themselves. Prohibiting such conflicts by injunction will not settle them. Intervention by the board will not tend to foster the self-discipline which organized labor must eventually have if it is to play its part in planning for economic welfare. Second, where there is no common machinery for settling conflicts between unions, the board has already stepped in. It has substituted its judgment and trial by ballot for trial by combat. This marks an advance whose effectiveness is to be judged by the hundreds of peacefully conducted elections between competing unions. Third, the public acceptance of the board's work might be improved if it were to allow employers as well as unions to appeal for investigation and possible settlement of jurisdictional conflicts.

Sympathetic strikes are those in which one group of workers stops work in order to help another group which has walked out. They are usually confined to one industry, but sometimes occur in different industries in the same community. They are a visible expression of the idea of solidarity among workers. Belief in their prevalence is frequently the basis for opposition by employers to dealing with outside unions. The fear that national officers will call a strike of a local which is having no trouble with the employer in order to support striking workers elsewhere often persuades employers to resist the advances of affiliated unions. Though this fear may be real, the basis for it is slight. Less than one per cent of all strikes called in any normal period are sympathetic strikes.[9] How important is this issue?

Much has been made of it in attacks on the N.L.R.A. based on comparisons between British and American labor law. It has been repeated almost endlessly by columnists and editorial writers that the British Trades Disputes Act of 1927 prohibited sympathetic strikes. Students of labor who have insisted that this simply was not true have made little headway. The report of the President's committee to study British labor relations, however, has now given wide publicity to the following facts: The Trades Disputes Act does not forbid sympathetic strikes in one industry. Sympathetic strikes in different industries are not forbidden unless they are designed to bring pressure to bear upon the government. No suit has been brought against a British trade union under this law in the eleven years it has been on the books. In the years 1923, 1924, and 1925 there were forty-three sympathetic strikes involving 71,000 workers, while in the years 1934, 1935, and 1936 there were thirty-nine involving 120,000.[10] This reference to British law and experience may not prove much, but at least the Trades Disputes Act cannot be cited as a reason for adopting a prohibition of sympathetic strikes in this country.

Sympathetic strikes are rarely used in a competitive industry because they are bad strategy. If a union has called a strike against one producer it is no more than good sense to keep his competitor going in order to hasten the collapse of the strike-bound employer. Prohibition of sym pathetic strikes in these cases would simply compel unions to adopt good strategy. This is probably not what is intended by supporters of a ban on sympathetic strikes.

Strikes which cover an entire industry at once are usually called general strikes. In so far as any strikes are socially valuable, these "sympathetic" strikes in competitive industries are perhaps most valuable of all. Their object is to impose standard wage and hour conditions throughout the whole industry at once. This is often the only way in which standardization can be accomplished. The employers who provide the best wage, hour, and working conditions often welcome such strikes since they are designed to bring their less provident or efficient competitors into line. The chief hope of peaceful collective bargaining rests upon its adoption upon an industry-wide basis. General strikes in one industry are a step in this direction. Bargaining between the representatives of different interests in a whole industry may not eliminate strikes altogether, but all British experience and such experience as we have had in the railroad, clothing, coal, and a few other industries suggest that it at least diminishes the frequency, duration, and violence of industrial conflicts.

The most common and effective form of sympathetic strike is that which resembles a boycott. Workers in one industry sometimes strike against the handling of "hot" goods from another nonunion or antiunion industry.[11] If the "hot" goods come from an antiunion industry there would seem to be little question about the desirability of allowing organized workers in another industry to help defeat antiunionism. Such strikes are means of helping to enforce national policy. As antiunionism disappears, these strikes will disappear. If, however, the "hot" goods come from an industry that is merely unorganized, the problem is different.

It would appear to be a shortsighted policy to attempt to organize a nonunion industry by striking against its products in an organized industry. Stable unionism rests upon the reasoned acceptance by workers of the idea of collective action. Some compulsion of individuals or small groups is always involved in collective action. The greater and more violent the compulsion, however, the less stable the collective action based upon it. Thus far labor leaders have made negligible use of this method of organizing nonunion industries.[12]

The National Labor Relations Act specifically permits unions to demand and secure the *closed shop* provided that the unions making or securing this demand are freely chosen by a majority of the workers in an appropriate unit and provided that there is no evidence of collusion between an employer and a union in establishing the closed-shop relationship.[13] By implication, therefore, strikes for the closed shop are also legalized as far as the act is concerned. Should the act be amended to delegalize strikes whose major objective is to impose the closed shop upon an employer and upon nonunion workers? This question is of much greater importance than the question of sympathetic strikes since about 10 per cent of all strikes are directed toward the closed shop, as compared with less than 1 per cent of sympathetic strikes.[14]

The distinction between a closed shop and a *closed union* should be made clear. A closed-shop agreement simply requires that all workers hired by the employer shall join the union at the time of hiring or within a stated period afterward. It leaves the choice of workers up to the employer. He can hire whomever he pleases and fire whomever he pleases, as far as a closed-shop agreement is concerned. The closed shop does not create a monopoly of the labor supply by the union since the employer can expand or contract his labor force at will. The closed shop is not itself a hardship on the employer, except to the extent that it increases the union's bargaining power. The chief effect of the closed shop is upon the minority of workers who are unwilling to join the union.

When the closed shop is combined with a closed union, however, a tight monopoly is created which may injure the employer, nonunion workers, and consumers. That is, if the union seriously restricts membership, the effect upon costs of production, prices, sales, and employment is indistinguishable from the effect of any other monopoly—a small minority gains at the expense of the great majority.

The demand for the closed shop rests upon two motives: the desire to prevent a minority of nonunion "chiselers" from securing, free of charge, the advantages for which the union members have paid; and a desire to prevent the employer from defeating the union by gradually transforming a nonunion minority into an antiunion majority.

The first motive is understandable enough to anyone who has ever taken part in group activity. The majority, especially if it is a large majority, almost always feels that the minority ought to pay "its share of the freight." Even individualistic employers sometimes agree with this point of view. In a small New England factory an employer was recently conferring with C.I.O. union representatives about the renewal of their contract. The employer said that he was satisfied with the contract except that he hated to see a "small bunch of workers who were perfectly able to pay, riding on the coat tails of the rest of the men."

There was no possible taint of collusion in this case since the union in question had a large majority, had worked hard for its bargaining status, and was entirely unopposed by any other competing union.[15]

More often, however, the employer takes the position that he will close down his plant before he will permit a minority of his men to be coerced by a majority. In these cases, the union frequently persists in its demand because of a strong suspicion that the real intention of the employer is to get rid of the union altogether as soon as possible. At this point the conflict tends to arrange itself around two unreal symbols: the "closed" shop *vs.* the "open" shop.

Neither side means exactly what it says. The union may be content with less than a closed shop if it can be assured of a secure position. In demanding an "open" shop the employer frequently wants so large a proportion of non-union men that the union is powerless as a bargaining agent. This is perfectly apparent when the "open shop" is accompanied by the other antiunion policies of employers who make the greatest stir over the closed-shop issue. The real matter at stake is not the open *vs.* the closed shop, but unionism *vs.* antiunionism. When a union is not even asking for the closed shop and the employer persists in condemning the union publicly for demanding it, the closed-shop issue becomes perfectly transparent. This was the case, for example, in the Little Steel strike of 1937.

Should the act be amended to meet this complex situation? It may be expected first that, as antiunionism diminishes in power, the closed-shop issue will become less important. This appears to have been the British experience. But antiunionism in this country has been more bitter and persistent than in England. It may, therefore, take longer to overcome its effects. On the other hand, the reaction against the extremes of antiunionism in this country took the form of the N.L.R.A. The act affords a degree of protection from employers' opposition which British unions have never enjoyed. This may accelerate the disappearance of the strikes for the closed shop which are motivated by a fear of antiunionism.

In any case, there is little reason for amending the act to prohibit closed-shop strikes. Such an amendment would be an invitation to antiunion employers to continue raising the spurious closed-shop issue when the real issue was antiunionism. The total number of strikes would not necessarily be decreased since unions would still strike against antiunionism when that was the issue. The task of the board in reducing the number of strikes against antiunionism would still remain, and its work would be increased by the necessity for distinguishing between real and false "closed shop" strikes.

Finally, there is the question as to whether the closed shop should not be allowed as a means to compelling the "chiselers" to pay their way. Does a minority have the right to enjoy the benefits provided by the majority without paying for them? A variety of analogies suggests a negative answer. Fraternity members are often compelled to pay a dance tax whether they attend the dance or not. College faculty members frequently are induced by social compulsions to support the faculty club whether they use it or not. College undergraduates are frequently required to pay athletic taxes even if they never attend a game or set foot on a playing field. Towns, states, and national governments insist upon the payment of taxes by people who do not enjoy proportional benefits. If people are compelled to pay in these instances when they do not accept the benefits paid for, should not workers be expected to pay union dues when they cannot help accepting the benefits of collective bargaining?

In each case the argument is, "If you don't like this outfit, you can go somewhere else." By the same token, union members say, "If you don't like our arrangements, you can work elsewhere." The fact that the fraternity member, teacher, student, citizen, or worker usually cannot go somewhere else doesn't seem to make much difference. His only real alternative, in a democracy, is to persuade the majority to change its policies. Is there any abstract rule of justice indicating that the N.L.R.A. should prevent unions from doing what other human associations do? If not, there is no more reason for preventing strikes for the closed shop than strikes for any other reason.

There remains the question as to whether the closed shop combined with the closed union should be discouraged by outlawing strikes to enforce this demand. This question and the problem of strikes in defiance of an existing contract raise an important issue. How far should the government go in regulating the internal affairs of labor unions? If particular unions appear to be irresponsible, racketized, corrupt, monopolistic, or autocratic, should the government interfere? There is no general answer. Each disease is different. The virulence of the disease determines whether the doctor should be called in to administer drugs or whether, after careful observation and a little advice, nature should be allowed to take its course.

No individual can be held responsible for his actions unless he has some control over them. No human association can be held responsible for its acts or agreements unless it is sufficiently organic in structure to have a head capable of controlling its members. There is a general disposition to attribute an organic quality to associations of men. It makes for better headlines and fewer headaches to think of John L. Lewis, Alfred P. Sloan, and J. P. Morgan as synonymous with C.I.O., General Motors, and capitalism, respectively. The impression thus created is that each of these structures is as internally cohesive as a pyramidal monolith.

The fact is that each is in some respects more like a heap of stones or a colony of cells. Many American business leaders have discovered to their surprise since the passage of the N.L.R.A. that although their organizations might be monolithic in financial or sales policies, they had no personnel policy whatever, or no control over such policy as they had. Each separate plant superintendent did as he pleased. And within each plant, foremen and supervisors frequently did as they pleased. Under such circumstances, talk of responsibility or irresponsibility of management is meaningless. There can be no responsibility unless there is a system each part of which has a definite relation to other parts.

In the absence of such system, the president of a company might sign an agreement with a national union in perfectly good faith and, if he took no other steps, be dismayed to find that no one paid much attention to him. Plant superintendents might disregard the agreement to slow the assembly line, and foremen might continue to fire men wearing union buttons. If our press were not what it is, editors would cry out against this evidence of "irresponsibility" and the company president would have to take the blame.

Without editorial help, many business leaders have been busy during the last two years in revamping their organizations to meet obligations under contracts they have signed. This has involved the sending out of instructions to subordinates, the use of training courses in industrial relations, discharging subordinates who could not swallow the bitter pill, and coöperating with unions in setting up joint machinery for interpreting and enforcing the agreement.

In some instances this revamping has resulted in valuable by-products. A major oil company, for example, sent a messenger to all of its tanker captains telling them about its agreement with the National Maritime Union and what was expected of them under this agreement. The captains were so pleased to discover that the company knew of their existence that they coöperated much better with the company in matters unrelated to unionism than had previously been the case.[16]

The companies which have little or no trouble in the observance of union contracts, such as United States Steel and General Electric, have been the companies which have created systems in which responsibility was possible. The companies which have had the most trouble have been those that have signed agreements and then done nothing else about it except to supply press releases about the irresponsibility of the C.I.O.

All of this applies also to unionism, except that it is harder and takes more time to create a system from a democracy of 400,000 workers than from an oligarchy of 500 company officials. Responsible observance of contracts requires education, discipline, patience, and tact, as well as systematic relationships and machinery for enforcement and interpretation. These things are of slow growth. They cannot easily develop in an atmosphere of conflict. Talk of "irresponsibility" when there is not even a written agreement, let alone a system of applying and interpreting it, is patently ridiculous.

Since unions exist primarily for the maintenance of certain working conditions while business responsibility for the observance of labor contracts is widely diffused throughout the entire management, and business is anxious to cut costs, it would not be surprising if there were fewer infractions by unions than management. Such evidence as there is points to this conclusion.

Before the advent of the Steel Workers' Organizing Committee in the steel industry, *Steel Facts,* a paper published by steel managements, pointed with pride to the fact that under company-union agreements covering about 80 per cent of the workers in the steel industry in 1936, 75 per cent of grievance claims were settled in favor of the workers. This was intended to show how satisfactory the company unions were. But since the awards were made under agreements between managements and company unions, these figures also show that in 75 per cent of the cases it was management which was responsible for infractions of the agreement.[17] Similar evidence of a relatively high degree of union "responsibility" may be observed in the experience of the National Mediation Board. Here again it has been found that in 69 per cent of the conflicts referred to mediators for settlement, it is management which is primarily responsible for infractions.[18]

Outright repudiation of contracts, which is a different matter, is much more rare than infraction. The record of unions in observing contracts is certainly as good as, perhaps better than, that of management. There are already legal precedents making trade agreements enforceable in the courts upon both labor and management. Violations may be prevented by the injunctive process. Such court orders create or perpetuate a conflict situation, however, which does not improve matters much. Layoffs by the employer or sabotage by the union may easily be the compensation for suppressing a conflict rather than removing its causes.

It is difficult to see how any change in the N.L.R.A. could create or promote responsibility in industrial relations when such responsibility is the product of so complex an arrangement of factors. The greatest contribution which government can make is already well under way in the form of the educational and mediation work being carried on informally by the board and a variety of state and federal mediatory agencies.

Racketeering is not peculiar to labor organizations. It attacks small businesses and other associations of people which are relatively weak and helpless. Rackets usually offer a service of some sort, but exact in return a tribute out of proportion to the service rendered. They depend for their existence upon violence and terror. Competition from without is crushed by force, while differences of interests within are ruthlessly destroyed.

It is difficult to draw a logical line between the racket which exacts plate-glass "insurance" from a florist under threat of throwing bricks through his show window, the racket which demands tribute from workers for "job insurance" and from employers for "strike insurance," and the racket which extorts tribute from Jewish industrialists under a guarantee that they may keep their heads a little while longer.

Rackets in the labor movement have appeared chiefly in the building and service trades.[19] They have been imposed by racketeers from the outside and they have developed from within as a result of the policies of labor misleaders. The service offered by the racketeer has usually been the guarantee of a job to the worker, and freedom from labor trouble to the employer. The tributes exacted have been "kickbacks" from wages or excessive charges for dues and working permits on the one hand, and "donations" from employers on the other.

Labor rackets have been fostered by the connivance of employers and the protection of politicians. They are nurtured by the excessively "business" point of view of reactionary labor leaders, some of whom are still high in the councils of labor leadership. They are encouraged by the narrowly monopolistic policies of a few craft unions. They are protected by the "nonpartisan" politics of an older labor movement which began in good faith and ended in the corrupt political machines of metropolitan centers. They may spring from the nature of a society in which human ambitions, malformed by early environment and thwarted by the absence of legitimate economic opportunity, are diverted into extra-legal channels. They have never been characteristic of mass industrial unionism and there is no evidence of their development in this field today.

In the long run, therefore, the elimination of labor racketeering would appear to depend upon the further development of mass industrial unionism, democratic control within these unions, the training of labor leaders whose strictly business point of view is saturated with working-class ideals, the substitution of coöperation for collusion in industrial relations, the progress of labor politics with a program and constituency sufficiently distinct to free it from the corruption of older political machines, the improvement of adolescent environment, and the provision of adult economic opportunity.

Toward many of these objectives the work of the N.L.R.B. makes an important contribution. In the meantime, the punitive surgery of such public prosecutors as Thomas Dewey appears to be the most effective program available. While such surgery does not get at the cause of the disease, it removes the most malignant symptoms. If the federal government must be called upon for aid, the Department of Justice would appear to be a more appropriate agency than the N.L.R.B.

The idea that compulsory incorporation of trade unions would cure either labor "irresponsibility" or labor racketeering appears to have lost favor even among those business groups which originally advanced it. Both the opponents of incorporation among labor groups and the proponents in the business world are beginning to concede that the controversy has been something of a tempest in a teapot. Labor now feels that it has less to fear from incorporation than it originally supposed.[20] Antiunion business has almost decided that incorporation would give it less of a hold on labor than it hoped.[21] And the public has been fully informed that compulsory incorporation has almost no relation either to the problem of irresponsibility or racketeering.

Incorporation is a method of limiting liability rather than extending it. Corporate shareholders are liable only to the extent of their investment. Under precedents set by the Supreme Court, unions are now liable as entities and members are liable as individuals for union acts.[22] If an employer won a suit for damages against a union for violating a contract or engaging in unlawful restraint of

trade, the entire resources of the union and its individual members (if these precedents were followed) could be
attached in settlement of the claim. By incorporating,
unions could limit their liabilities to the par value of their
stock and thus be *less* responsible, if they wanted to, in the
observance of contracts.

Moreover, a national union, like the United Mine Workers, could set itself up in a series of holding companies.
The top holding company could hold the no-par-value
voting shares of its subsidiaries. It could thus control the
union with a minimum of attachable assets. It could sign
and violate contracts every day and have nothing attachable except the control of the union. If an employer attempted to attach this power of control in satisfaction of
a damage claim, he would be violating the N.L.R.A. as
it now stands. No one has yet suggested that the act be
amended to allow employers to take over unions and operate them for personal benefit. The idea that the magic
spell of responsibility can be cast over 600,000 coal miners
by the legal abracadabra of incorporation is just fantastic
enough to make it a seven days' wonder, like flag-pole
sitting.

The case is similar with respect to incorporation as an
antidote for union racketeering. When a sovereign state
like New York is for years unwilling or unable to apply
basic criminal law against racketeers whose victims lie
riddled in the gutter or encased in cement at the bottom
of the East River, how can it be expected that the state's
power to inspect the accounts of incorporated businesses
or unions would suddenly liberate the punitive processes
of the law?

To proposals that voluntary, rather than compulsory,
federal incorporations of unions be permitted, "as in Eng-

land," the following reply may be interesting to collectors of curiosities. Until recently there was on the books a federal law permitting voluntary incorporation of unions. It was passed in the 'eighties in response to requests from union leaders that their organizations be allowed to become socially respectable. For about fifty years no union took advantage of this privilege. Suddenly a little flock of "Home" and "Family" unions appeared on the books as incorporated under this act. Upon investigation, they turned out to be divorce-insurance companies from Texas whose legal personalities had fled from that state and sought shelter under the federal law permitting voluntary incorporation. This sanctuary was rudely shattered, however, by the unsentimental thrust of an act to repeal.[23]

There remain the questions of the alleged monopolistic practices, corruption, and autocracy of unionism. Should the act be amended in various ways to protect American workers from these practices?

Unquestionably, some unions by restricting membership and production have practiced and still practice monopolistic policies. Should not the board become a kind of Federal Trade Commission in the labor field? Again, the answer is probably in the negative. First of all, the whole present drive of the labor movement is in the direction of expanding rather than contracting membership. This is attested not only by the phenomenal growth of the C.I.O. but also by the expansion of independent railroad unionism and the rapid increase in membership of all but a few A. F. of L. affiliates.[24] Second, the impact of modern power-driven and specialized machinery upon trade-union policy is far too great to be withstood by a more powerful labor movement than we have today. The ability to restrict the output of these machines lies less in the hands of labor than in those of ownership and management. Third, the self-interests of a mass labor movement do not lie in the direction of restriction of production except to the extent that shortening of the working hours and diminishing the speed of production provide leisure and prolong life. It is the self-interest of a minority which leads toward monopoly. The labor movement and its dependents are driving toward a majority status as fast as the means and the inclination to organization will allow. Finally, although it is true that monopolistic policies are practiced in a few crafts of such industries as construction, the guarantee of an annual living wage by the construction industry with the aid of government subsidies in return for the surrender of these policies would seem to be a more suitable method of meeting the situation than procedures under doctrines of restraint of trade.[25]

What about corruption? Labor leaders are sometimes corrupted by employers in an attempt to weaken or divert the power of a union. The board is doing the best it can to eliminate such corruption as well as other methods of interference by employers in union affairs. In the Remington Rand case, for example, the board fully exposed the attempt of a labor spy hired by the management to bribe influential labor leaders connected with the Remington Rand strike.[26]

Labor leaders are sometimes corrupted by their own carelessness or greed which results in the absence of financial accounts, padding of expense allowances, and defalcation of funds. Most unions require the bonding of their officers and the issuance of detailed and periodic accounts. Many unions make these public. Almost all have them certified by public accountants. A few local unions, either racketized or thoroughly corrupted, have no financial reports at all. Should not the act be amended to require at least the annual publication of financial reports by all unions making use of the board's services?

There is a slight danger that such reports might strengthen the hand of employers against unions by showing when the union was financially weak enough to diminish its bargaining power. Employers can and do obtain such information, however, through the use of spies and stool pigeons. There would be a great deal to recommend such an amendment to the act, particularly if it were also applied to employers' associations, company unions, "independent" unions, citizens' committees, and back-to-work movements. The glimpses which the La Follette Committee has given of the financial affairs of these groups suggest that further information would be more useful to enthusiastic believers in democracy than additional information about the financial affairs of the labor movement. The labor movement would ultimately gain from information of both kinds.

Finally, there is the question of autocracy in the labor movement. As industrial unions increase in size and number, the labor movement as a whole becomes more democratic in relation to the entire class of gainfully employed citizens. But as unions increase in size, the problem of maintaining democracy within these unions becomes more difficult.

Democratic government progresses as a result of two forces: pulling by the leaders and pushing by the followers. In the very long run, the ultimate stability of democracy depends upon the second force. Final reliance cannot be placed upon the good will and intelligence of individual leaders. The genius of democracy lies in the hope or assurance that the education, energy, and self-discipline of the mass will enable it to develop and control leaders who will promote the good of the followers. Everything, therefore, ought to be done to encourage the education, self-reliance, and experience of the mass. This leads to the conclusion that the mass ought to be allowed to flounder in the educational morass of trial and failure until it finally wallows toward firmer ground.

On the other hand, the altruistic impulses of leaders and the paternalistic inclinations of government are just as much a part of the normal social pattern as the self-interests of the mass. There is no point in throwing away these valuable aids just because they do not fit into the ultimate scheme of an absolutely self-determined people. This is particularly true of the labor movement which, in its early stages, is a fighting organization unable to afford a town meeting every time a decision is called for. A degree of benevolent despotism is inescapable. The question is, how much? The answer is that it depends upon the circumstances.

The circumstances are such that the problem of autocracy in the American labor movement is not serious. There are all kinds of unions. Some appear to have too much democracy to get anywhere. Others look suspiciously like totalitarian states. Still others have developed a combination of democratic control and intelligent leadership which would be hard to duplicate this side of utopia. To a certain extent these unions rub against and help each other. The general drift of the huge new unions is in the right direction. Some bear evidence of internal disintegration through either too much or too little democracy. Others have developed excellent educational plans along with paternalistic leadership. Competition between the A. F. of L. and the C.I.O. and independent unions has its brighter side. The buyers are offered a choice of wares.

In view of this situation should the act be amended to provide for compulsory annual elections of bargaining agents under board auspices (to choose one example from many proposals)? One practical difficulty stands in the way. In the first three years of its existence the board had some difficulty in keeping up with elections in which 450,-842 valid votes were cast. If compulsory annual elections were adopted, the board would be compelled to handle 10,000,000 ballots a year. Its staff and funds would have to be considerably augmented.

Apart from this practical consideration, in the face of present circumstances it may be possible to accept the board's dictum:

Self-organization of employees implies a policy of self-management. . . . The act envisages cohesive organizations well-constructed and intelligently guided. Such organizations will not develop if they are led to look elsewhere for the solution of their problems.[27]

CHAPTER VIII

THE BOARD AND THE COURTS

THE relation between the board and the judicial system has already been indicated. The board cannot enforce its orders without recourse to the courts. Anyone aggrieved by an order of the board may appeal to the courts for relief. In this respect the N.L.R.B. follows the pattern long since established by Congress in the case of the Interstate Commerce Commission, the Federal Trade Commission, the Securities Exchange Commission, the Federal Communications Commission, and other administrative agencies of the federal government.

These federal commissions have developed during a period covering fifty years. Each one successively, beginning with the I.C.C., has been bitterly opposed by the economic interests upon which regulation has been imposed. They have been set up and their powers expanded under Democratic and Republican administrations alike. They represent an adjustment to two fundamental economic developments: interdependence and complexity.

Increasing interdependence of all parts of economic society has compelled the federal government to assume regulatory responsibility since it alone has sufficiently wide jurisdiction to meet the scope of the problems. Complexity has compelled regulation to assume an administrative character since no one but an expert can hope to deal with the intricate questions in each field.

Stated negatively, this means that neither states nor judges are competent by themselves to deal with modern economic life. The states are subject to geographic and the judges to human limitations. States cannot regulate industry which pays no attention to state boundaries. Judges cannot be expected to turn from problems of freight rates to problems of trade practices, capital issues, wave lengths, and appropriate units. Even judges would deny that judicial robes endow their wearers with omniscience as well as impartiality.

Consequently, administrative agencies have developed several characteristics which follow logically from the complexity of the problems with which they deal. Important among the characteristics of the N.L.R.B. are the following: (1) It cannot be enjoined by federal district courts from carrying out its regulatory responsibilities. (2) It is allowed greater freedom in the admission of evidence during its hearings than is generally the case in jury trials. (3) In appeals to the circuit court for relief from the board's orders, the court must accept the findings of the board if supported by evidence. (4) Agents of the board in its formal hearings act in the capacities of both prosecutors and judges.

Each of these characteristics has given rise to attacks upon the N.L.R.B. which have been even more bitter than those directed against other administrative agencies in their time. The board has been variously described as "a kangaroo court," "a drumhead court-martial," "a French revolutionary tribunal," "Public Enemy No. 1," "Fascistic," "Communistic," "bureaucracy run rampant," the "American Inquisition." [1] The extent to which these opinions conform to the facts may be judged by a discussion of the administrative characteristics of the N.L.R.B.

When the board proceeds against an employer for unfair practices it cannot be enjoined by federal district courts from carrying on any of the activities which are necessary and permissible under the act. A district court cannot prohibit the board from subpoenaing persons and records, from holding hearings, presenting evidence, making findings, and issuing orders.[2]

There are two reasons for this. The first is the question of the amount of time involved in injunction proceedings. In matters of industrial relations, time is important to both the worker and the employer. If an employer is accused of discriminatory discharge, the sooner the matter is settled the less the back wages the employer has to pay if he loses the case, or the sooner the worker can start looking for another job if he loses the case. Injunctions and appeals from them delay matters interminably with resulting loss to either party.

The second reason is that injunction proceedings are likely to develop into full-fledged hearings in themselves. This defeats the whole idea of removing intricate problems from the ordinary courts and putting them in the hands of specialists in the field concerned. If the board loses an injunction case, the courts have successfully retained control over a matter delegated by Congress to trained administrators. If the board wins an injunction case, it has to go through the whole thing again in its own hearings.

Injunctions are supposed to be granted only when irreparable damage is threatened. There is a good deal of difference between a situation in which a boycott is about to destroy the trade name of a company, and a situation in which the board is about to obtain the facts which will enable it to decide whether or not to order the reinstatement of a discharged worker. In the first case, if the injunction is not granted, business good will may be wrongfully and irreparably destroyed. In the second case, the worst that can happen is that the board order the reinstatement of the worker. If the facts support this conclusion, it is neither a wrongful nor an irreparable damage. The best that can happen, from the employer's point of view, is that he be exonerated from the charge.

If it is urged that even exoneration is an irreparable damage because no one reads about acquittals, it must be replied, first, that this is true of any court action against an accused person and, second, that the board's own regulations provide every opportunity for settlement of complaints in private conferences which entirely avoid such odium as may attach to public hearings.[3] It is difficult to see how employers can suffer from the absence of injunctive relief in board cases. If they feel aggrieved after the board has made its decision, they may appeal to the circuit court for relief.

In spite of this explicit prohibition of injunctions, the board was swamped with injunction cases during its first two years. The early injunctive actions were stimulated by the National Lawyers' Committee of the Liberty League which proclaimed that the act was unconstitutional. Each succeeding plea for an injunction fed on the language of its predecessor. By the time that these documents had grown to mature and standardized forms, broadcast with the assistance of employers' associations, a fabulous conception of the board and its work had been created.[4] The language of court decisions in some of these cases suggests that the judges themselves were startled by the contrast between the language of the act and the monstrosity conjured from legal brief cases by the incantations of corporate medicine men.

In an injunction suit brought in the Eastern District of Virginia before Federal District Judge Way,[5] for example, the judge stated:

It is the duty of the Court in approaching questions of this kind to try to meet them with an open mind, not influenced by the discussions that occur in the public press and on the hustings. I never read this Act of Congress until a few days ago. *I am frank to say, gentlemen, that I was surprised to find that so much care has been exercised by the Congress* in providing for review of the proceedings by the National Labor Relations Board. . . .

A point that impresses me greatly is the fact that the Board is powerless to enforce any orders it makes without the aid of the Circuit Court of Appeals . . . and the Court has practically un-limited power to modify, set aside, or affirm the order as it may deem just and proper.

This case before Judge Way was one of a total of ninety-seven injunction suits brought against the board and its agents in the early months of the board's efforts to enforce the act. The board finally won out in every one. Of the first ninety-five cases, seventy-three were won outright in the district courts when the issue was first presented. Thirty-six cases were appealed to the circuit courts either by employers or by the board. Of these cases the board won all but two. Losing employers appealed from the circuit court to the Supreme Court in fourteen cases, but were granted a hearing in only one instance. This case was lost by the employer. The board appealed to the Supreme Court in two cases and won in both. The board therefore won 77 per cent of its injunction cases in the district courts, 94 per cent in the circuit courts, and 100 per cent in the Supreme Court.[6]

It would appear, therefore, that if its freedom from the injunctive process makes the board a "kangaroo court,"

Courtesy of Elderman and the *Washington Post.*

PARENTAL AUTHORITY

the entire judicial system of the United States, with an unusual degree of unanimity, is abetting the board in its nefarious work.

The second common characteristic of a federal administrative agency is the greater freedom in the admission of evidence during its hearings than is allowed in jury trials. This characteristic, which is shared by the N.L.R.B., has been made the basis for the most violent of the verbal attacks on the board. It is nothing new in the history of administrative agencies. It is a freedom granted by Congress and repeatedly upheld by the courts. In the case of the N.L.R.A., Section 10 (b) says in part, "In any such proceeding the rules of evidence prevailing in courts of law or equity shall not be controlling."

Congress has not granted nor have the courts sustained this freedom out of pure whimsicality. This may be supported by observing the basic reason for the development of "rules of evidence" in *jury* trials. There are two of these reasons. Jury trials are expensive and long-drawn-out at best. There is no reason for allowing the taxpayers' money to be wasted and the processes of justice delayed by the admission of evidence which is irrelevant and immaterial to the point at issue. Attorneys must be able to show that there is some connection between the testimony which they are offering and the thing they are trying to prove. If the relevancy of testimony is questioned, it is up to the judge to decide whether or not to allow time to be consumed by continuing a certain line of questioning. There is no fixed rule that determines whether a matter is relevant or not. One of the reasons for having a judge on hand during a jury trial is to have him use his judgment.

In a hearing before a trial examiner or before the board itself, exactly the same thing is true. Time and money are at stake, even though there is no jury to be paid. If either the attorney for the board or the employer protests against the admission of evidence on the ground that it is irrelevant, it is up to the trial examiner or the board to make a ruling. If the trial examiner refuses to sustain an objection from an employer's attorney, the attorney may take exception to this ruling. This exception is subject to review by the board and by the circuit court, if the employer cares to appeal the case.

Thus, the employer has the same right of appeal from a trial examiner's ruling that he has from the ruling of a judge in a lower court. In the meantime the trial examiner is enabled to admit a volume of evidence for the assistance of the board in making its orders. A strict interpretation of "relevancy" in the original hearing might prevent the board from obtaining valuable general information or compel members of the board to waste time and money in rehearing the case in person.

The second reason for laying down rules of evidence in jury trials is to prevent attorneys from influencing the jury by presenting testimony which is incompetent or prejudicial. The jury is a group of citizens who have no special training in sifting evidence or making judgments. By the choice of derogatory words, by the use of vague hearsay testimony, by introducing opinions and beliefs rather than objective facts or statements, a skilful attorney may construct a damning case out of thin air.

It is the task of opposing attorneys to prevent each other from doing this. If they clash over the question of the competence of testimony, it is up to the judge to decide between them. The judge's ultimate task is to protect the jury from prejudice. The judge is supposed to have the training necessary to distinguish between that which is valid and that which is prejudicial. If there is difficulty in deciding, the jury is sometimes asked to leave the room, or the judge and the attorneys engage in *sotto voce* asides while the matter is argued out. Obviously, the whole point of these proceedings is to protect the jury from prejudice inside the courtroom just as it is protected outside the courtroom by sequestration during the trial.

If a hearing takes place before a judge or referee without a jury, the "rules of evidence" need not be strictly adhered to, except as a timesaver. There is no particular point in protecting the judge from himself. He is considered competent to sift the facts, throw out those that are irrelevant, incompetent, immaterial or prejudicial, and pass judgment upon the remainder.

For example, during the recent case of the People of the State of New York *vs.* James Hines, which ended in the declaration of a mistrial by Justice Pecora, the point at issue was not whether an improper question put to a witness by Prosecutor Dewey had prejudiced the judge against the defendant. The issue was whether this question had prejudiced the *jury*. If there had been no jury, there would have been little sense in Justice Pecora's taking three days off to decide whether *he* had been prejudiced against the defendant.

Precisely the same thing is true of a hearing before a trial examiner. There is no jury present. The trial examiner is an expert on legal or labor matters who is supposed to be able to protect himself from the eloquence or trickery of those who practice before him. If strict observance of the "rules of evidence" were required, the interesting question would arise as to who was to interpret them.

If it were the trial examiner's task, he would simply do

in public what he now does in his own office; that is, sift out the relevant and competent testimony as a basis for his decision. If this is not satisfactory, however, there is an alternative. That is to send the trial examiner out of the room and call in someone else. This is approximately what now happens under the act. Although the trial examiner is not sent out of the room, the record of the case is sent to Washington. There it is examined by the board and the trial examiner's rulings are affirmed or denied. If the employer appeals the case, the circuit court and perhaps the Supreme Court go through the same process, if the respondent still objects to rulings which have been made.

It is of some importance to note in this connection that even the great jurists sometimes disagree as to what evidence is or is not relevant. In the Friedman–Harry Marks Clothing Company case, for example, the board admitted evidence, as it always must, tending to show that the business of the company affected interstate commerce. When the case reached the Supreme Court, Chief Justice Hughes surveyed this evidence in detail and concluded that it supported the findings of the board as to the interstate nature of the business. Mr. Justice McReynolds, however, in reviewing the same evidence in a dissenting opinion, said, "During hearings held at Richmond and Washington, *unfettered by rules of evidence,* it received a mass of testimony *largely irrelevant.* Much related to the character of the respondent's business, general methods used in the clothing industry, the numbers employed and the general effect of strikes therein." [7] Chief Justice Hughes thought that the "character of the respondent's business" and the "effect of strikes therein" were essential to proof of the

constitutionality of the board's case. Mr. Justice Mc-
Reynolds dismissed this as "largely irrelevant."

A third reason for relaxation of the rules of evidence in
the case of board hearings, which is not necessarily true
of other administrative agencies, is that some of the evidence necessary to its decisions could not be admitted
under the rulings prevailing in many jury trials. Suppose,
for example, that a part of an employer's antiunion
program consists of a whispering campaign against an outside union. This campaign might be carried on by foremen, company-controlled workers, or professional spies.
If it were possible to show the receipted bills paid by the
company to the spy agency, or if an employer would testify
that he had directed foremen to say the company would
move out of town if the workers joined the union, the
board's attorney might rest the case upon this evidence.

But such evidence may be entirely unavailable. There
might, however, be a hundred workers who would testify
that they had *heard* that the company would move; or a
score of workers who had been told by a foreman that he
believed the company would move; or a dozen clerks and
timekeepers who gave it as their *opinion* that the company
would move out of town if the workers signed up.

The company's attorney would surely object to this
testimony as "hearsay, matters of opinion and belief,
prejudicial, incompetent, irrelevant and immaterial." The
trial examiner, however, might admit the evidence for his
own information and that of the board. If it were supported by other evidence of antiunionism the board might
order the employer to desist from his unfair practices.

If relaxation of the rules of evidence in board hearings
transforms them into "French revolutionary tribunals,"

grave concern must surely be felt over the fact that common sense, as well as judges and referees sitting without a jury, and other federal administrative agencies all support or enjoy the same revolutionary license. Such anxiety as will be aroused by this thought, however, may perhaps be soothed by keeping in mind that for many years the Supreme Court has been able to retain its composure in the face of this situation.

The fact that press criticism of board procedure is unsupported by fact, common sense, administrative precedent, or judicial opinion is unfortunately not the end of the matter. This and other attacks on the board have worried many employers into believing that board hearings are likely to open with an ominous roll of drums and close with the swish of a guillotine. At one recent board hearing the company's attorney rose at the opening and announced, "I fully expect to have every objection I make overruled during the course of this hearing." [8]

In another, a hypersensitive employer on the witness stand behaved as though a spiritual rack were stretching every moral ligament of his being. It took nearly two days of persuasion, soothing, and cajolery to elicit any facts as to the nature of his business. So disturbed was this employer that he threw the board's subpoenas out his window and locked his doors against its agents. Even the Jersey City police were less upset than the employer in this case, and came to the aid of the board's agents in securing the employer's attendance at hearings. [9]

This is exactly the result which is to be expected from the hundreds of columns of press attack on board procedure. It is presumably what is intended by these attacks, since they have no verifiable basis in fact. The enforceability of the act depends upon its acceptance by the great majority of well-intentioned employers. If this acceptance can be destroyed by creating a hysterical attitude among the majority, the minority will have won the battle. Neither the board's agents nor law-abiding employers can coöperate under the tension produced by day-in, day-out descriptions of the board as a Spanish Inquisition.

The third characteristic which the board has in common with many other administrative agencies is that, in case of appeal from its decisions, the board's findings of fact are to be accepted as final if supported by evidence. This is also true of appeals by the board to the courts for enforcement of its orders.

The relevant sections of the act cover the following details: (1) No objection which has not been urged before the board shall be considered by the court. (2) "The findings of the board as to the facts, if supported by evidence, shall be conclusive." (3) If either the board or the employer wish to raise new objections or to bring in additional evidence, they must prove that there were good grounds for not having raised these objections or adduced the evidence in the original hearings. (4) If the court gives leave to bring in new evidence, the case goes back to the board, the evidence is introduced, the board may modify its findings or orders, and the case returns, if necessary, to the court. (5) The court may enforce, modify, or set aside in whole or in part the order of the board.[10]

A few examples of the terms used in this summary of the procedure of appeal may be useful.

"Objections" mean protests by employer's attorneys against any detail of board procedure or any rulings affecting the admission or rejection of evidence. If the board denies a motion for six weeks' postponement until a company executive returns from Europe, the employer's attorney may "object" to this ruling. If the board omits to provide the employer with a copy of the trial examiner's report, or refuses to hear additional evidence in Washington after testimony has been taken before a trial examiner in the employer's city, or accepts "hearsay" testimony, or refuses to accept the testimony of workers outside the appropriate unit, the company's attorney may "object" to these actions or rulings of the board.

"Evidence" means, for example, that a discharged worker was the highest paid and most skilful man in the shop, had been regularly employed for fifteen years, had been warned to stop "talking union," and had been discharged the day after presiding at the first organizing meeting of a union; or that a company buys 60 per cent of its raw materials and sells 70 per cent of its finished products in interstate commerce; or that an employer repeatedly urged the formation of a company union, paid all its expenses, and furnished time and a place for meetings.

"Findings of fact" mean, for example, that an employer discharged a worker for his union activities; that a company is engaged in interstate commerce; that a certain group of workers constitutes a labor organization; that an employer did bargain in good faith with the accredited representatives of his workers; and that a certain craft is an appropriate unit for bargaining purposes.

"Orders" mean, for example, that an employer must reinstate a discharged worker with back pay from the time of discharge minus any earnings he may have made in the meantime; that an employer must desist from a variety of antiunion practices, or reinstate a group of strikers, or post a notice for thirty days saying that he has complied with the board's order, or write to the board within ten days saying what steps he has taken to comply with other orders of the board.

In the light of these illustrations, the board's relation to courts of appeal may again be summarized: (1) All *objections* are subject to review by the courts. (2) The *orders* of the board may be modified or set aside in part or in whole. (3) The setting aside or modification of board orders may be based upon the upholding by the court of the employer's *objections* to board procedure or rulings. (4) Or the setting aside of board orders may be based on the court's conclusion that *evidence* does not support the board's *findings of fact*.

About the first three of these points there is absolutely no doubt. The fourth, however, is veiled in uncertainty. If the courts may review the board's evidence to see whether it supports the findings of fact, what point is there in saying that the board's findings of fact shall be conclusive? How can anything be "conclusive" that is immediately conditioned by a very large "if"?

The answer in common practice is that this phraseology throws the burden of proof upon the courts to show that the board's evidence does not support its findings. Only in extraordinary cases may a court find that the evidence does not support the findings. Under all ordinary circumstances the court must accept the findings of an administrative agency as established by the evidence in the record of the case.

There are two clear reasons for this procedure. It restricts the introduction of new evidence, and it compels the court to give way to the specialized training of administrative agents in questions of fact.

First, suppose that an employer either refuses to obey a board order or appeals from a board order to the circuit court. In both cases the entire record of the case is transferred from the board to the court. The court must base its decision on the written material in its possession and on such oral exposition as the attorneys concerned feel necessary. If the court were freely allowed to accept new testimony, employers could escape the jurisdiction of the board altogether simply by refusing testimony in board hearings and reserving it for the court of appeal.

Since the employer's testimony would not be available to the board under these circumstances, the judgment of an unspecialized court would be substituted for the judgment of trained specialists. Congressional intentions would be completely defeated and the board might as well close shop whenever an employer refused compliance.

Consequently, Congress has made it difficult to introduce new evidence in the court of appeal. If the court does grant permission to introduce new evidence, the case is remanded to the board for hearing of the evidence in question. There is, therefore, no incentive for the employer to refuse testimony at the original hearing, and provision is made for extraordinary cases in which injustice might be done if new evidence were flatly refused.

Secondly, even though the evidence is confined to the record of the board hearing, the court might interpret this evidence in a manner different from the board. Congress therefore gives precedence to the judgment of the board over that of the court in the specialized field concerned. The permission of the court to pass upon the findings of fact is limited to extraordinary cases of tyranny or stupidity on the part of the administrative agent. In ordinary cases the court is expected to confine itself to questions of procedure, rulings on admission of evidence, constitutionality, and the appropriateness of orders.

These are merely the facts about the common relation between administrative agencies, including the N.L.R.B., and courts of appeal. This relation has long since become well settled and its constitutionality repeatedly established. The issue has been reopened, however, by critics of the board. In the supercharged atmosphere of contemporary conflict, battles rage over three-letter words. Critics of the act point out that it does not even say *"the"* evidence. It just says "if supported by evidence." They urge that this means *any* evidence at all, and that the act ought at least to say "the" evidence, if not "substantial" evidence or "preponderant" evidence.[11]

Although few cases can be pointed out in which the board has not amassed so great a volume of evidence that a good deal more patience is required to read it than is ordinarily possessed by the board's critics, it is urged that there is nothing to stop the board from running amok. It *might,* for example, order the reinstatement of a worker just because he was a very active union man even though he was thoroughly incompetent and a source of constant loss to his employer. Such an order by the board is conceivable but this scarcely justifies the conclusion that the board is in fact a "drumhead court-martial."

The opinions of members of the judiciary, in this matter, may not take precedence over those of newspaper columnists, but they are worth citing for the effect of contrast.

In Agwalines, Inc. *vs*. N.L.R.B., Judge Hutcheson of the Fifth Circuit Court of Appeals said:

The Board's findings of fact are set forth in great detail. They consist of a careful and accurate *summary* of the facts testified to, and the Board's conclusions as to the meaning of these facts. A test of this summary by a careful reading and analysis of the long *record* discloses that the picture it presents of the background and setting of the scenes and actions under review, of the characteristics and circumstances of the various actors and of the actions themselves, is, though in miniature, full, fair and accurate. Nothing seems out of focus, nothing distorted.[12]

It is apparent that the Justice read not only the summary but also the record itself, and balanced this evidence against the findings of fact before making his decision upholding the board's orders.

The care with which the courts may scrutinize the board's procedure and do scrutinize its evidence is suggested by Chief Justice Hughes in N.L.R.B. *vs.* Jones and Laughlin Steel Corporation.

The procedural provisions of the Act are assailed. But these provisions, as we construe them, do not offend against the constitutional requirements governing the creation and action of administrative bodies. The Act establishes standards to which the Board must conform. There must be complaint, notice and hearing. The Board must receive evidence and make findings. The findings of fact are to be conclusive but only if supported by evidence. The order of the Board is subject to review by the designated court, and only when sustained by the court may the order be enforced. Upon that review all questions of the jurisdiction of the Board and the regularity of its proceedings, all questions of constitutional right or statutory authority are open to examination by the court. None of the rules of administrative agencies appears to have been transgressed in the instant case. Respondent was notified and heard. It had opportunity to meet the charge of unfair labor practice upon the merits, and by withdrawing from the hearing it declined to avail itself of that opportunity. The *facts* found by the Board *support its order* and *the evidence* supports the *findings*. Respondent has no just cause for complaint on this score.[13]

It will be noticed that Chief Justice Hughes introduced the article "the" before "evidence" without benefit of statutory amendment. It is possible that this was no more than a matter of literary compulsion.

Speaking for a unanimous court, Mr. Justice Roberts, in Washington, Virginia, and Maryland Coach Company *vs.* N.L.R.B., went even further in defending the board, however, by allowing the word "substantial" to come to the aid of "evidence."

> . . . We should not review the facts, since . . . "the findings of the Board as to the facts, if supported by evidence, shall be conclusive," and there was *substantial* evidence to support the findings. . . . We have refused to review the evidence or weigh the testimony [in other similar cases] and have declared we will reverse or modify the findings only if clearly improper or not supported by *substantial* evidence.[14]

Although apparently Mr. Justice Roberts had difficulty with the somewhat metaphysical task of accepting the findings as conclusive without weighing the evidence and then taking a peek at the evidence to see that it was substantial, the point is clear enough. The burden of proof is on the courts to show that the board is wrong in its findings of fact. The judgment of an expert is given more weight than the judgment of a jack-of-all-justice, however impartial and well informed. Congress proposes this arrangement because of the complexity of administrative tasks. The Supreme Court passes upon it favorably and regularly. The board has not yet become sufficiently tyrannical under this license to attract the attention of the great majority of lower courts, although they take a good look at the evidence in every case, just to make sure.

Only in the Consolidated Edison Company case has the Supreme Court questioned the board's findings of fact. In this case the board's order was modified partly because of slight procedural defects in the calling of witnesses and amending of complaints. Beyond this, however, the Court held that the board's conclusion that the existing contracts between the company and the union should be invalidated was "entirely too broad to be sustained." The Court agreed with the board that there was "substantial" evidence of attempts by the company to coerce its workers into the International Brotherhood of Electrical Workers. It concluded, however, that this coercion was not sufficient to justify the abrogation of the contracts. While the board and two members of the Court, Justices Black and Reed, held that the contracts were the logical culmination of a long list of coercive acts and that therefore the contracts were as invalid as the coercion was illegal, the majority of the Court held that the board had not presented sufficient evidence that the workers themselves were unwilling to abide by the agreements.

Students of industrial relations may have considerable difficulty in agreeing with the Court that coercion of workers into a union is not sufficient ground for invalidating a contract between that union and the employer who applies the coercion. As experts in industrial relations, the members of the board experienced this difficulty. The Court substituted its judgment for that of the board. In so doing it came very close to reversing the positions stated by Chief Justice Hughes and Mr. Justice Roberts less than two years previously.

In any case, this decision illustrates the extent to which the board's orders are subject to judicial review even in matters of weighing evidence and in spite of express limitations placed by the N.L.R.A. upon the judiciary. This should give comfort to those who fear the arbitrary exercise of power by the board. It may well cause alarm, however, among those who regard the judiciary as the

Maginot Line of conservatism past which no real liberalization of the legal status of organized labor can advance.

Mr. Dooley might have had some pleasure in observing that the Consolidated Edison decision came one month after the New Deal election reverses of November, 1938. He might suggest further that critics of the board should be encouraged to demand amendments to the act requiring that board findings and orders be supported not merely by "the" evidence or "substantial" evidence, but that the words "preponderant," "incontestable," and "overwhelming" be added in order to relieve the courts from the necessity of falling back upon such cumbersome phrases as "entirely too broad to be sustained."

Lacking Mr. Dooley's powers of expression, it should be sufficient to recall that the whole tradition of the American judiciary has been as unsympathetic toward unionism in practice as it has recently been enthusiastic about it in principle. Generous statutory words have given the principle of unionism to American workers and parsimonious judicial words have taken it back. The history of unionism in this country abounds in illustrations of this conflict. Many of them were cited earlier in this book.

This judicial practice is by no means defunct. While the Supreme Court has, until the present, almost entirely upheld the intent of Congress, the circuit courts are not as yet so nearly unanimous in their enthusiasm for the act. One or two of the ten circuit courts have repeatedly blocked the will of Congress, first by affirming or granting injunctions and later by decisions modifying or setting aside board orders after disregarding the board's findings of fact. Until the legality of collective bargaining is as firmly established in the courts in practice as it is in principle, there is no valid reason for inviting the fate of the Clayton

Act, Section 7a, and Public Resolution No. 44 by providing shelter in the act for the remnants of judicial antiunionism.

The record of the board in the circuit courts is of interest in this connection. Between the beginning of its litigation record and the fall of 1938, the board appeared in the circuit courts in 144 cases involving enforcement of its orders. Sixty-five cases were petitions by employers to the courts for review of the board's orders. Seventy-nine cases were petitions by the board to the courts for enforcement of its orders. Of the 144 cases in which the board had been involved, fifty-seven had been definitely settled. Of these fifty-seven the board had won forty-three and lost fourteen. But of the forty-three won by the board, only thirty-four were finally settled in the circuit courts. In nine cases, decisions by the Supreme Court were necessary before the board's orders could be enforced. Of the fourteen cases lost by the board in the circuit courts, four have been appealed by the board to the Supreme Court and will eventually be decided there. The board's heaviest losses were in the third and seventh circuits in each of which it lost two out of three cases. The other cases lost by the board were scattered throughout seven of the remaining eight circuits.[15]

In contrast to this 71 per cent record of victories in the circuit courts, the board has won outright nine of the cases dealing with the enforcement of its orders which were appealed to the Supreme Court. In the Consolidated Edison case its orders were modified in one important respect. The Supreme Court has also denied four petitions by employers for a hearing. These nine victories in the Supreme Court are in addition to the three Supreme Court decisions in which the board's freedom from injunctive action was upheld.[16]

The board has won one other important victory in the Supreme Court. After months of hearings and preparation of findings in the cases of the Republic Steel Company and the Ford Motor Company, the board decided to take these cases under its own wing and make its decisions without the issuance of a trial examiner's report. After serving its decisions upon the companies and being met with refusals to comply, the board turned to the circuit courts for enforcement of its orders.

Just as the board was handing these cases to the circuit courts, the Supreme Court rendered a decision on April 25, 1937, which had an indirect bearing upon the board's procedure in the Republic and Ford cases. In Morgan vs. United States, the Supreme Court held that the failure of the administrator of the Packers and Stockyards Act to issue a trial examiner's report contributed to a denial of a "fair hearing" to the company. Because of this procedural defect, the case fell to the ground.

This placed the board in a quandary. Should it continue to press the Republic and Ford cases in spite of its omission of the trial examiner's report? Or should it withdraw the case from the court, remedy the possible defect, and then return to the courts?

There were good reasons for each policy. Against withdrawal from the courts were the following reasons: (1) Whereas in the Morgan case the company had not been provided originally with a written complaint to which it could make a formal reply, the board invariably serves such a complaint and had done so in the Ford and Republic cases. (2) The absence of a trial examiner's report in the Ford and Republic cases, therefore, did not deny the companies a fair hearing, since they had already filed objections and denials at the time of the issuing of the original complaint. In this respect the Ford and Republic cases differed sharply from the Morgan case in which the original complaint as well as the trial examiner's report had been omitted. (3) Nothing in the N.L.R.A. can be construed as requiring the issuance of a trial examiner's report. (4) The board's regulations specifically state that the trial examiner's report may be omitted. (5) In a number of circuit court and Supreme Court decisions in cases in which the board had not issued a trial examiner's report, the courts had upheld the board without raising the issue of the missing trial examiner's report.

On the other hand, these two cases were so important that the board was unwilling to have them tried in the courts on the procedure involved rather than on their merits. The board therefore sought to remove these cases from the courts in order to perfect any possible procedural defects.[17]

The companies then behaved in a manner which was absurd in logic but brilliant in publicity strategy. They protested vigorously against allowing the board to withdraw the cases from the courts. Logically, this protest meant that the companies were refusing to be given a fair hearing, since one reason for a trial examiner's report is to allow the company another chance to protest. From a publicity point of view, however, it gave the companies a splendid opportunity to proclaim that the board had a bad conscience, had been caught stealing eggs, and was trying to sneak out. Counsel for the Ford Company coupled this proclamation with a list of questions which was packed with innuendoes of misconduct by board officials. For a few days the almost unanimous voice of the press cried out against the board, describing the withdrawal of the cases as guilt and accepting innuendoes as facts.[18]

Then the headlines turned to other matters and subsequent events were scarcely reported. The subsequent events were: (1) Three weeks after the Morgan case, the Supreme Court in N.L.R.B. *vs.* Mackay Radio and Telegraph Company, on May 16, upheld the board in a case in which no trial examiner's report was issued. Mr. Justice Roberts noted the absence of the trial examiner's report, remarked that it was not necessary to a "fair hearing," denied the company's plea for dismissal on this ground, and drew attention to the contrast between the board's procedure and that involved in Morgan *vs.* United States. This decision received scant publicity, yet it was a complete answer to the allegations of Ford counsel. (2) On May 31, 1938, the Supreme Court rendered a decision which in effect directed the Third Circuit Court to return the Republic Steel case to the board.[19] Until this time, on the plea of the company, the court had refused to allow the board to resume jurisdiction. (3) On June 11 the Sixth Circuit Court of Appeals returned jurisdiction over the Ford case to the board but at the same time issued a stay which prevented the board from reopening the case while the company appealed to the Supreme Court against the circuit court's order. Since the Supreme Court was not in session, this delayed the board for months more. In December, 1938, the Court's decision had not been handed down.[20]

In summary of this case it may be said, however, that the Supreme Court refused to allow the Republic Company to demand what it had itself described as an "unfair hearing." At the same time, in the Mackay decision, the Supreme Court announced that the board's procedure in omitting trial examiner's reports in both cases was *not* an "unfair hearing." But for the intervention of the

Supreme Court, however, the board would have been compelled to allow important cases in which there was the possibility of a slight procedural defect to begin their journey through the courts. The chief fault of the board, if it was a fault, lay in being overscrupulous in the technical preparation of its cases. One could scarcely have guessed this, however, from the newspapers. The antiboard barrage was so intense during this period that even staunch defenders of the board were alarmed.[21]

The fourth major characteristic of many federal administrative agencies, including the N.L.R.B., is that they may be said to combine under one head the functions of judge, prosecutor, and jury. The board has been attacked upon this ground in the following details: The board's formal hearings are held before a trial examiner who is appointed and paid by the board. Evidence supporting the charge is developed and presented by an attorney who is also paid and appointed by the board. Testimony is often introduced by witnesses who are in fact legal or economic specialists employed by the board. The recommendations and rulings of the trial examiner are surveyed by the board and compared with the record of the case which is summarized by legal technicians employed by the board. In important cases, the board may also take testimony in person at Washington or in the field. The board then makes its own findings of fact, bases its orders on its own findings, and demands that the employer obey these orders.

All this is believed to be so great a travesty upon justice that conservative business groups, now supported by the A. F. of L. executive council, demand the separation of the judicial from the administrative powers of the board. In New York state an exactly similar effort was made in

Courtesy of Herbert Johnson and the *Saturday Evening Po[st]*

"GOSH! AND I MADE IT MYSELF!"

the proposed new constitution. If these suggestions were adopted, and the example were followed, federal and state administrative agencies would become fact-collecting errand boys for the courts. The courts would have resumed or assumed control over t' e intricate special problems of economic life which the whole trend of the last fifty legislative years has granted to trained administrators.[22]

The analogy between the board's procedure and the judge-jury-prosecution triangle is a half truth at best. In some respects the board is more like a traffic policeman whose powers include the making of charges against traffic offenders, the collection of evidence as to the speed at which a car is traveling, making a finding that the car's speed under the conditions legally constitutes "speeding," and (in many jurisdictions) the levying and collection of a fine. Usually the policeman's acts are subject to judicial review. The judge, however, generally accepts the officer's findings of fact as conclusive. The burden of proof is certainly upon the driver to show that the policeman's findings are wrong. The court may suspend or modify sentence.

The difference between the board and a policeman is that the task of the board in dealing with industrial relations is usually much more complicated than that of a policeman dealing with misdemeanors. The organization of the board, therefore, must be more elaborate and must involve a greater degree of specialization of function among its personnel. As this specialization develops, the executive, prosecuting, and judicial functions informally performed by a policeman are, in the case of the board, allotted to separate persons.

In its simple and informal cases, the field examiner of a regional office acts almost exactly like a good policeman. Charges from workers are turned over by the regional office to a field examiner. The field examiner makes a preliminary investigation. On the basis of his findings and the recommendation of the regional director the board decides whether a complaint should be issued. If a complaint is issued, the principals meet with the field examiner, and evidence is taken simply by having the employer and the workers discuss the matter. The workers' agent acts as prosecutor, the employer's agent as defense counsel, and the field examiner as referee, technical adviser, and informal special police in following up the results of the discussion.

Even in its important and complicated cases, the board might avoid the charge of being judge, jury, prosecutor, and chief witness by dropping altogether the formal analogy to courtroom procedure. It could summon the respondents to Washington, closet itself with them in a private room, get the whole story, and make its findings and issue its orders on the spot. It would thus be acting simply as trained industrial police whose orders were subject to review by the courts, but whose judgment as to the facts of the case was generally given the benefit of any possible doubt.

Considerations of efficiency and justice, however, compel the board to adopt a more formal and complicated procedure involving public hearings and specialized functions among board personnel. The board must hire not only stenographers and clerks, but economists to investigate the broad historical background of cases so that they may be placed in their proper perspective, legal technicians to sift and summarize evidence, and statisticians to tabulate the result of board actions so that its general policies may become apparent to the public and to parties concerned with the act.

Having done this, the board is faced with the necessity for deciding what form its hearings shall take. Should they be public? Yes, not only because the public receives an important education from the conduct of open hearings, but principally because the public provides an extremely critical jury which makes star-chamber procedure impossible. The public is represented by newspaper reporters. The newspapers are at present generally hostile to the act and the board. By allowing newspaper reporters to take down everything which goes on in a hearing (whether on or off the official record) the board and its agents subject themselves to the severest sort of scrutiny.

Having decided that the hearings should be public, the next question is, "What form should the hearings assume? Should they follow the analogy of courtroom procedure?" There are some reasons against this. Courtroom behavior tends to overdramatize problems. The essential elements of a situation frequently become lost in the technical theatrics of the leading actors. The play is the thing and dramatic art supersedes scientific investigation. Round-table discussions in the presence of a stenographer would minimize the theatrics and might arrive nearer the truth.

On the other hand, there are advantages of courtroom procedure which have been recognized by the hundreds of years of its continuous usage. Someone has to preside, even at a round-table discussion, if order is to be preserved. The presiding officer can be seen and heard better if he sits on a raised platform between the two groups of participants. If there must be a presiding officer who has to be paid, he might as well be a man trained in the law or in labor relations who can not only keep order in the room but also sift evidence, draw conclusions, and make recommendations to help earn his keep while maintaining order.

So the board hires trial examiners to perform these tasks.

Even in round-table discussions, the two groups of interested participants tend to line up on opposite sides of the table. They thus avoid rubbing shoulders with people they don't like, at least for the time being, and it makes it easier to tell which side is speaking. Thus the next step toward a courtroom setting is taken. The two groups sit on different sides of the trial examiner's dais. Having divided into two groups, spokesmen for each group are recognized in the form of the attorney for the respondent on the one hand and the attorneys for the board and the workers on the other. The scene tends, therefore, to look more and more like a courtroom.

But why should the workers have two attorneys, one paid by the board and one by the union? Why not have just a union attorney and an employer's attorney? First of all, the union attorney is necessary because he knows the union's case. A proceeding in which a union was vitally interested could not very well be held if the union were not represented. The board's attorney might and often does act alone for the union in unimportant cases. But if the case is complicated, it is much easier to have a legally trained and recognized representative of the union easily accessible in the room than to have the board's attorney call up the union on the phone or confer with union officers every few minutes on details about which information is needed.

But, in the second place, the board's attorney is necessary because the board must bear the ultimate responsibility. It has to present somehow the information which its experts have prepared dealing with the historical background of a case, its legal aspects, and its broader context which the union may not know. But could not the trial examiner perform this function for the board? To some extent he does. Just as a judge often questions witnesses when he thinks that the cause of justice will be furthered by so doing, the trial examiner often reserves a period in which to question the witness. But there are two good reasons for not compelling the trial examiner to perform the functions of both prosecutor and judge.

First, it is mechanically difficult for the trial examiner to sit in the middle of the room and keep order and at the same time be at the side of the room conferring with his advisers or questioning witnesses. Furthermore, the trial examiner would cease to be of much use to the board as a sifter of evidence and as a maker of recommendations if he were himself prosecuting the case. The board, or some other agent of the board, would have to take over this function. Since it has to be performed by someone, it is better done in the hearing room where the behavior of witnesses can be observed at first hand.

The second reason for giving the functions of trial examiner and prosecutor to two separate persons is that justice is more likely to be served by having one person act as a check upon the other. The board's attorney and the trial examiner tend to develop opposite sets of interests. The prestige and self-esteem of the attorney depend upon his ability to win cases which he has accepted, while the prestige, self-esteem, and perhaps the tenure of the trial examiner depend upon developing a reputation for having his recommendations sustained by the board and the courts. This compels the trial examiner to be more circumspect about the admission of board or union evidence and to give more freedom to the respondent's witnesses than a prosecutor would.

For example, in a recent board hearing the employer's

attorney asked the employer (who was on the witness stand) whether he had accepted a salary reduction himself before a company union in his plant had accepted a wage cut for the workers. Strictly speaking, this question was irrelevant since the point at issue was whether the company union was company dominated, and the employer's salary reduction had nothing to do with that. The board's attorney promptly objected to the question on the ground stated above. The witness turned inquiringly toward the trial examiner. The trial examiner said, "The witness may answer the question." While the board's attorney was concerned with the fact that the next day's local newspaper headlines would probably say, in effect, "COMPANY OFFICIAL ACCEPTED SALARY REDUCTION BEFORE WORKERS' WAGES WERE CUT," the trial examiner recognized that the answer to the question could not hurt the board's case since the matter was irrelevant, while a refusal to allow the witness to answer "yes" might influence a circuit justice unfavorably if the case came up for judicial review.[23] The board encourages separation of interest between the trial examiner and counsel for the board by appointing trial examiners from Washington who move all over the country, while counsel is attached to a regional office.

Suppose that there should be both a trial examiner and an attorney for the board; why should the board also call as witnesses its own paid economic and legal experts? The answer is that this is one way of getting their information upon the record of a case. If the history of industrial relations in an industry seems essential to a decision as to what the appropriate bargaining unit should be, for example, the board has its experts make a study and draw up a report. This report might simply be given privately to the trial examiner or to the board for its own information. Such studies might thus become a part of the record of the case if it were subjected to judicial review.

But another and perhaps better method of introducing this report is to make it a part of the evidence at the hearing. First, the public obtains a clearer picture of the whole situation in this way. Second, the employer or the unions concerned are given a much better idea of the nature of the case for or against them. They are provided with an opportunity to dispute the evidence developed by the experts and to adjust their case to fit it. If this evidence is to be presented to the public and to the interested parties, rather than simply to the board, who is better prepared to present the evidence than the experts who developed it?

Well, why should not the board go even further in the separation of its functions by appointing a federal district judge to act as trial examiner? If by this it is meant that the recommendations of the district judge would be subject to review by the board just as the trial examiner's recommendations now are subject to review, the only change effected by this proposal would be the substitution of a judge without industrial training but with a gown for an examiner with special training but without a gown. In making its findings, the trial examiner's special training is likely to be of more use to the board than the judge's robes.

The trial examiners might, of course, take to wearing gowns. As many of them have extended academic experience, their hoods might add a touch of color to the room. Since both federal district judges and board trial examiners are appointed and paid by the federal government, it would appear that the only thing needed to make the trial examiners just as impartial as the district judges is the adoption of an archaic form of attire. The board feels, however, that it has gone far enough in dramatizing its hearings. Having adopted the general plan of court-room procedure, the board urges its representatives to act as little as possible like the characters in a detective story and as much as possible like people interested in getting at the truth. Robes are therefore ruled out without any reflection upon the customs of the judicial branch of the government.

But should not the judicial functions of the board itself be given to the circuit courts? Federal circuit-court justices, like the members of the board, are appointed by the federal executive. Both are paid by the federal government from congressional appropriations. The circuit justices are appointed by the President, if not for political reasons, then because of their experience and record in administering general, unspecialized justice. Their appointments are subject to the advice and consent of the Senate. The members of the board are appointed by the President on the basis of their experience and special training in matters of both law and labor relations. Their appointments are subject to the advice and consent of the Senate.

Who can believe that industrial justice is better to be served by unspecialized judges than by specialized experts when the circumstances surrounding their respective appointments are identical except that thus far political considerations have played little part in the selection of board members? What end is to be gained by calling a man a judge, dressing him in a gown, and putting him behind a bench if no provision is made for his special training? Why not substitute a board for a bench, a business suit for a robe, and a technical knowledge of the subject at hand for general legal learning?

If, finally, it is urged that specialists in economic affairs are all right but specialists in impartiality are indispensable, let it be emphasized once more that the administrative system does not supplant the judicial system of our government. Every detail of board procedure is subject to judicial scrutiny. The statutory authority and the constitutionality of acts of the board are fully reviewable by the courts. The board's findings of fact must be supported by evidence. The courts may scrutinize the board's evidence. They have already exercised this prerogative to an extent which not only should assuage alarm over the advance of administrative powers, but may even arouse concern among those who feel that judicial review is in danger of being carried to excess.[24]

CHAPTER IX

THE N.L.R.B. AND DEMOCRACY

CONTEMPORARY European developments have compelled Americans to reëxamine their faith in democracy. Much of this reëxamination has been of the Fourth of July variety. From a pyrotechnical point of view it has been magnificent, although somewhat lacking in novelty. It has consisted chiefly of condemning all departures from the norms of our forefathers as Fascistic or Communistic.[1]

While the rockets of investigators and the indignant bombs of editors cast a red glare over the political landscape, thousands of other citizens, however, are moving toward a different conclusion. The danger to democracy does not lie in change. It lies in the failure of social institutions to adjust themselves to changes which have already taken place.[2]

The whole surge of economic development has been in the direction of centralization of power, interdependence of all parts upon each other, increasing complexity, and the inability of the individual to control his economic destiny. The individual worker cannot assure himself of employment, of freedom from industrial accident and disease, or of old-age independence.[3] The individual consumer cannot assure himself of decent quality or of a reasonable price of the goods he buys.[4] The individual investor cannot assure himself of the proper care of his funds.[5] The utmost expenditure of energy and initiative by the individual farmer or small businessman cannot assure him of a livelihood.[6] The years of training of profes-

sional specialists—engineers, doctors, lawyers, teachers—
do not assure them of employment or freedom to follow
their professions where their faiths may lead.[7] To just the
degree that economic life becomes vast, interdependent,
complex, and centrally controlled, the average citizen loses
his individual power to secure a livelihood.

Under these conditions, a good living can be assured
only by concerted action toward such common goals as employment, health, old-age independence, opportunity, and
professional freedom. If these objectives are to be reached,
however, the political institutions through which individuals attempt to control their economic lives must conform to the new economic society. One change which is
thus forced upon political institutions, not by conspiring
politicians of any particular party but by basic economic
evolution, is the growth of federal power at the expense of
state and local authority.

Wages, hours, and working conditions which are determined by interstate forces not only cannot be influenced
by the individual but are beyond the control of the state
except in limited fields. The prices and quality of goods
made and advertised by the peoples of a dozen states cannot be controlled by the people of any one state. The
safety of investments and savings affected by nationwide
business conditions cannot be guaranteed by individual
wisdom or state authority. Unemployment and old-age
dependence whose origin may lie thousands of miles from
the scene of their incidence are not only beyond prevention
by the state but frequently beyond its powers of adequate
relief. A whole section of the national community may be
so impoverished by forces beyond its control that nothing
short of a helping federal hand can relieve it from its futile
efforts to raise itself by its own bootstraps.[8]

Over a period of fifty years the federal government has been compelled by the force of economic developments to take over problems of railroading, the sale and advertising of goods, banking, trade practices, agriculture, unemployment, old-age dependence, investment, public-utility control, industrial relations, housing assistance, and wage and hour regulation. Each problem has usually not been taken over until the necessity for federal aid has been apparent for many years. Political adjustments have lagged behind economic change. This lag has been the result of the inertia of traditional thinking, the intense resistance of vested interests, and the honest fears of those who found greater potential danger in centralized federal power than in the present helplessness of the groups whose protection was sought.

The inertia of traditional thinking is to be expected and accepted—both as an obstacle to change and a medium through which change may be effected.[9] The resistance of vested interests is also to be expected. Sometimes these interests can be shown to be no more than apparent. Those who fight change frequently discover that they are better off after the change than before. In other cases, however, the majority is compelled to override the minority. But in the centralization of political power there lies a danger that the effort of the people to improve their economic lot through the instruments of government will itself destroy democracy. The immense weight of the federal administrative machinery may crush the people who brought it into being.[10]

Power granted by the mass of people to federal agencies may be turned against the people either by minority interests which capture the government or by the administrators themselves. Administrators tend to become bureaucrats. That is, they become interested in their own power and perquisites. These may frequently be at variance with the interests of the mass of people. What is to prevent bureaucrats from using the means of power against the people? Or what is to prevent those whose regulation is sought—bankers, utility magnates, industrialists, financiers, stockbrokers—from taking over the means of power and turning it against the people? [11] Or what is to prevent a combination of these two groups, supported by discontented masses, from accomplishing the same end?

The more complex, technical, and remote from the ordinary citizen that government becomes, the more difficult it is for the people to compel it to aid in improving the conditions of their economic life. Every step from the town meeting to the state legislature, from the state legislature to the federal Congress, and from Congress to federal administrative agencies is a step away from direct popular control. The defenses of the people against the possible tyranny of a remote federal administrator may become as weak as the defense of a worker against a remote employer, or a consumer against the massed power of advertising,[12] or a shareholder against a corporate holding company,[13] or the farmer against a starvation price, or all of us against unemployment and old-age dependence. Is the move toward federal regulation of economic life anything more than a leap from an unbearable frying pan into a consuming flame?

There are at least three logical courses of action which present themselves in response to this question. One is to go backward. Another is to sit down and hang on tight. The third is to take courage in hand and proceed as cautiously as possible.

Going backward may be a logical possibility, but it is

scarcely a social and economic possibility. To reverse more than forty years of federal regulative evolution and at the same time meet the problems that compel this evolution would require the reversal of the more than forty years of economic development which created the problems. The automatic protection of workers, consumers, investors, depositors, farmers, small businessmen, and professionals requires a very simple economic society. Free competition among small units of production, investment in local concerns, production for a local market, easy access to the land or to industrial opportunity, the possibility of self-employment with inexpensive tools or machines, simple commodities limited in quantity, the self-sufficiency of each community—these are some of the prerequisites of a society in which conscious social protection of individuals and groups is relatively unnecessary.

But this is scarcely an accurate picture of modern economic society. To recapture this older society would involve the surrender of geographical specialization, the breaking up of business combinations, and the abandonment of much of our specialized machinery. The result would be a heavy loss in the variety, quality, and quantity of commodities as well as of the population which creates and is sustained by these commodities. Railroads, telegraph, telephone and radio, electric power transmission, automobiles, steel bridges, modern cities, and super-highways are a few of the things which cannot be made without large-scale and specialized production. Even if the surrender of these things is considered by some to be a good idea, the possibility of reversing the rise of modern industry is slight.[14]

If economic evolution cannot be turned backward, the problems which it creates cannot be solved by thinking about the good old days. Perhaps, then, we should just sit still, try not to think about anything, close our eyes and ears to the sufferings of others, and yelp a little when the frying pan becomes warm in our corner. This program has its attractions, but the comfort of the frying pan and the perils of climbing out should not be overdone.

Millions of people are unemployed. Other millions, though employed, remain chronically at the verge of destitution.[15] Millions of people face the expectation of old-age dependence. Other millions are badly housed, under-schooled, or victims of accident and disease.[16] Thousands of people have lost their savings and investments through irresponsible corporate trusteeship. Thousands of people live in communities in which economic democracy is non-existent and political democracy is a farce.[17] These are some of the characteristics of the frying pan.

How stable is a democracy whose prestige is being undermined by the suffering and discontent of millions of people? Antidemocratic totalitarian states are not merely imposed from the top by greedy economic interests and grasping bureaucrats. They require mass support. They find it among the millions whose physical suffering, loss of hope, and distortion of judgment make them willing followers of anyone with a quick tongue and a messianic urge.[18] The difference between "thirty dollars every Thursday" and "the superiority of the Aryan race" is one of degree. People asking for bread are given a slogan. In exchange, they begin or complete the surrender of their democratic power to control their real well-being. There are as great dangers to democracy in federal inaction as there are in federal expansion.

Moreover, the threat to democracy comes from below in another sense. All over this country there are diseased spots in which dominant economic interests operating through corrupt political machines have effectively destroyed the civil liberties of speech, writing, assembly, and education upon which a democratic society is dependent for its existence. The danger that democracy will be destroyed by the encroachments of the federal government is at the moment far less than that these malignant spots will break into a rash. The federal government offers the means whereby the democratic pressures of some communities can be exerted for the protection of democracy in others. This pressure is exerted not only through the Supreme Court and such legislative bodies as the La Follette Committee, but also by federal administrative agencies. The combined action of the Department of Justice and the N.L.R.B., for example, has recently broken through the medieval defenses of Harlan County, Kentucky, and allowed a pale light of industrial democracy, at least, to fall upon its citizens.[19]

The frying pan, then, *is* a frying pan. And the alternative may not be the fire.

How can protection be assured against the possibility that federal administrators will fall a prey to powerful minority groups or to their own delusions of grandeur? There are in general two possible answers. First, that groups of people organize around their respective economic interests to obtain control over them outside political channels. Second, that when there are conflicts of group interests or problems beyond the scope of group control, these economic organizations actively participate in political government.

The most powerful economic interests are those of producers. Consumers, it is true, are interested in the price and quality of the goods they buy. But these interests are generally overshadowed by a more intense interest in the amount of income and the conditions under which it is earned. Most people think of themselves as consumers secondarily. They think and act primarily as wage earners, professionals, farmers, businessmen, and investors. People may and should organize to protect consumer interests. Much can be accomplished through consumers' coöperatives and advisory services. But within these consumers' organizations, the more powerful producer interests constantly assert themselves and conflicts of policy frequently result which are difficult to resolve within the consumer organization.[20]

Among producer groups, somewhat the same thing is true of investors. They may and do organize to protect themselves. But a very small minority of people has investments great enough to produce income equal to its wages or salaries. This small minority whose income from investments is greater than from salaries is already powerfully organized through corporate and banking devices. Their problem is not acute, to put it mildly.[21] The great majority of investors, however, is incapable of organization around investment interests and must organize, if at all, as wage or salary earners.

Farmers are an extremely important producer group which has a long tradition of collective action alongside its tradition of individualism. This collective action has been chiefly directed in the past toward general political objectives such as railroad regulation and tariff reduction. In the last ten years, however, growing farmers' organizations have directed their attention toward such particular economic ends as collective purchase of materials and sale of products. In the meantime, as a result of organized farmers' political pressure, the federal government has come to the farmers' aid to an unprecedented extent. This does not mean that the farmers have become dangerously dependent upon the federal government. Because of the virility of farmers' political organizations, the federal government has become dependent, to a large degree, upon the farmers.[22]

The farmers are acting through the federal machinery of government for the protection of their economic status. They are also acting directly through their buying and selling coöperatives. In both policies the farmers are being encouraged by the federal government. This advance of federal regulatory activity at the insistence of the farmers can hardly be described as authoritarian, destructive of democracy, or even paternalistic. On the contrary, it may be said that because the farmers are organizing to protect their economic interests both directly and through political channels, they are creating a democracy which conforms to modern economic life.

Small businessmen, also, have organized to protect themselves. Their most important organizations are concerned with immediate ends such as coöperative purchase of goods, common credit resources, local taxation or civic obligations, common advertising, exchange of technical information, trade practices, and price control. These organizations, of which there are scores of different types, have given to small business many of the advantages which could otherwise be enjoyed only by big business.[23] They are far more important than the efforts of small business to organize for political objectives. Such political organizations of small business as have appeared have tended to parrot the slogans and policies of big business whose interests in many respects are dissimilar.[24] But the pressure of small businessmen's organization is already a factor to be taken into account by federal legislators and administrators. Small businessmen also are adjusting the forms of democracy to the conditions of modern economic life.

Professionals—lawyers, doctors, teachers, among others —have long since been organized in an effort to regulate their working conditions. They don't call them working conditions, but professional training requirements, ethics, and freedom are the equivalent of union apprenticeship regulations, standards of production speed, and sanitary conditions. These organizations are rapidly spreading into such fields as engineering, technical service, insurance agencies, banking, and government. All of these professional organizations, from the lawyers down or up, are becoming more and more interested in exercising some control over the amount of their income, the standards of their work, the tenure of their jobs, and the conditions under which they work. Their efforts at control over these matters are being exerted both through bargaining on the job and through political pressures.[25]

Many doctors are interested in federally subsidized medicine both for the sake of the people's health and for the sake of their own economic skins. Engineers are interested in federal public works for similar reasons. Teachers are concerned with not only adequate education and academic freedom, but the regularity of pay day. Government workers are interested in hours and salaries as well as efficient public service. All of these groups are new forms of democracy. They attempt both to improve the economic lot of their members directly and to compel the federal government to do what the groups cannot themselves accomplish. Not only are they propelling the federal government forward into new fields but they constitute a democratic check upon possible authoritarian tyranny.

Fully two-thirds of our population is composed of wage workers and their dependents. Among them there are twenty-five to thirty million potential union members. There are perhaps eight million already in unions.[26] In their broadest aspect, these unions also represent an adjustment of democratic forms to modern economic life. Every local union is a miniature political society just as every town meeting used to be, and in some places still is. Many of the problems facing union members can be settled right in the local meeting. Others are so broad in scope that they have to be referred upward to the regional or national officers or conventions.

Just as the local and state governments have had to refer an increasing share of their problems upward to the federal government, so the local unions are compelled to delegate the handling of industry-wide bargaining, organizing, and strike control to national officers. The democratic control of union members over their officers is more direct, however, than is the control of the average citizen over his federal officials.

First, since unions are concerned with the most immediate and primary interests of their members, frequent and relatively well-attended meetings are possible. Town or other local political meetings, on the contrary, cover such a diversity of economic interests that it is difficult, if not impossible, to arouse interest in the issues before the meeting. Consequently people don't come. There is little direct and continuous check by the people upon their representatives. Such checks as exist are indirectly applied through letter writing and unofficial polls. Frequent and active union meetings (usually every two weeks) provide a continuous check upon the officers.

Second, since unions usually cover only one industry or

occupation, the issues are relatively simple and the members are united upon general ends which the officers may serve. Failure to serve these ends is soon apparent and results in dispensing with the officers' services. Selectmen, governors, Congressmen, and Presidents, on the contrary, serve geographical units including a great variety of economic interests, many of which are in conflict. Under these conditions it is often impossible for the politician to stand for anything without incurring the wrath of some group powerful in votes or funds. To be elected from such a constituency, free cigars, political favors, and Delphic utterances must be substituted for intelligent discussion of issues and objectives. Once elected, a representative has few definite commitments. He may, therefore, either do nothing at all or succumb to the pressures of group interests which are brought directly to bear upon him through channels not provided for in the constitution. Such pressure groups may represent small minorities of power and wealth whose interests are directly opposed to those of the great majority. Unless the majority is organized well enough to prevent representatives from giving in to the pressure of minorities, there is little to prevent the politician from doing so. The next election day is far away and simply repeats the free-cigar–baby-kissing–Delphic-utterance pattern.

Unions, therefore, may be regarded as democracy adapted to industrial life. They make possible both the continuous, direct scrutiny of leaders' actions and the simplification of issues in a complex society. They take their place with organizations of farmers, businessmen, and professionals as efforts to apply group power to the solution of individual problems.

But none of these organizations, including wage workers' unions, can expect to deal with problems which lie outside its jurisdiction. Organized economic groups therefore turn to local, state, and federal governments for aid. Local civil liberties, state unemployment relief, federal old-age annuities, housing assistance, health insurance, and abolition of sweatshop wages and hours are all questions in which organized labor is interested but which to varying degrees lie beyond its powers of direct control. To secure these objectives, labor turns toward the government, and particularly the federal government.

It is true that the existence of the National Labor Relations Board serves to strengthen the influence of the federal government over the economic life of the nation. But the reason for the existence of the board is to encourage the development of unionism by removing the antiunion obstacles in its path. To just the extent that unionism is encouraged, the means of democratic control over the federal government are enhanced. Although the board is a federal agency, its task is to hasten the advance of local industrial democracy and democratic political checks upon federal power. Through the N.L.R.A., the federal government is atoning for its concentration of power by assisting the progress of a check upon itself.

This policy is a flat contradiction of the policies of authoritarian governments abroad. One of the first steps of a totalitarian government is to crush the independent labor movement out of existence. The obvious reason for this is that an independent labor movement, as well as independent religious, fraternal, and political groups, challenges the dominance of the totalitarian authority. It is difficult to imagine a policy more completely at variance with despotic ambitions than the encouragement provided by the N.L.R.A. to an independent labor movement.

The existence of a strong labor movement not only acts as a check upon the bureaucratic ambitions of administrative officers but also serves to forestall the capture of governmental machinery by organized economic minorities.[27] As has been suggested, the confusion of economic issues which arises within territorial political units increasingly tends to transfer the formation of governmental policy from the ballot box to the arena of pressure politics.[28] In legislative lobbies and administrative offices the representatives of economic groups attempt to secure the adoption and enforcement of policies which serve the interests of their constituencies. The forms of territorial democracy remain. The content, however, becomes increasingly economic. Political representatives tend to become the mouthpieces of economic representatives who stand at their shoulder.

This process is so nearly universal that it cannot be dismissed or condemned as a corruption of democracy. It is, rather, an adjustment of democracy to modern specialized economic life. It might be more logical to abandon territorial representation in favor of a guild congress composed of representatives of various economic interests.[29] This, however, is neither likely, necessary, nor, perhaps, desirable. It is not likely because traditional methods of doing things have so powerful a hold upon public thinking and action that nothing short of revolution can bring about the great symbolic changes involved in a reorganization of the forms of government. It is not necessary as long as group-pressure politics can give modern economic content to ancient political forms. It is perhaps not desirable since the territorial units of town, county, district, and state continue to provide representation to citizens who do not easily or quickly fall into organized economic groups.

The chief danger of group-pressure politics is that the better-organized minority groups may exercise greater pressure upon government policy than the looser organizations of majority interests. In extreme form this superior pressure of minority groups might result in their complete domination of the machinery of government and the suppression of the organizations of opposed economic interests. Organized pressure groups of bankers, public-utility managements, stock traders, and large taxpayers, for example, although representing a small minority of the total population, may outweigh the pressures of workers, farmers, professionals, and small businessmen.

Protection against this danger lies in spreading the economic and political organization of the groups which compose the vast majority of citizens. The progress of such organization has already been noted. To just the extent that the National Labor Relations Act promotes the organization of workers, it serves to prevent the capture of governmental machinery by minority interests.

To the original question, "What can be done to prevent the centralization of federal power from destroying effective democracy?" these possible answers were given: to reverse the trend of economic change, to stand still and do nothing, and to proceed with caution. The first of these answers was dismissed as impossible. The second was thrown out as being more dangerous to the stability of democracy than further centralization of federal power. The third has been discussed in terms of the kind of caution which the federal government now displays in proceeding toward further centralization of administrative control.

It has been indicated that by strengthening the economic organizations of workers and farmers the federal government is broadening the path of democracy in its rear before blazing a trail farther into the wilderness. This suggests a rough definition of "caution" in the extension of federal power. In military terms, the federal government should not advance beyond the point of maintaining adequate support from the democratic reinforcements at the rear. If it does, it may be cut off by the raiding parties of minority interests on its flanks. In engineering terms, the federal government should not erect a superstructure of control upon an inadequate democratic foundation. If it does, the superstructure may fall and obliterate the foundation. In terms of industry, the federal government should not proceed further in the regulation of relations between management and labor than the progress of industrial democracy will allow.

The National Labor Relations Act is concerned almost exclusively with the progress of industrial democracy. Should the federal government now go further in the direction of centralized control by substituting compulsory regulation of wages, hours, and working conditions for the settlement of these matters through collective bargaining? Curiously enough, those who view with the greatest alarm the advance of federal power as exemplified in the N.L.R.A. are often those who are most insistent in urging that labor and (occasionally) management be shorn of their economic power to settle matters of industrial relations. To propose that labor's right to strike or use other forms of economic pressure against management be legally limited, and that management's right to close down its plants or use other forms of economic pressure against labor be similarly restricted, would solve no problems of industrial relations unless something else were substituted for these economic weapons. The obvious substitute is compulsory arbitration. Since the great bulk of modern business is interstate in character, the task of carrying out compulsory arbitration would fall chiefly to the federal government. The assumption of this task would involve an extension of federal regulatory power far greater in scope and significance than any single previous advance.

The National Labor Relations Board cannot be condemned, therefore, simply because it represents an extension of federal power if at the same time it is proposed further to extend federal control over wages, hours, and working conditions. If the National Labor Relations Act and compulsory federal arbitration are to be discussed in relation to each other, they must both be recognized as extensions of federal power, but with very different objectives. The major objective of the N.L.R.A. is to increase the democratic control by workers and management through collective bargaining over industrial life. An indirect effect is to enhance the political power of labor over matters in which it is interested but which do not fall within the scope of particular organizations. The main objective of compulsory arbitration, on the contrary, is to reduce the importance of industrial self-government by turning over to federal administrators powers which would otherwise be exercised by organized management and labor. In some respects, therefore, the two objectives are flatly opposed. The N.L.R.A. encourages the assumption of industrial problems by the organizations of labor and management. Compulsory arbitration surrenders the solution of these problems to a relatively remote federal authority.

Having recognized that limitations upon the use of the economic power of labor and management to bring about industrial settlements are a move in the direction of compulsory arbitration, and having recognized that this would involve a vast increase in federal regulatory power, it must be said that compulsory arbitration has its attractions. There is nothing particularly inviting about strikes and lockouts, however sacred the right to strike and lock out may be. There is little that is scientific about resort to economic force even though a prohibition of its use may be said to result in involuntary servitude for workers or the denial of employers' right to go out of business.

Compulsory arbitration might, indeed, become a very scientific instrument of national economic planning. By reference to living standards, prices, industrial earnings, profits, salaries, and industrial trends, government arbitrators not only might arrive at more equitable solutions of industrial conflicts, but also might be able to fit the plans of one industry into those of the nation as a whole.

Against this view of compulsory arbitration, however, objections must be urged. The first is that centralized control tends toward rigidity of policy. The dynamic quality of industry demands flexibility.[30] Such flexibility can be achieved only by encouraging initiative and responsibility on the part of representatives of management and labor who are in the field. Some uniformity of policy is, of course, essential. Uniformity is beginning to develop as a result of collective bargaining, first on a local, and then on an industry-wide basis. Wherever collective bargaining has been practiced, industrial policies tend to become uniform over larger and larger economic areas, but at the same time a balance is worked out between uniformity in general policies and flexibility in their application. Such a balance is best developed slowly by the people who are intimately concerned. The ultimate outcome of collective bargaining may be the development and acceptance of industrial policies so uniform and widespread in scope as to approach the kind of economic planning involved in compulsory arbitration.

But collective bargaining is in its infancy in this country. Management and labor are just beginning to develop methods of dealing with each other. They are far from the adoption of uniform policies leading toward industrial equity and peace. To propose to leap from the present stage of industrial relations to their probable ultimate conclusion is to impose regulations from above without adequate preparation from below. Such regulation is likely to be arbitrary, rigid, and unenforceable. Compulsory arbitration can do little more than clarify and apply the policies and decisions toward which the principals are themselves moving and which they are willing to accept. When collective bargaining on a democratic basis has developed sufficiently to render compulsory arbitration relatively unnecessary, that may be the time to invoke compulsory arbitration! Some American industries, such as the railroads, and to a less degree clothing and mining, are approaching this situation.[31] Others are years or decades removed from the logical end of present developments.

The second objection to compulsory arbitration is suggested by the first. Unless compulsory arbitration takes place against a well-developed background of democratic collective bargaining, the *source* of conflict is not likely to be removed. The conflict itself is simply transferred from the industrial to the political arena. In order to win the fight, management and labor are compelled to enter politics to select or influence the arbitrators. Industrial struggles simply become political struggles. Victory in politics is little more likely to produce economic justice and peace than victory in economic warfare. No real believer in the processes of democracy can be enthusiastic about compulsory arbitration until collective bargaining in industry and organized action by labor in politics have developed sufficiently to prevent government regulation of industrial relations from being merely an arbitrary imposition of the policies of powerful economic and political minorities.

The reverse of this is that those who are opposed to democratic methods and majority rule in industry should work for the repeal of the National Labor Relations Act, the imposition of compulsory arbitration (under the guise of shearing labor of its powers to strike and picket), and the placing of obstacles in the path of political action by labor.

Labor politics now takes the form of direct lobbying by labor representatives in the legislatures, efforts in party primaries to influence the selection of party nominees, the swinging of votes from one party to another to affect the outcome of elections, and the formation of independent labor parties or farmer-labor parties which give their support either to their own candidates or to preferred nominees of other parties. These forms of labor politics represent varying degrees of adjustment of political action to economic change. The development of independent labor politics marks a somewhat more clear-cut formulation of group economic interests than is occurring in the gradual reshuffling of the older parties into liberal and conservative alignments. It is a thoroughly democratic development in the sense that political action by wage workers covers the largest single economic group interest in the country—one which contains an overwhelming potential majority of all voters.

The advance of democratic action by workers in politics is being as bitterly opposed as has been the guarantee of industrial democracy through collective bargaining under the N.L.R.A. When, for example, John L. Lewis visited the Speaker of the House in an effort to dislodge a proposed amendment to the Walsh-Healy Act from the Rules Committee, his action was denounced as "dictatorship," "an invasion," "effrontery," and so on. This condemnation was offered in spite of the fact that the similar and frequently more effective comings and goings of lobbyists for all sorts of minority interests [32] usually attract little attention, and in spite of the fact that a very small minority of the House occupying a strategic position in the Rules Committee was blocking action desired by the administration, by majorities in both houses of Congress, and by millions of organized workers and their sympathizers.

More important than this disapproval of labor lobbying is the demand that the N.L.R.A. be amended to prohibit contributions by unions for political purposes.[33] Such a proposal is designed to hamstring labor parties or restrict the support given by labor to the party it favors in a particular area. Hands were raised in horror at the fact that the United Mine Workers contributed approximately $500,000 to the 1936 campaign of the Democratic party and that the American Labor party in New York state raised about $85,000 for the support of its candidates. Little attention was directed toward the fact that the average contribution of a member of the miner's union was less than a dollar, and the average contribution of American Labor party supporters was twenty-six cents. As between contributions of this size and contributions of thousands or tens of thousands of dollars by wealthy individuals or families, the greater degree of democracy would appear to rest with the former rather than with the latter, as long as union members retain democratic control over union expenditures.

This and other similar efforts to use the N.L.R.A. as a weapon against labor politics are an attack upon the adjustment of democratic forms to fit modern industrial society. In whatever guise they may be cloaked, such attacks represent the effort of minority interests to stem the rising political power of a labor movement which is moving toward a majority status. The immediate objective of the National Labor Relations Act is the encouragement of collective bargaining as a means toward industrial peace. Its more remote objectives include the improvement of the lot of American workers not only through collective bargaining in industry but also through encouragement to industrial and political democracy in local and national life.[34] In the contemporary conflict between democracy and dictatorship, whether political or industrial, the National Labor Relations Board is in the center of the struggle. Its influence and power are wholly on the side of democracy.

NOTES AND BIBLIOGRAPHY

CHAPTER I

1. On December 30, 1936, Justice McCook of the New York State Supreme Court handed down a decision in the Blue Dale Dress Co. case which ordered two companies to return to New York City from Archbald, Penn., where they had gone to escape from the I.L.G.W.U. The Justice held that the concerns had violated the terms of their contract, that they must move their machinery back to New York City, pay damages in the form of back wages to discharged workers, and reinstate their former employees. (*New York Times*, Nov. 17, 1936, p. 50, col. 2; Dec. 31, p. 1, col. 6.)
2. All of the cases described in Chapter I are taken from the files of regional offices of the National Labor Relations Board with the exception of the Memphis Furniture Company case. In all except the Memphis Furniture Company case, the names of companies, union representatives, and employers are fictionalized in order to protect the anonymity of the participants. These cases, however, are restored as accurately as possible from notes, memoranda, documents, and correspondence exchanged among the principals.
3. N.L.R.B., *National Labor Relations Act Signed Three Years Ago Today (July 5th)*, Press Release No. R-1032.
4. *Ibid.*
5. *Ibid.*
6. Memphis Furniture Manufacturing Co. and Furniture Workers' Local Union No. 1174, United Brotherhood of Carpenters and Joiners of America. 3 N.L.R.B. 26.

CHAPTER II

BIBLIOGRAPHY

THE most condensed and up-to-date statement of the background of the legal status of organized labor is contained in:

DAUGHERTY, CARROL R., *Labor Problems in American Industry* (revised ed. New York, Houghton Mifflin, 1938), chaps. 22, 23, and 24.

Other standard reference works of value in this connection are:

COMMONS, J. R., and ANDREWS, J. B., *Principles of Labor Legislation* (4th ed. revised. New York, Harper, 1936).

FRANKFURTER, FELIX, and GREENE, NATHAN, *The Labor Injunction* (New York, Macmillan, 1930).

National Labor Relations Board (the first board), *Decisions of the National Labor Relations Board* (U. S. Government Printing Office, 1935), Vols. I and II.

National Labor Relations Board (the present board), *Governmental Protection of Labor's Right to Organize,* Division of Economic Research, Bulletin No. 1 (U. S. Government Printing Office, 1935).

SWAZEE, CLEON O., *Contempt of Court in Labor Injunction Cases* (New York, Columbia University Press, 1935).

United States Senate, *Hearings Before the Committee on Education and Labor,* 74th Congress, 1st Sess., on S. 1958 (U. S. Government Printing Office, 1935).

WITTE, EDWIN E., *The Government in Labor Disputes* (New York, McGraw-Hill, 1932).

NOTES

1. Commonwealth *vs.* Hunt, 4 Metcalf Reports, III, Mass., 1842.
2. Especially in interpreting the interstate commerce clause.
3. Cf. Allen, Robert, and Pearson, Drew, *The Nine Old Men* (Garden City, N. Y., Doubleday, Doran, 1936).
4. Hitchman Coal and Coke Co. *vs.* Mitchell, 245 U.S. 229, 1917.
5. Gompers *vs.* Buck Stove and Range Co., 221 U.S. 418, 1911.
6. Lawler *vs.* Loewe, 235 U.S. 522, 1915.
7. Lehigh Structural Steel Co. *vs.* Atlantic Works, 92 N.J. Eq. 131, 1920. Stearns Lumber Co. *vs.* Howlett, 260 Mass. 45, 1927. Moore Drop Forging Co. *vs.* McCarthy, 243 Mass. 554, 1923. Reynolds *vs.* Davis, 198 Mass. 294, 1908.
8. Butterick Publishing Co. *vs.* Typographical Union, 50 Misc., N.Y. 1, 1906.
9. Atchison, Topeka & Santa Fe Railway Co. *vs.* Gee, 139 Fed. 582.
10. Bedford Cut Stone Co. *vs.* Journeyman Stone Cutters' Association, 274 U.S. 37, 1927.
11. Gompers case, *supra.*
12. *In re* Debs, 158 U.S. 564, 1895.
13. Loewe *vs.* Lawlor, 208 U.S. 274, 1908.
14. Gompers case, *supra.*
15. Duplex Printing Co. *vs.* Deering, 254 U.S. 349, 1921.

16. American Steel Foundries *vs.* Tri-City Central Trades Council, 257 U.S. 344, 1922.
17. United Mine Workers *vs.* Coronado Coal and Coke Co., 259 U.S. 344, 1922; 268 U.S. 295, 1925.
18. Bedford case, *supra.*
19. A recent instance is provided by the case of Organizer William Sentner of the C.I.O.'s United Radio, Electrical, and Machine Workers of America who, on July 6, 1938, was arrested in St. Louis, Mo., on a charge of assembly for promoting criminal syndicalism. His offense was alleged to be that of urging strikers to ignore an injunction against picketing. He and two other officers of the union were fined $500 and sentenced to six months in jail. The judge offered to suspend the sentences if the officers called off the strike. *Life,* July 18, 1938, p. 18; *Time,* July 25, p. 10.
20. Jersey City, N.J., provides the most informative current examples of this practice.
21. New Orleans vigilantes and police authorities in the summer of 1938 broke loose in a campaign of terrorism against the local C.I.O. organizing program. *The Nation,* July 9, pp. 30–31.
22. DAUGHERTY, *op. cit.,* pp. 899–900.
23. City Trust Co. *vs.* Waldhauer, 95 N.Y. Sup. 222, 1905.
24. Adair *vs.* United States, 208 U.S. 161, 1908.
25. DAUGHERTY, *op. cit.,* pp. 899–900.
26. In July, 1938, Justice Cotillo of the Supreme Court of New York handed down a decision in the Busch Jewelry Company case which threatened New York's "little Norris-LaGuardia Act" and all other similar acts. In spite of express prohibition by the act, Justice Cotillo enjoined *all* picketing by the union on the ground that *some* pickets had committed fraudulent and violent acts. *The Nation,* July 16, 1938, pp. 58–59.
27. The only southern state with an anti-injunction statute is Louisiana. In addition to the remaining southern states, South Dakota, Nebraska, Iowa, Kansas, Missouri, Nevada, Vermont, New Hampshire, Connecticut, Rhode Island, and Montana are the other states without anti-injunction laws.
29. For a discussion of the other forces which limited the expansion of organized labor during this period, see BROOKS, ROBERT R. R., *When Labor Organizes* (New Haven, Yale University Press, 1937), pp. 57–63.
30. In the Matter of Houde Engineering Corporation *and* United Automobile Workers' Federal Labor Union No. 18, 839. Decided Aug. 30, 1934.

31. Under the authority of the Railway Labor Act of 1934, the National Mediation Board was established to carry out the policies which were later included in the N.L.R.A. This board developed a valuable body of experience and precedents which the N.L.R.B. was able later to use as a guide.

CHAPTER III

1. BONNETT, CLARENCE E., *Employers' Associations in the United States* (New York, Macmillan, 1922). "Employers' Associations," *Encyclopedia of Social Sciences* (New York, 1931), Vol. V. PERLMAN, SELIG, and TAFT, PHILIP, *History of Labor in the United States, 1896–1932* (New York, Harper, 1935), IV, chaps. 12, 28, 37.

2. BROOKS, ROBERT R. R., *When Labor Organizes* (New Haven, Yale University Press, 1937), chaps. 3 and 5. *Hearings Before a Subcommittee of the Committee on Education and Labor*, U. S. Senate, pursuant to S. Res. 266 (74th Congress), on "Violations of Free Speech and Rights of Labor." *Report of the Committee on Education and Labor*, pursuant to S. Res. 266 (74th Congress), Nov. 16, 1937, on "Industrial Espionage."

3. N.L.R.B., Muskin Shoe Co. and United Shoe Workers of America. 8 N.L.R.B. No. 1; *Second Annual Report* (U. S. Government Printing Office, 1937), pp. 65–68; *Speech of Edwin S. Smith at American Communications Association Convention, New York*, July 22, 1938, Press Release R-1082; *Statement of J. Warren Madden*, Dec. 12, 1937, Press Release R-479.
Constitutional Educational League, Inc. (New Haven, Conn.), *Communism's Iron Grip on the C.I.O.; Join the C.I.O. and Help Build a Soviet America; Stop Lewis and Smash Communism; The Hell of Herrin Rages Again.*

4. *New York Times*, July 12, 1938, editorial; on this subject see also Frankfurter and Green, *op. cit.*, p. 98.

5. Ford Motor Co. and United Automobile Workers of America, 4 N.L.R.B. 621.

6. STEIN, ROSE M., "Ernest T. Weir *vs.* The United States Government," *The C.I.O. News*, July 22, 1938.

7. Cf. Virginian Railway Co. *vs.* System Federation No. 40, 300 U.S. 515; also Associated Press *vs.* N.L.R.B., 301 U.S. 103.

8. Club Troika, Inc., and Hotel and Restaurant Employees' Alliance, Local 781, 2 N.L.R.B. 90.

9. Tidewater Express Lines, Inc., and Locals 355 and 430, Brotherhood of Teamsters, 2 N.L.R.B. 560.

10. N.L.R.B., *Second Annual Report,* pp. 70–76.

11. Omaha Hat Corp. and United Hatters' Union, Locals Nos. 7 and 8, 4 N.L.R.B. 878.

12. Cf. Cardinale Trucking Corp. and International Association of Machinists, 5 N.L.R.B. 220; Standard Lime and Stone Co. and Quarry Workers' Union, Branch No. 175, 5 N.L.R.B. 106. In this case eight workers guilty of crimes in connection with a strike were not reinstated.

13. N.L.R.B., *Second Annual Report,* pp. 76–78.

14. *Idem,* p. 77.

15. Mackay Radio and Telegraph Co. and American Radio Telegraphists' Association, 1 N.L.R.B. 201. The Supreme Court sustained the board in this decision. Mackay Radio and Telegraph Co. *vs.* N.L.R.B., 304 U.S. 333.

16. N.L.R.B., Press Release No. R-1032, July 5, 1938.

17. *Ibid.*

18. *Ibid.*

19. Hopwood Retinning Co., Inc., and Monarch Retinning Co. and Metal Polishers' Union, Local No. 8, and Teamsters' Union, Local No. 584, 4 N.L.R.B. 922. The Second Circuit Court of Appeals sustained the board in this case. N.L.R.B. *vs.* Hopwood Retinning Co., Inc., 98 Fed. (2d), 97.

20. Atlas Bag and Burlap Co. and Milton Rosenberg, Organizer, United Textile Workers, Local No. 2469, 1 N.L.R.B. 292.

21. Remington Rand, Inc., and Remington Rand Joint Protective Board, 2 N.L.R.B. 626.

22. Ansin Shoe Manufacturing Co. and Shoe Workers' Protective Union, Local No. 80, 1 N.L.R.B. 929.

23. Brown Shoe Co., Inc., and Boot and Shoe Workers' Union, Local No. 655, 1 N.L.R.B. 803.

24. See notes 11 and 19, Ch. III.

25. S and K Knee Pants Co., Inc., and Amalgamated Clothing Workers, 2 N.L.R.B. 940.

26. N.L.R.B., *Second Annual Report,* pp. 62–65.

27. U. S. Dept. of Labor, Bureau of Labor Statistics, *Characteristics of Company Unions,* April, 1935, Bulletin No. 634, May, 1937.

28. National Association of Manufacturers, *Independent Unions: an Analysis and a Survey,* Labor Relations Bulletin No. 23, July 23, 1937.
    N.L.R.B., Division of Economic Research, *Statistical Analysis of 85 "Independent" Unions and Readapted Company Unions,* March, 1938.

29. Saposs, D. J., *Memorandum to Staff*, N.L.R.B., Division of Economic Research, Z-207, pp. 22–23.

30. N.L.R.B., *Summary of All N.L.R.B. Elections from October, 1935*, Press Release R-1073.

31. In cases of collusion between an employer and either A. F. of L. or C.I.O. unions, although the board does not order the disestablishment of the union it has in several cases set aside the contract which was the result of this collusion. For examples of A. F. of L.–employer collusion, see: Stone Knitting Mills Co. and A. F. of L., Bamberger Reinthal Co., Federal Knitting Mills Co., and International Ladies' Garment Workers' Union, 3 N.L.R.B. 257. National Electric Products Co. and United Radio Workers, Local No. 609, 3 N.L.R.B. 475. Consolidated Edison Co. of N.Y., Inc., and United Radio Workers, 4 N.L.R.B. 71. Lenox Shoe Co., Inc., and United Shoe Workers, 4 N.L.R.B. 72. For reference to C.I.O.–employer collusion, see statement of J. Warren Madden in *Hearings Before a Subcommittee of the Committee of the Judiciary*, U. S. Senate on S. Res. 207, pp. 63–64. See also Chapter IV, below.

32. From the author's experience.

33. National Association of Manufacturers, *A Community Organizes*, Labor Relations Bulletin, July 20, 1936, p. 5.

34. *Idem*, No. 22, July 15, 1937.

35. Issued by the N.A.M. in August, 1937.

36. Distributed during Gulf longshoremen's strike, Mobile, Ala., 1935.

37. Handbill issued in Sunshine Mining strike, Kellogg, Idaho, 1937.

38. For material on antiunionism in general, see the *Hearings* fully cited in note 2, Ch. III.

39. *New York Times*, July 21 and 22, 1938.

40. *Idem*, July 21, 1938.

41. See especially the *Hearings* on Johnstown Citizens' Committee. Full citation in note 2.

42. In fighting a six-day strike in 1935, Republic Steel supplied $8,804 worth of tear gas and guns to the police.

43. One day's shooting of 15 persons by company guards cost Republic Steel $8,971.99. Total payments for personal damage claims during the six days of the strike were $42,228.

44. 2 N.L.R.B. 626.

45. 4 N.L.R.B. 621.

46. 9 N.L.R.B. No. 33.

47. For example, 5 N.L.R.B. 106 cited in note 12.

48. Anderson, Paul Y., "Where Murder Is Overlooked," *The Nation*, July 30, 1938.

CHAPTER IV

1. ANDERSON, PAUL Y., "California's Blackshirts," *The Nation*, Aug. 8, 1938, p. 122.
2. Section 1 of the N.L.R.A.
3. Cf. Houde Engineering Corp. and United Automobile Workers of America, Federal Labor Union No. 18,839.
4. The word "employer" is defined in the act as "any person acting in the interest of an employer directly or indirectly" and the word "person" is defined so as to include "one or more associations."
5. N.L.R.B., *Second Annual Report*, pp. 122–140.
6. *Ibid.*, for references to cases.
7. *Idem*, p. 110.
8. Letter from an agent of the board to the author. See also 8 N.L.R.B. 54.
9. 1 N.L.R.B. 164.
10. 2 N.L.R.B. 168.
11. N.L.R.B., *Second Annual Report*, pp. 114–117.
12. N.L.R.B., *Summary of All N.L.R.B. Elections from October, 1935*, Press Release R-1073.
13. N.L.R.B., *N.L.R.B. Directs First Run-Off Election*, Press Release R-530.
14. *Ibid.*
15. See note 12.
16. *Ibid.*
17. *Ibid.*
18. N.L.R.B., *Second Annual Report*, pp. 108–110.
19. N.L.R.B., *Certifications on Proof of Majority Rather Than by Election*, memorandum from the board to the author, Aug. 25, 1938.
20. Cf. President William Green's speech at the convention of the Massachusetts Federation of Labor in August, 1938, or his speeches at the October, 1938, convention of the A. F. of L. On one occasion President Green is reported to have said, "We will mobilize all our political and economic strength in an uncompromising fight until this Board is driven from power." *Fortune*, October, 1938.
21. 4 N.L.R.B. 71.
22. N.L.R.B., *Analysis of Labor Board Decisions Involving Contracts with Labor Organizations, from the Beginning of the Board's*

Operations to August 29, 1938, memorandum from the board to the author.

23. 3 N.L.R.B. No. 47; 4 N.L.R.B. No. 54; 5 N.L.R.B. Nos. 66, 73; 7 N.L.R.B. Nos. 28, 145; 8 N.L.R.B. Nos. 14, 33, 57, and 66.

24. 4 N.L.R.B. 46.

25. e.g., Tennessee Electric Power Co., 7 N.L.R.B. No. 7.

26. The Supreme Court, however, has granted a petition by the employer to review this case.

27. N.L.R.B., *Second Annual Report,* pp. 80–90.

28. *Idem,* p. 86.

29. *Idem,* p. 81.

30. Cf. La Follette Committee *Hearings* cited in full in Chapter III, note 2.

31. Inland Steel Co. and Steel Workers' Organizing Committee, 9 N.L.R.B. No. 73.
Case No. C-252.

32. *Ibid.*

33. SAPOSS, D. J., *Written Agreements in Collective Bargaining,* Digest of Testimony in Inland Steel Case, N.L.R.B., Division of Economic Research, Memorandum No. 2, Z-228, April, 1938.

34. *New York Times,* Aug. 12, 1938, p. 6, col. 5.

CHAPTER V

1. United States Department of Labor, Bureau of Labor Statistics, *Analysis of Strikes in April, 1938,* Serial R. 805.

2. BURKE, EDWARD R., *We Must Amend the Wagner Act* (pamphlet reprint of speech delivered in the U. S. Senate, April 5, 1938), p. 4.

3. Quoted in *Hearings Before a Subcommittee of the Committee of the Judiciary,* U. S. Senate, 75th Congress, 3d Sess., on S. Res. 207, p. 77.

4. *Analysis* (cited in note 1), p. 1.

5. *Hearings* (cited in note 3), pp. 120–121.

6. *Idem,* p. 115; cf. also N.L.R.B., *Speech of J. Warren Madden at Harvard Business School,* June 18, 1938, Press Release No. R-984. See Chapter VIII, below.

7. N.L.R.B., *Litigation Record of the N.L.R.B.,* Press Release No. R-756.

8. *Hearings* (cited in note 3), pp. 116–117.

9. 5 N.L.R.B. 172.

10. BROOKS, ROBERT R. R., *When Labor Organizes* (New Haven, Yale University Press, 1937), pp. 172–173.

11. N.L.R.B., *Summary of All N.L.R.B. Elections from October, 1935; N.L.R.B. Handled 14,207 Cases to May 1, 1938,* Press Releases Nos. R-1073 and R-899, respectively.
12. N.L.R.B., *N.L.R.B. Handled 3,852 Cases to June 1, 1937; N.L.R.B. Handled 14,207 Cases to May 1, 1938,* Press Releases Nos. R-260 and R-899, respectively.
13. N.L.R.B., *N.L.R.B. Handled 15,561 Cases to July 1, 1938,* Press Release No. R-1126.
14. The last case in Chapter I.
15. According to tables printed on p. 119 of the *Hearings* cited in note 3 as compared with figures given in the *Analysis* cited in note 1.
16. *Analysis* (cited in note 1), *February, 1938,* Serial No. 766, p. 6.
17. *Ibid.*
18. *Idem,* p. 8.
19. BROOKS, ROBERT R. R., *op. cit.,* chaps. 3, 7, 9.
20. *Ibid.* Cf. also SEIDMAN, HAROLD, *Labor Czars, A History of Labor Racketeering* (New York, Liveright, 1938).
21. *Hearings* (cited in note 3), p. 119.
22. *Idem,* p. 114.

CHAPTER VI

1. Especially in the case of jurisdictional conflicts between the Carpenters' Union and others.
2. 1 N.L.R.B. 530.
3. 1 N.L.R.B. 604, 614.
4. N.L.R.B., *Summary of All N.L.R.B. Elections from October, 1935,* Press Release No. R-1073, p. 2.
5. 7 N.L.R.B. No. 120, discussed in Chapter IV. For a good summary of this case, see N.L.R.B. Press Release No. R-994. For a statement of other factors in the Pacific coast situation, see the series of articles by Russell B. Porter in the *New York Times.* See also LEVINSON, EDWARD, "Conflicts on the Waterfront," *The New Republic,* Sept. 14, 1938.
6. On Aug. 18, 1938, for example, the general counsel of the A. F. of L. said that the amendments to the act proposed by the executive council "would make it impossible for the board to consider a whole plant as an industrial unit." *New York Times,* Aug. 19, 1938, p. 1.
7. e.g., in the case of the six crafts in the Allis Chalmers Co. 4 N.L.R.B. 159.

8. e.g., in the Allis Chalmers Co. case the board set aside as an appropriate unit the industrial engineers and draftsmen. In order to simplify the issues, this craft is not mentioned in the text.

9. e.g., 3 N.L.R.B. 294; 4 N.L.R.B. 246, 535.

10. *New York Times,* Aug. 23, 1938, p. 21, col. 1.

11. See note 7.

12. 5 N.L.R.B. 61.

13. *New York Times,* Aug. 23, 1938, p. 9.

14. BROOKS, ROBERT R. R., *When Labor Organizes* (New Haven, Yale University Press, 1937), pp. 55–63.

15. U. S. Dept. of Labor, Bureau of Labor Statistics, *Monthly Labor Review,* July, 1938, rearranged from material on p. 35.

16. By the author's count. Of the 196 election contests between Jan. 1 and Sept. 1, 1938, the C.I.O. won 114 and the A. F. of L. 71. Two were tied and in 9 cases neither union won. Of the C.I.O.'s victories, 37, however, were by the C.I.O. National Maritime Union over the almost defunct A. F. of L. International Seamen's Union. If the C.I.O.'s 37 victories and the A. F. of L.'s 11 victories in these shipping elections are subtracted from the total victories won by each, the result leaves the two organizations close to each other in the board election race.

17. From a memorandum sent to the author by the board, *Appropriate Unit Decisions in Cases Where Unions Affiliated with A. F. of L. and C.I.O. Participated.*

18. U. S. Dept. of Labor, Bureau of Labor Statistics, *Analysis of Strikes in November, December, 1937, February, March, 1938.* Serial Nos. R-728, R-746, R-766, and R-781, respectively.

19. A letter to the author from Mr. Paul Herzog, a member of the New York State Labor Relations Board, states that 25 of these 46 petitions involved conflict between A. F. of L., C.I.O., or independent outside unions. Five cases involved conflict between one of these three groups and company unions. In 16 cases it appeared that employers were attempting to force a premature election. Thirty of the 46 cases were settled without formal hearings and many of these 30 cases resulted in recognition of a union as bargaining agent. Four certifications after elections and one based on membership cards resulted from the cases formally handled. The New York Labor Relations Act does not allow the S.L.R.B. to hold elections *solely* on the appeal of an employer; that is, if in the board's judgment the situation does not require an election, it need not be held simply because an employer has requested it.

20. In the 1938 session of Congress, Senator Vandenberg introduced

a series of proposed amendments to the act, one of which provided for appeal by employers to the board for elections. The language of Senator Vandenberg's proposed amendments actually would grant to the board no more power or impose upon it no greater obligation to hold elections at employers' requests than the present version of the act. Senator Vandenberg's proposal uses the word "may." Under the act as it stands, the board *may* give ear to employer petitions. Compare Senate Bill 2712, 75th Congress, 1st Sess., p. 4, ll. 4–20, with Section 9 (c) of the N.L.R.A.

CHAPTER VII

1. See almost any newspaper for the last eighteen months, but particularly the editorials of the *New York Times* and the speeches of Senators Burke, Bridges, Nye, and Vandenberg, and Representatives Hoffman and Rankin.
2. *Supra,* Chapter II.
3. Cf. Douglas, Paul H., "American Labor Relations Acts," *American Economic Review,* Vol. XXVII, No. 4, December, 1937.
4. Cf. the account by Mrs. Elinore Herrick of elections in the east coast shipping industry given to the Senate Committee on Commerce, released by the N.L.R.B. as *Statement on East Coast Maritime Situation,* Press Release No. R-582.
5. N.L.R.B., *Second Annual Report,* p. 109.
6. *Hearings Before a Subcommittee of the Committee on the Judiciary,* U. S. Senate, 75th Congress, 3d Sess., on S. Res. 207, "Investigation of the National Labor Relations Board," pp. 87–89. Standard Lime and Stone Co. and Quarry Workers' Union, Branch No. 175, 5 N.L.R.B. 106. In this case eight workers guilty of crimes during a strike were not reinstated.
7. *Infra,* Chapter VIII.
8. Section 13.
9. The percentages of sympathetic strikes in November and December, 1937, and February and March, 1938, were 0.9, 1.6, 0.7 and 0, respectively. U. S. Dept. of Labor, Bureau of Labor Statistics, *Analysis of Strikes in November, December, 1937, February, March, 1938,* Serial Nos. R-728, R-746, R-766, and R-781.
10. *New York Times,* Sept. 2, 1938, p. 8, cols. 7–8. Note that although the *Times's* subheadline says, "Unions Not Immune to Suits for Strikes," the fine print immediately below the commission's report says that unions remain immune to suits in spite of the Act of 1927 for all nonpolitical strike purposes.

11. e.g., the 1936 strike of east coast seamen in sympathy with the west coast longshoremen.

12. Apparently a threatened boycott was used by the A. F. of L. in the National Electric Products case to persuade the workers to vote for the A. F. of L. and against the C.I.O. LEVINSON, EDWARD, *Labor on the March* (New York, Liveright, 1938), pp. 231–232.

13. Section 8 (3).

14. See note 9.

15. As related to the author by one of the union leaders concerned.

16. Told to a group of which the author was a member by Mr. William Leiserson, Chairman of the National Mediation Board

17. *Steel Facts,* No. 15, September, 1936, p. 1.

18. SPENCER, W. H., "The National Railroad Adjustment Board," *The Journal of Business* (University of Chicago), Vol. XI, No. 2, p. 50.

19. SEIDMAN, HAROLD, *Labor Czars, a History of Labor Racketeering* (New York, Liveright), 1938.

20. A high official of the A. F. of L. recently expressed this opinion to the author.

21. SAPOSS, DAVID J., *Union Responsibility and Incorporation of Trade Unions,* N.L.R.B., Division of Economic Research, Z-194, Feb. 2, 1938.

22. Loewe *vs.* Lawlor, 208 U.S. 274; Coronado Coal Cases, 259 U.S. 344 and 268 U.S. 295.

23. See note 16, Chapter VII.

24. Both the A. F. of L. and the C.I.O. have apparently continued to grow during the 1937 depression. In October, 1938, the announced membership of the A. F. of L., including unemployed nondues-paying members, was given as approximately five million. Although this is probably a generous figure, the number of workers under A. F. of L. influence cannot be far from this number. The combined membership of the C.I.O. and standard national independents probably constitutes another five million persons under strong union influence. The number of workers closely associated with unionism is, therefore, probably close to ten millions. Taken with their dependents, they compose from a quarter to a third of the total population. This is a remarkable change from the situation in 1929 and indicates a trend which may be described without great inaccuracy as "a drive toward a majority status."

25. Federal authorities have repeatedly, although not recently, proposed such an arrangement. Cf. *New York Times,* Nov. 12, 1938, p. 8, col. 2.

26. 2 N.L.R.B. 626.
27. 1 N.L.R.B. 530. On the general question of regulation of trade unions consult the speech of Edwin S. Smith before the International Juridical Association, Jan. 15, 1938, and the speech of Chairman Madden before the General Council of the National League of Women Voters, May 5, 1938. N.L.R.B., Press Releases Nos. R-542 and R-212.

CHAPTER VIII

1. N.L.R.B., *The Drive against the National Labor Relations Board*, speech by Edwin S. Smith, Press Release No. R-904.
2. This interdict against injunctions has been established by court decisions rather than by specific provision in the act.
3. Mr. Justice Brandeis thoroughly covered this point in A. Howard Myers et al. *vs.* Bethlehem Shipbuilding Corp.
4. N.L.R.B., *First Annual Report*, pp. 46–50.
5. Newport News Shipbuilding and Dry Dock Co. *vs.* Bennett F. Schauffler et al. Italics supplied.
6. The figures and percentages in this paragraph are based on the first ninety-five injunction cases. About the disposition of the other two cases the author has no information except that they were eventually won by the board. N.L.R.B. *Second Annual Report*, pp. 31, 36–40; *Litigation Record of the N.L.R.B.*, Press Release No. R-973.
7. National Labor Relations Board *vs.* Friedman–Harry Marks Clothing Co., 301 U.S. 58. Italics supplied.
8. N.L.R.B., *The Drive against the National Labor Relations Board*, speech by Edwin S. Smith, Press Release No. R-904.
9. From the court transcript of a case to which the author had access in the files of a regional office.
10. Section 10 (e), (f).
11. From the experience of the author during public speeches describing the board's work.
12. Italics supplied.
13. Italics supplied.
14. Italics supplied.
15. Memorandum from the board to the author based on the period ending Aug. 25, 1938.
16. A. Howard Myers et al. *vs.* Bethlehem Shipbuilding Corp. A. Howard Myers et al. *vs.* Charles McKenzie et al. Newport News Shipbuilding and Dry Dock Co. *vs.* Bennett F. Schauffler et al.

17. N.L.R.B., *Statement of J. Warren Madden,* Press Release No. R-859. See also note 8, above.
18. See note 8, above.
19. In the Matter of the Petition of the National Labor Relations Board for a Writ of Prohibition and a Writ of Mandamus.
20. N.L.R.B., Press Releases Nos. R-940 and R-966.
21. Cf., for example, PAUL Y. ANDERSON, in *The Nation,* May 7, 1938, p. 525; May 21, p. 580; June 4, p. 634.
22. Cf. JOHN T. FLYNN, in *The New Republic,* Aug. 31, 1938, p. 103.
23. From the author's experience.
24. LANDIS, JAMES, *The Administrative Process* (New Haven, Yale University Press, 1938). In this book the Dean of Harvard Law School and former chairman of the Securities and Exchange Commission discusses many of the problems which have been more briefly treated in this chapter.

CHAPTER IX

1. Cf. the activities of Attorney General A. Mitchell Palmer twenty years ago; the continuing policies of the Daughters of the American Revolution and large sections of the American Legion; the perennial appearance of new crops of "patriotic" organizations rallying to the defense of the much-beleaguered Constitution; and the contemporary efforts of the Dies Committee to expose "un-American" activities in the C.I.O. and the New Deal.
2. For an able exposition of this thesis consult SOULE, GEORGE, *The Coming American Revolution* (New York, Macmillan, 1934).
3. Cf. EPSTEIN, ABRAHAM, *Insecurity: A Challenge to America* (3d [revised] ed. New York, Random House, 1936).
4. Cf. HARDING, T. SWAN, *The Popular Practice of Fraud* (New York, Longmans, Green, 1935). LAMB, RUTH DE F., *The American Chamber of Horrors* (New York, Farrar & Rinehart, 1936).
5. Cf. BRANDEIS, LOUIS D., *Other People's Money* (New York, Stokes, 1932). FLYNN, JOHN T., *Security Speculation* (New York, Harcourt Brace, 1934), and *Graft in Business* (New York, Vanguard, 1931). LOWENTHAL, M., *The Investor Pays* (New York, Knopf, 1933). WINKLER, M., *Foreign Bonds, an Autopsy* (Philadelphia, Roland Swain, 1932).
6. EZEKIAL, M., and BEAN, L. H., *Economic Bases for the Agricultural Adjustment Act,* U. S. Department of Agriculture, 1933.
7. COREY, LOUIS, *The Crisis of the Middle Class* (New York, Covici Friede, 1935).

8. United States National Emergency Council, Report on *Economic Conditions of the South* (Government Printing Office, 1938).

9. ARNOLD, THURMAN W., *The Folklore of Capitalism* (New Haven, Yale University Press, 1937).

10. This point of view has been extensively developed by Walter Lippmann and Dorothy Thompson. Cf. LIPPMANN, WALTER, *The Good Society* (Boston, Little, Brown, 1937).

11. The mechanics of this process have been best observed and reported by LINCOLN STEFFENS in his *Autobiography* (New York, Harcourt Brace, 1931).

12. RORTY, JAMES, *Our Master's Voice: Advertising* (New York, John Day, 1934).

13. BERLE, A. A., and MEANS, G. C., *The Modern Corporation and Private Property* (New York, Macmillan, 1934).

14. CHAMBERLAIN, JOHN, *Farewell to Reform* (New York, Liveright, 1932). STRACHEY, JOHN, *The Coming Struggle for Power* (New York, Covici Friede, 1933).

15. United States National Resources Committee, *Consumer Incomes in the United States: Their Distribution in 1935–36* (Government Printing Office, 1938).

16. *Ibid.* POST, LANGSON W., *The Challenge of Housing* (New York, Farrar & Rinehart, 1938). EPSTEIN, A., *op. cit.*

17. Cf. the La Follette Committee Reports cited in full in earlier chapters.

18. Cf. SCHUMAN, FREDERICK L., *The Nazi Dictatorship* (revised ed. New York, Knopf, 1936).

19. *The C.I.O. News*, Sept. 3, 1938.

20. WARBASSE, J. P., *Coöperative Democracy* (New York, Harper, 1936). WEBB, SIDNEY and BEATRICE, *The Consumers' Coöperative Movement* (New York, Longmans, Green, 1921).

21. LUNDBERG, FERDINAND, *America's Sixty Families* (New York, Vanguard, 1937).

22. There are at present six strong farmers' organizations whose activities are great enough to influence governmental policy. Consult Labor Research Association, *Labor Fact Book III* (New York, International, 1936), chap. 7.

23. FRAIN, H. L., *An Introduction to Economics* (Boston, Houghton Mifflin, 1937), pp. 254–256.

24. Cf. newspaper accounts of the convention of "small" businessmen called by President Roosevelt in February, 1938. For accounts of subsequent activities of this group see the *New York Times Index*, 1938, under "Businessmen's Ass'n., National Small, Inc."

25. There are at present five professional unions affiliated with the

C.I.O., five affiliated with the A. F. of L., and one independent which are on a strictly trade-union basis. In addition to these unions there are more than a score of professional organizations whose interests lead them increasingly toward the assumption of national political functions as well as the democratic method of handling many of their own economic affairs.

26. Exact figures of dues-paying membership are difficult to obtain. There are probably about ten million workers under strong union influence of whom somewhat less than eight million are in good standing.

27. If it be urged that the labor movement is itself a minority which "captures governmental machinery" it can only be replied that the labor movement is by far the largest organized minority group in the country, that the larger the minority the more likely its interests are to coincide with those of the community as a whole, that the labor movement is at present trying as hard as its funds, energies, and leadership capacities will allow to become a majority, and that the election of 1936 suggests that the labor movement is already a powerful force supporting political movements which are strongly opposed to the influence of economic minorities upon governmental policy.

28. Cf. THOMPSON, C. D., *Confessions of the Power Trust* (New York, Dutton, 1932).

29. Cf. COLE, G. D. H., *Guild Socialism, a Plan for Economic Democracy* (New York, Stokes, 1921).

30. One aspect of the Australian experience with compulsory arbitration has been that wage rates set by arbitration awards tend to remain rigidly fixed over long periods of time during which both the general productivity of an industry and the relationship among the different classes of workers within it may undergo marked alterations. Although this is also true of wage rates fixed by custom or by trade agreements, both the degree and the duration of rigidity are likely to be less than when control is relatively remote from the scene of action. This objection does not apply with equal force against *minimum* wage fixation by federal authority since wide latitude for differentials and for variation is allowed above the relatively rigid minimum.

31. Cf. "Report of the President's Commission of Industrial Relations in Great Britain," *New York Times*, Sept. 2, 1938, p. 8.

32. *Time*, Aug. 20, 1938, p. 3, col. 1.

33. Cf. Amendments to the N.L.R.A., proposed by Senator Vandenberg, Senate Bill 2712, 75th Congress, 1st Sess., p. 3, ll. 10–12.

34. For an excellent statement of the board's own conception of its

relation to the labor movement and to political and economic democracy, see *The National Labor Relations Act: Guardian of Democracy*, a speech by Edwin S. Smith, member of the N.L.R.B., before the Carolina Political Union, Durham, N.C., March 30, 1938, N.L.R.B. Press Release No. R-755.

APPENDIX

NATIONAL LABOR RELATIONS ACT

(49 Stat. 449)

AN ACT

To diminish the causes of labor disputes burdening or obstructing interstate and foreign commerce, to create a National Labor Relations Board, and for other purposes.

Be it enacted by the Senate and House of Representatives of the United States of America in Congress assembled,

FINDINGS AND POLICY

Section 1. The denial by employers of the right of employees to organize and the refusal by employers to accept the procedure of collective bargaining lead to strikes and other forms of industrial strife or unrest, which have the intent or the necessary effect of burdening or obstructing commerce by (a) impairing the efficiency, safety, or operation of the instrumentalities of commerce; (b) occurring in the current of commerce; (c) materially affecting, restraining, or controlling the flow of raw materials or manufactured or processed goods from or into the channels of commerce, or the prices of such materials or goods in commerce; or (d) causing diminution of employment and wages in such volume as substantially to impair or disrupt the market for goods flowing from or into the channels of commerce.

The inequality of bargaining power between employees who do not possess full freedom of association or actual liberty of contract, and employers who are organized in the corporate or other forms of ownership association substantially burdens and affects the flow of commerce, and tends to aggravate recurrent business depressions, by depressing wage rates and the purchasing power of wage earners in industry and by preventing the stabilization of competitive wage rates and working conditions within and between industries.

Experience has proved that protection by law of the right of employees to organize and bargain collectively safeguards commerce from injury, impairment, or interruption, and promotes the flow of commerce by removing certain recognized sources of industrial strife and unrest, by encouraging practices fundamental to the friendly adjustment of industrial disputes arising out of differences as to wages, hours, or other working conditions, and by restoring equality of bargaining power between employers and employees.

It is hereby declared to be the policy of the United States to eliminate the causes of certain substantial obstructions to the free flow of commerce and to mitigate and eliminate these obstructions when they have occurred by encouraging the practice and procedure of collective bargaining and by protecting the exercise by workers of full freedom of association, self-organization, and designation of representatives of their own choosing, for the purpose of negotiating the terms and conditions of their employment or other mutual aid or protection.

DEFINITIONS

Sec. 2. When used in this Act—

(1) The term "person" includes one or more individuals, partnerships, associations, corporations, legal representatives, trustees, trustees in bankruptcy, or receivers.

(2) The term "employer" includes any person acting in the interest of an employer, directly or indirectly, but shall not include the United States, or any State or political subdivision thereof, or any person subject to the Railway Labor Act, as amended from time to time, or any labor organization (other than when acting as an employer), or anyone acting in the capacity of officer or agent of such labor organization.

(3) The term "employee" shall include any employee, and shall not be limited to the employees of a particular employer, unless the Act explicitly states otherwise, and shall include any individual whose work has ceased as a consequence of, or in connection with, any current labor dispute or because of any unfair labor practice, and who has not obtained any other regular and substantially equivalent employment, but shall not include any individual employed as an agricultural laborer, or in the domestic service of any family or person at his home, or any individual employed by his parent or spouse.

(4) The term "representatives" includes any individual or labor organization.

(5) The term "labor organization" means any organization of any kind, or any agency or employee representation committee or plan, in which employees participate and which exists for the purpose, in whole or in part, of dealing with employers concerning grievances,

labor disputes, wages, rates of pay, hours of employment, or conditions of work.

(6) The term "commerce" means trade, traffic, commerce, transportation, or communication among the several States, or between the District of Columbia or any Territory of the United States and any State or other Territory, or between any foreign country and any State, Territory, or the District of Columbia, or within the District of Columbia or any Territory, or between points in the same State but through any other State or any Territory or the District of Columbia or any foreign country.

(7) The term "affecting commerce" means in commerce, or burdening or obstructing commerce or the free flow of commerce, or having led or tending to lead to a labor dispute burdening or obstructing commerce or the free flow of commerce.

(8) The term "unfair labor practice" means any unfair labor practice listed in section 8.

(9) The term "labor dispute" includes any controversy concerning terms, tenure or conditions of employment, or concerning the association or representation of persons in negotiating, fixing, maintaining, changing, or seeking to arrange terms or conditions of employment, regardless of whether the disputants stand in the proximate relation of employer and employee.

(10) The term "National Labor Relations Board" means the National Labor Relations Board created by section 3 of this Act.

(11) The term "old Board" means the National Labor Relations Board established by Executive Order Numbered 6763 of the President on June 29, 1934, pursuant to Public Resolution Numbered 44, approved June 19, 1934 (48 Stat. 1183), and reestablished and continued by Executive Order Numbered 7074 of the President of June 15, 1935, pursuant to Title I of the National Industrial Recovery Act (48 Stat. 195) as amended and continued by Senate Joint Resolution 133 * approved June 14, 1935.

NATIONAL LABOR RELATIONS BOARD

SEC. 3. (a) There is hereby created a board, to be known as the "National Labor Relations Board" (hereinafter referred to as the "Board"), which shall be composed of three members, who shall be appointed by the President, by and with the advice and consent of the Senate. One of the original members shall be appointed for a term of one year, one for a term of three years, and one for a term

* So in original.

of five years, but their successors shall be appointed for terms of five years each, except that any individual chosen to fill a vacancy shall be appointed only for the unexpired term of the member whom he shall succeed. The President shall designate one member to serve as the chairman of the Board. Any member of the Board may be removed by the President, upon notice and hearing, for neglect of duty or malfeasance in office, but for no other cause.

(b) A vacancy in the Board shall not impair the right of the remaining members to exercise all the powers of the Board, and two members of the Board shall, at all times, constitute a quorum. The Board shall have an official seal which shall be judicially noticed.

(c) The Board shall at the close of each fiscal year make a report in writing to Congress and to the President stating in detail the cases it has heard, the decisions it has rendered, the names, salaries, and duties of all employees and officers in the employ or under the supervision of the Board, and an account of all moneys it has disbursed.

SEC. 4. (a) Each member of the Board shall receive a salary of $10,000 a year, shall be eligible for reappointment, and shall not engage in any other business, vocation, or employment. The Board shall appoint, without regard for the provisions of the civil-service laws but subject to the Classification Act of 1923, as amended, an executive secretary, and such attorneys, examiners, and regional directors, and shall appoint such other employees with regard to existing laws applicable to the employment and compensation of officers and employees of the United States, as it may from time to time find necessary for the proper performance of its duties and as may be from time to time appropriated for by Congress. The Board may establish or utilize such regional, local, or other agencies, and utilize such voluntary and uncompensated services, as may from time to time be needed. Attorneys appointed under this section may, at the direction of the Board, appear for and represent the Board in any case in court. Nothing in this Act shall be construed to authorize the Board to appoint individuals for the purpose of conciliation or mediation (or for statistical work), where such service may be obtained from the Department of Labor.

(b) Upon the appointment of the three original members of the Board and the designation of its chairman, the old Board shall cease to exist. All employees of the old Board shall be transferred to and become employees of the Board with salaries under the Classification Act of 1923, as amended, without acquiring by such transfer a permanent or civil service status. All records, papers, and property of the old Board shall become records, papers, and property of the Board, and all unexpended funds and appropriations for the use and maintenance of the old Board shall become funds and appropriations available to be expended by the Board in the exercise of the powers, authority, and duties conferred on it by this Act.

(c) All of the expenses of the Board, including all necessary traveling and subsistence expenses outside the District of Columbia incurred by the members or employees of the Board under its orders, shall be allowed and paid on the presentation of itemized vouchers therefor approved by the Board or by any individual it designates for that purpose.

SEC. 5. The principal office of the Board shall be in the District of Columbia, but it may meet and exercise any or all of its powers at any other place. The Board may, by one or more of its members or by such agents or agencies as it may designate, prosecute any inquiry necessary to its functions in any part of the United States. A member who participates in such an inquiry shall not be disqualified from subsequently participating in a decision of the Board in the same case.

SEC. 6. (a) The Board shall have authority from time to time to make, amend, and rescind such rules and regulations as may be necessary to carry out the provisions of this Act. Such rules and regulations shall be effective upon publication in the manner which the Board shall prescribe.

RIGHTS OF EMPLOYEES

SEC. 7. Employees shall have the right to self-organization, to form, join, or assist labor organizations, to bargain collectively through representatives of their own choosing, and to engage in concerted activities, for the purpose of collective bargaining or other mutual aid or protection.

SEC. 8. It shall be an unfair labor practice for an employer—

(1) To interfere with, restrain, or coerce employees in the exercise of the rights guaranteed in section 7.

(2) To dominate or interfere with the formation or administration of any labor organization or contribute financial or other support to it: *Provided*, That subject to rules and regulations made and published by the Board pursuant to section 6 (a), an employer shall not be prohibited from permitting employees to confer with him during working hours without loss of time or pay.

(3) By discrimination in regard to hire or tenure of employment or any term or condition of employment to encourage or discourage membership in any labor organization: *Provided*, That nothing in

this Act, or in the National Industrial Recovery Act (U. S. C., Supp. VII, title 15, secs. 701–712), as amended from time to time, or in any code or agreement approved or prescribed thereunder, or in any other statute of the United States, shall preclude an employer from making an agreement with a labor organization (not established, maintained, or assisted by any action defined in this Act as an unfair labor practice) to require as a condition of employment membership therein, if such labor organization is the representative of the employees as provided in section 9 (a), in the appropriate collective bargaining unit covered by such agreement when made.

(4) To discharge or otherwise discriminate against an employee because he has filed charges or given testimony under this Act.

(5) To refuse to bargain collectively with the representatives of his employees, subject to the provisions of section 9 (a).

REPRESENTATIVES AND ELECTIONS

Sec. 9. (a) Representatives designated or selected for the purposes of collective bargaining by the majority of the employees in a unit appropriate for such purposes, shall be the exclusive representatives of all the employees in such unit for the purposes of collective bargaining in respect to rates of pay, wages, hours of employment, or other conditions of employment: *Provided*, That any individual employee or a group of employees shall have the right at any time to present grievances to their employer.

(b) The Board shall decide in each case whether, in order to insure to employees the full benefit of their right to self-organization and to collective bargaining, and otherwise to effectuate the policies of this Act, the unit appropriate for the purposes of collective bargaining shall be the employer unit, craft unit, plant unit, or subdivision thereof.

(c) Whenever a question affecting commerce arises concerning the representation of employees, the Board may investigate such controversy and certify to the parties, in writing, the name or names of the representatives that have been designated or selected. In any such investigation, the Board shall provide for an appropriate hearing upon due notice, either in conjunction with a proceeding under section 10 or otherwise, and may take a secret ballot of employees, or utilize any other suitable method to ascertain * such representatives.

(d) Whenever an order of the Board made pursuant to section

* So in original.

10 (c) is based in whole or in part upon facts certified following an investigation pursuant to subsection (c) of this section, and there is a petition for the enforcement or review of such order, such certification and the record of such investigation shall be included in the transcript of the entire record required to be filed under subsections 10 (e) or 10 (f), and thereupon the decree of the court enforcing, modifying, or setting aside in whole or in part the order of the Board shall be made and entered upon the pleadings, testimony, and proceedings set forth in such transcript.

PREVENTION OF UNFAIR LABOR PRACTICES

SEC. 10. (a) The Board is empowered, as hereinafter provided, to prevent any person from engaging in any unfair labor practice (listed in section 8) affecting commerce. This power shall be exclusive, and shall not be affected by any other means of adjustment or prevention that has been or may be established by agreement, code, law, or otherwise.

(b) Whenever it is charged that any person has engaged in or is engaging in any such unfair labor practice, the Board, or any agent or agency designated by the Board for such purposes, shall have power to issue and cause to be served upon such person a complaint stating the charges in that respect, and containing a notice of hearing before the Board or a member thereof, or before a designated agent or agency, at a place therein fixed, not less than five days after the serving of said complaint. Any such complaint may be amended by the member, agent, or agency conducting the hearing or the Board in its discretion at any time prior to the issuance of an order based thereon. The person so complained of shall have the right to file an answer to the original or amended complaint and to appear in person or otherwise and give testimony at the place and time fixed in the complaint. In the discretion of the member, agent, or agency conducting the hearing or the Board, any other person may be allowed to intervene in the said proceeding and to present testimony. In any such proceeding the rules of evidence prevailing in courts of law or equity shall not be controlling.

(c) The testimony taken by such member, agent or agency or the Board shall be reduced to writing and filed with the Board. Thereafter, in its discretion, the Board upon notice may take further testimony or hear argument. If upon all the testimony taken the Board shall be of the opinion that any person named in the complaint has engaged in or is engaging in any such unfair labor practice, then the Board shall state its findings of fact and shall issue and cause to be served on such person an order requiring such person to cease and desist from such unfair labor practice, and to take such affirmative action, including reinstatement of employees with or without back pay, as will effectuate the policies of this Act. Such order may further require such person to make reports from time to time showing the extent to which it has complied with the order. If upon all the testimony taken the Board shall be of the opinion that no person named in the complaint has engaged in or is engaging in any such unfair labor practice, then the Board shall state its findings of fact and shall issue an order dismissing the said complaint.

(d) Until a transcript of the record in a case shall have been filed in a court, as hereinafter provided, the Board may at any time, upon reasonable notice and in such manner as it shall deem proper, modify or set aside, in whole or in part, any finding or order made or issued by it.

(e) The Board shall have power to petition any circuit court of appeals of the United States (including the Court of Appeals of the District of Columbia), or if all the circuit courts of appeals to which application may be made are in vacation, any district court of the United States (including the Supreme Court of the District of Columbia), within any circuit or district, respectively, wherein the unfair labor practice in question occurred or wherein such person resides or transacts business, for the enforcement of such order and for appropriate temporary relief or restraining order, and shall certify and file in the court a transcript of the entire record in the proceeding, including the pleadings and testimony upon which such order was entered and the findings and order of the Board. Upon such filing, the court shall cause notice thereof to be served upon such person, and thereupon shall have jurisdiction of the proceeding and of the question determined therein, and shall have power to grant such temporary relief or restraining order as it deems just and proper, and to make and enter upon the pleadings, testimony, and proceedings set forth in such transcript a decree enforcing, modifying, and enforcing as so modified, or setting aside in whole or in part the order of the Board. No objection that has not been urged before the Board, its member, agent, or agency, shall be considered by the court, unless the failure or neglect to urge such objection shall be excused because of extraordinary circumstances. The findings of the Board as to the facts, if supported by evidence, shall be conclusive. If either party shall apply to the court for leave to adduce additional evidence and shall show to the satisfaction of the court that such additional evidence is material and that there were reasonable grounds for the failure to adduce such evidence in the hearing before the Board, its member, agent, or agency, the court may order such additional evidence to be taken before the Board, its member, agent, or agency, and to be made a part of the transcript. The Board may modify its findings as to the facts, or make new findings, by reason of additional evidence so taken and filed, and it shall file such modified or new findings, which, if supported by evidence, shall be conclusive, and shall file its recommendations, if any, for the modification or setting aside of its original order. The jurisdiction of the court shall be exclusive and its judgment and decree shall be final, except that the same shall be subject to review by the appropriate circuit court of appeals if application was made to the district court as hereinabove provided, and by the Supreme Court of the United States upon writ of certiorari or certification as provided in sections 239 and 240 of the Judicial Code, as amended (U. S. C., title 28, secs. 346 and 347).

(f) Any person aggrieved by a final order of the Board granting or denying in whole or in part the relief sought may obtain a review of such order in any circuit court of appeals of the United States in the circuit wherein the unfair labor practice in question was alleged to have been engaged in or wherein such person resides or transacts business, or in the Court of Appeals of the District of Columbia, by filing in such court a written petition praying that the order of the Board be modified or set aside. A copy of such petition shall be forthwith served upon the Board, and thereupon the aggrieved party shall file in the court a transcript of the entire record in the proceeding, certified by the Board, including the pleading and testimony upon which the order complained of was entered and the findings and order of the Board. Upon such filing, the court shall proceed in the same manner as in the case of an application by the Board under subsection (e), and shall have the same exclusive jurisdiction to grant to the Board such temporary relief or restraining order as it deems just and proper, and in like manner to make and enter a decree enforcing, modifying, and enforcing as so modified, or setting aside in whole or in part the order of the Board; and the findings of the Board as to the facts, if supported by evidence, shall in like manner be conclusive.

(g) The commencement of proceedings under subsection (e) or (f) of this section shall not, unless specifically ordered by the court, operate as a stay of the Board's order.

(h) When granting appropriate temporary relief or a restraining order, or making and entering a decree enforcing, modifying, and enforcing as so modified or setting aside in whole or in part an order of the Board, as provided in this section, the jurisdiction of courts sitting in equity shall not be limited by the Act entitled "An Act to amend the Judicial Code and to define and limit the jurisdiction of courts sitting in equity, and for other purposes," approved March 23, 1932 (U. S. C., Supp. VII, title 29, secs. 101–115).

(i) Petitions filed under this Act shall be heard expeditiously, and if possible within ten days after they have been docketed.

INVESTIGATORY POWERS

Sec. 11. For the purpose of all hearings and investigations, which, in the opinion of the Board, are necessary and proper for the exercise of the powers vested in it by section 9 and section 10—

(1) The Board, or its duly authorized agents or agencies, shall at all reasonable times have access to, for the purpose of examination, and the right to copy any evidence of any person being investigated or proceeded against that relates to any matter under investigation or in question. Any member of the Board shall have power to issue subpenas requiring the attendance and testimony of witnesses and the production of any evidence that relates to any matter under investigation or in question, before the Board, its member, agent, or agency conducting the hearing or investigation. Any member of the Board, or any agent or agency designated by the Board for such purposes, may administer oaths and affirmations, examine witnesses, and receive evidence. Such attendance of witnesses and the production of such evidence may be required from any place in the United States or any Territory or possession thereof, at any designated place of hearing.

(2) In case of contumacy or refusal to obey a subpena issued to any person, any District Court of the United States or the United States courts of any Territory or possession, or the Supreme Court of the District of Columbia, within the jurisdiction of which the inquiry is carried on or within the jurisdiction of which said person guilty of contumacy or refusal to obey is found or resides or transacts business, upon application by the Board shall have jurisdiction to issue to such person an order requiring such person to appear before the Board, its member, agent, or agency, there to produce evidence if so ordered, or there to give testimony touching the matter under investigation or in question; and any failure to obey such order of the court may be punished by said court as a contempt thereof.

(3) No person shall be excused from attending and testifying or from producing books, records, correspondence, documents, or other evidence in obedience to the subpena of the Board, on the ground that the testimony or evidence required of him may tend to incriminate him or subject him to a penalty or forfeiture; but no individual shall be prosecuted or subjected to any penalty or forfeiture for or on account of any transaction, matter, or thing concerning which he is compelled, after having claimed his privilege against self-incrimination, to testify or produce evidence, except that such individual so testifying shall not be exempt from prosecution and punishment for perjury committed in so testifying.

(4) Complaints, orders, and other process and papers of the Board, its member, agent, or agency, may be served either personally or by registered mail or by telegraph or by leaving a copy thereof at the principal office or place of business of the person required to be served. The verified return by the individual so serving the same setting forth the manner of such service shall be proof of the same, and the return post office receipt or telegraph receipt therefor when registered and mailed or telegraphed as aforesaid shall be proof of service of the same. Witnesses summoned before the Board, its member, agent, or agency, shall be paid the same fees and mileage that are paid witnesses in the courts of the United States, and witnesses whose depositions are taken and the persons taking the same shall severally be entitled to the same fees as are paid for like services in the courts of the United States.

(5) All process of any court to which application may be made under this Act may be served in the judicial district wherein the defendant or other person required to be served resides or may be found.

(6) The several departments and agencies of the Government, when directed by the President, shall furnish the Board, upon its request, all records, papers, and information in their possession relating to any matter before the Board.

SEC. 12. Any person who shall willfully resist, prevent, impede, or interfere with any member of the Board or any of its agents or agencies in the performance of duties pursuant to this Act shall be punished by a fine of not more than $5,000 or by imprisonment for not more than one year, or both.

LIMITATIONS

SEC. 13. Nothing in this Act shall be construed so as to interfere with or impede or diminish in any way the right to strike.

Sec. 14. Wherever the application of the provisions of section 7 (a) of the National Industrial Recovery Act (U. S. C., Supp. VII, title 15, sec. 707 (a)), as amended from time to time, or of section 77 B, paragraphs (1) and (m) of the Act approved June 7, 1934, entitled "An Act to amend an Act entitled 'An Act to establish a uniform system of bankruptcy throughout the United States' approved July 1, 1898, and Acts amendatory thereof and supplementary thereto" (48 Stat. 922, pars. (1) and (m)), as amended from time to time, or of Public Resolution Numbered 44, approved June 19, 1934 (48 Stat. 1183), conflicts with the application of the provisions of this Act, this Act shall prevail: *Provided,* That in any situation where the provisions of this Act cannot be validly enforced, the provisions of such other Acts shall remain in full force and effect.

Sec. 15. If any provision of this Act, or the application of such provision to any person or circumstance, shall be held invalid, the remainder of this Act, or the application of such provision to persons or circumstances other than those as to which it is held invalid, shall not be affected thereby.

Sec. 16. This Act may be cited as the "National Labor Relations Act."

Approved, July 5, 1935.

INDEX

ADJUSTED charges, 10–16
Administrative agencies, 236 *et seq.; see* Courts
Agreements, union trade, *see* Contracts, union
Agwalines Inc. *vs.* N.L.R.B., case involving board procedure, 217
Allis Chalmers Co., case on appropriate unit, 160–161
Aluminum Co. of America, 149
Aluminum Workers, National Council of, 149
Amendments to N.L.R.A., proposed, 158–159, 162, 166–170, 171, 181–182, 199, 201, 233–234, 256
American Bankers' Ass'n, 47
American Federation of Labor (A. F. of L.), on Norris-LaGuardia Act, 33; and collusive contracts, 100–107; and interunion conflicts, 145–166; hostility to board, 156–162; on amending N.L.R.A., 158–159, 162, 166–170; on craft union issue, 163–165; in appropriate unit cases, 165
"American Inquisition," 203
American Labor Party, 256
American Liberty League, 122; National Lawyers' Committee of, 205
American Railway Union, 27
American Steel and Iron Institute, 75–76
Anarchists, 30
"Anti-injunction laws," Norris-LaGuardia Act, 33–36; state laws, 36, n. 27 Ch. II
Antiunionism, 45–80; judicial, 24–29, 73, 221–222; legal, 30, *see* Unions, legality of; local ordinances, 30, 43, 172, 173; criminal, 30, 49, 54, 77–79, 171; military, 30; economic, 31–32, 37, 39, 53–67; open shop, 32; propaganda, 32, 40, 48–49, 54–55, 72, 75–76, 171; company unions, 32, 40, 68–72, 132–135, 171; black lists, 33, 40, 55, 61, 62–63, 171; discriminatory discharge, 9, 11, 14, 17–20, 32, 40, 51, 55, 56–62, 126, 129–130; espionage, 32, 40, 67–68, 171; strikebreakers, 32, 40, 124; history of, 47–49; welfare work, 49; "yellow-dog" contracts, 25, 32, 55, 63, 64, 171; "runaway" plants, 1–6, 55, 64–67; "independent" unions, 69–70, 74; citizens' committees, 49, 72, 171; back-to-work movements, 72, 171; vigilantism, 73–75; Mohawk Valley Formula, 73–76, 79; motives for, 133–136
Appeals from board orders, 202, 203, 213, 218
Appropriate bargaining unit, 88–92, 144, 151, 152–166
Arbitration, compulsory, 112, 138, 251–255
Artificial Limbs Co., fictionalized case illustrating adjusted charges, 13–16
Attorneys for the board, 230–233
Autocracy, union, 172, 189, 201
Automobile Workers, United, 141, 160
Axton-Fisher Tobacco Co., case involving interunion conflict, 150–151

Back-to-work movements, 72, 171
  Balleisen contracts, 63–64
Beating, see Criminal antiunionism
Beck, Dave, 153
Bethlehem Shipbuilding Corp., case illustrating legal delays, 123
Big business, 27
Black, Mr. Justice, 220
Black Bill, 38
Black list, 33, 40, 55, 61, 62–63, 171
Black Shoe Co., fictionalized case illustrating dismissed charges, 1–7
Blacksmiths' Union, 145
Boilermakers' Union, 161
Bolshevists, 30
Boycotts, legality of, 26, 27–28, 29; unfair practices of labor, 172, 177, 184
Brewery Workmen, United, 145
Bridges, Harry, 153
British Trades Disputes Act, on sympathetic strikes, 183
Brooklyn Chamber of Commerce, 63–64
Brown Shoe Co., case illustrating legal delays, 122–123, 125
Businessmen, small, 244–245
Butcher Workmen's Union, 141

Carpenters, United Brotherhood of, 17, 141, 144
  Centralization, 236 et seq.; of economic life, 236–238, 240–241; of
  political power, 238–239
Certification, see Elections
Charges, illustrated, 1–16
Citizens' Committee, 49, 72, 171
Clayton Act, 28–29, 36, 221–222
"Clean hands," 34
Closed shop, confusion with majority rule, 86; legality under N.L.R.A.,
  87, 185; in Little Steel strikes, 112–113; strikes for, 130, 172, 180, 182,
  188–189; with closed union, 185–186; reasons for, 186–187
Clothing Workers, Amalgamated, 142, 145
Collective bargaining, 81–117; refusal of, 18, 20; defense of, 44, 81;
  definition of, 81, 88; social background, 81–82; economic background,
  82–84; Congressional view of, 85; majority representation, 87–99, 144;
  certification, 99; recognition, 99–100; validity of contracts, 100–107;
  definition of bargaining, 108–117; written contracts, 111–116; as economic planning, 181
Collusion, A. F. of L. and employers, 104–105; C.I.O. and employer,
  105–106
Combinations, of businessmen, 23, 28–29, 37–38; of workers, see Unions,
  legality of
Combustion Engineering Co., case involving problem of appropriate unit,
  161–162
Committee for Industrial Organization (C.I.O.), and collusive contracts,

100–107; in interunion conflicts, 145–148, 152–166; hostility to board, 156; acceptance of board, 158; election results, 163–165; in appropriate unit cases, 165

Common law affecting unions, 23–27, 47

Communists (and "Communists"), 30, 50, 71, 113, 145, 153

Company unions, 32, 40; under the N.L.R.A., 68–72; characteristics of, 69, 135; reasons for, 132–135; inadequacy of, 136

Complaints, illustrated, 16–17

Conflict, interunion, 140–170; causes, 140–143; examples, 141; craft *vs.* craft, 144; craft *vs.* industrial, 145, 155–159; industrial *vs.* industrial, 145, 153–155; solution, 145–146; within A. F. of L., 146, 148–151; within C.I.O., 147; C.I.O. *vs.* A. F. of L., 147, 153–155, 156–159; board policies toward, 147–163; election results in cases involving, 163–164; strikes resulting from, 166, 172, 180, 181, 182; employer's position in the face of, 167–169

Consolidated Edison Co., case involving collusive contracts, 100–103; review of evidence, 219–221, 222

Conspiracy in restraint of trade, *see* Unions, legality of

Constitutional Educational League, Inc., 50

Constitutionality, of N.L.R.A., 20, 44, 69, 120, 125, 171; of N.I.R.A., 41

Consumers, 242–243

Contracts, union, enforceability of, 1; validity of, 100–107; collusive, 100–107; company, 103–104; written, 111–116; extent of, 136–137; strikes against, 172, 180–182; observance of, 171, 172, 189–193

Coopers' Union, 145

Corruption, union, 172, 189, 198–199

Coughlin, Father, 86

Courts, the board and the, 202–235; appeals, 202, 203, 213, 218; injunctions, 203–207; rules of evidence, 203, 207–213; review of evidence, 203, 213–227; prosecution, judge, jury triangle, 203, 226–235; board's record in the courts, 222; intermediate reports, 223–226

Craft unions, *vs.* craft unions, 144; *vs.* industrial unions, 145, 155–159

Criminal action against employer, none under N.L.R.A., 44

Criminal antiunionism, 30, 49, 54, 77–79, 171

Criminal law affecting unions, 30, 43, 173–174

Criminal syndicalism, 30

Crucible Steel Co., 126

D AMAGE suits, against unions, 29, 43; against employers, 1
  Debs, Eugene V., 27

Degeneracy, industrial, 142–143

Democracy, and the board, 235–257; renewed scrutiny of, 236; centralized economic and political life under, 236 *et seq.;* dangers to, 239, 241–242; group action under, 243–247; territorial representation under, 247, 249; pressure politics in a, 247, 249, 250; and compulsory arbitration, 251–255; and labor politics, 255–257

Department of Justice, 41, 195, 242

Dewey, Thomas, 195, 209
Discriminatory discharge, alleged, 9, 11, 14; illustrated, 17–20, 51; pre-N.R.A. legality of, 32, 55; under Section 7a, 40; under the N.L.R.A., 56–62; workers reinstated after, 61–62, 126; strikes against, 129–130
Dismissed charges, 1–7, 10, 16
Dooley, Mr. (Peter Finley Dunne), 221
Dun & Bradstreet, 5

Economic antiunionism, 31–32, 37, 39, 55–67
   Elections, appropriate unit for, see Appropriate unit; time of, 92–93; nature of, 93–97, 164; results of, 95, 97, 98, 163–164; form of ballot for, 95–96; run-off, 96–97; certification without, 98–99; number conducted, 126; opposition to, 152; appeal for by employer, 167–169; effect of on intimidation, 178–179; compulsory annual, 201
Electrical Workers, International Brotherhood of, 101–103, 141, 160, 220
Electrical Workers, United Radio and, 93–95, 101–103, 141
Employer appeals to board for elections, 167–169
Employers' associations, 32, 47–49
Employer's position in the face of interunion conflict, 167–169
Enamel Workers' Union, 123–125
"Equal loss," 34–35
Espionage, 32; under Section 7a, 40; board policy toward, 67–68, 171
Evidence, review of, 203, 213–227; illustrated, 214; rules of, 203, 207–213; new, 213, 214–216; the, 217, 218, 221; any, 217; substantial, 217, 219, 221; preponderant, 217, 221; incontestable, 221

Farmers, group action, 243–244; relation to government, 244
   Fedders Mfg. Co., case involving run-off elections, 96–97
Federal Communications Commission, 202
Federal Trade Commission, 197, 202
Field examiner, duties illustrated, 2–16
Financial reports, union, 199
Findings of fact, illustrated, 214; supported by evidence, 215, 218; review of, 213, 215, 218
Firemen's and Oilers' union, 161
Ford, Henry, 54
Ford Motor Co., case illustrating criminal antiunionism, 54, 77, 80; board's procedure, 223–226
Formal cases, 16, 21
Free speech, 48, 49–55
Friedman-Harry Marks Clothing Co., case involving rules of evidence, 210
Furniture Workers' Union, 16–21, 127

Garment Workers, International Ladies', 142, 147
   Garment Workers, United, 142
General Electric Co., 191
General Motors Co., 190

Girdler, Tom, 116
Glass Bottle Blowers' Union, 141
Granite Cutters' Union, 141
Green, William, 162
Group action, economic, 243–247
Guild congress, 249

Harlan County, 242
  Hearings, illustrated, 17, 20
Hines, James, 209
Hoffmann, Representative, 50
Hoover administration, 38
Hopwood Retinning Co., case illustrating "yellow-dog" contracts, 63–64, 66
Houde Engineering Co., case involving majority rule, 42
Hughes, Chief Justice, 210–211, 218, 220
Hutcheson, Judge, 217

Incorporation of unions, suability of unincorporated unions, 29; compulsory, 195–197; voluntary, 197
Independent national unions, 164
"Independent" unions, 69–70, 74
Industrial unions, vs. craft unions, 145, 155–159; vs. industrial unions, 145, 153–155
Industrial Workers of the World (I.W.W.), 89, 90, 141, 145
Informal cases, 1–16; procedure exemplified, 1–16; dismissed, 1–7, 10, 16; withdrawn, 7–9, 10, 16; adjusted, 10–16
Injunctions, under Sherman Act, 27; under Clayton Act, 28; based on "yellow-dog" contracts, 32, 55; under Norris-LaGuardia Act, 33–36; under N.L.R.A., 43; in free speech cases, 53; against N.L.R.B., 122, 203–207; use against unions illustrated, 24; in jurisdictional strikes, 167
Inland Steel Co., case involving written contracts, 113
Intermediate report, trial examiners', 17, 175, 223–226
Interstate Commerce Commission, 202
Intimidation, by unions, 26, 171, 172–175, 177, 178–179
Investors, group action of, 243
"Irresponsibility" of unions, 26, 29, 113, 171, 172, 189–193

Jones and Laughlin Steel Corp., case illustrating discriminatory discharge, 62
Jones and Laughlin Steel Corp. (vs. N.L.R.B.), case illustrating board procedure, 219
Judicial antiunionism, 24–29, 73, 221–222
Jurisdiction, of board, 20, 103
Jurisdictional conflict, see Conflict, interunion
Jurisdictional strikes, 166, 172, 180

K IDNA PING, *see* Criminal antiunionism
Ku Klux Klan, 74–75

L A FOLLETTE Civil Liberties Committee, 54, 67, 75, 116, 199, 242
Leatherworkers' Union, 7–9
Legal antiunionism, 30, *see* Unions, legality of
Lewis, John L., 53, 190, 256
Liberty League, American, 122; National Lawyers' Committee of, 205
Little Steel strike, 112–113, 137
Local ordinances affecting unions, 30, 43, 172, 173
Lockout, 32
Longshoremen's Union, 153
Lovestoneite, 87

M ACHINISTS' Union, 145, 150, 160, 161
MacKay Radio and Telegraph Co., case illustrating black list, 61; involving intermediate reports, 225
McReynolds, Mr. Justice, 210
Majority representation, *vs.* proportional, 86–87; appropriate unit, 88–92, 144, 151, 152–166; time of elections, 92–93; definition of majority, 93–97
Marine Engineers' Beneficial Association, 141
Mechanics' Educational Society, 86
Memphis Furniture Co., case illustrating formal procedure, 16–21, 127
Military antiunionism, 30
Mine B. Coal Co., case involving collusive C.I.O. contract, 106
Mine Workers, Progressive, 106, 141, 145
Mine Workers, United, 106, 141, 145, 196, 256
Mohawk Valley Formula, 73–76, 79
Molders' Union, 160, 161
Monopoly, union, 172, 186, 189, 197–198
Monumental Mfg. Co., fictionalized case illustrating withdrawn charges, 7–9
Morgan, J. P., 190
Morgan, *vs.* U.S., case affecting board procedure, 223
Murder, *see* Criminal antiunionism
Muskin Shoe Co., case involving free speech issue, 49–51

N ATIONAL Ass'n of Manufacturers, 47, 73, 75
National Industrial Recovery Act (N.I.R.A.), 38, 41, 42
National Labor Board, 40–42, 43
National Labor Relations Act (N.L.R.A.), informal procedures under, 16; acceptance of, 21, 46, 62, 136; events leading to, 39–43; general aspects of, 43–44; constitutionality of, 44, 118, 120, 127; provisions against antiunionism, 46, *see* Antiunionism; economic background, 82–85; collusive contracts under, 100; on majority rule, 87; effect of, on unionism, 121–122, on interunion conflict, 143; proposed amendments to, 162, 166–170, 171, 181–182, 199, 201, 233–234, 256; "one-sided" character of, 171–

201; no criminal procedure under, 174; on strikes, 181; on closed shop, 185; as reaction against antiunionism, 188; effect of, on managerial responsibility, 190–191, on rules of evidence, 207; procedure under, *see* Courts; on intermediate reports, 224; and democracy, 236–257

National Labor Relations Board (the old board), 41–42, 43, 86

National Labor Relations Board (N.L.R.B.), informal procedures of, 1–16; formal procedures of, 16–21, 79–80, 174–176, *see* Courts; jurisdiction of, 20, 103; acceptance of, 21–22, 158; opposition to, 21, 46–47, 48, 49, 54, 80, 119, 120, 122, 124, 156–162; "partiality" of, 45; problem of free speech, 48; reinstatement of discharged workers, 61–62, 126; cease and desist orders, 62; on blacklisting, 62–63; on "yellow-dog" contracts, 63–64; on "runaway" plants, 64–67; on company unions, 68–72; on "independent" unions, 69–70; on Mohawk Valley Formula, 73–76; on reinstatement of workers convicted of major offenses, 79; on collective bargaining, 88–117; A. F. of L. hostility to, 100, 104–105, 155, 159; on strikes, 118–139; and injunctions, 122, 203–207; in litigation, 122–123; on interunion conflict, 143–170; on unfair practices of labor, 171–201; on criminal offenses of labor, 179–180; and the courts, 202–235; and democracy, 236–257

National Maritime Union, 191

National Mediation Board, 43, 159, 192

National Metal Trades' Association, 47

National Recovery Administration (N.R.A.), 41

New Deal, 38–39, 171

New York State Labor Relations Board, 168

New York Times, on free speech, 49–51, 53

Norris-LaGuardia Act, 33–36, 55–56, 63, 167

OBJECTIONS, illustrated, 17, 213–214; review of, 213, 215
Omaha Hat Corp., case involving discriminatory discharge, 57–59, 66

"Open shop," 32

Opposition to board, 21, 46–47, 48, 49, 54, 80, 119–120, 122, 124

Orders, illustrated, 20–21, 214–215; cease and desist, 62; review of, 213, 215, 218; appeal from, 202, 203, 213, 218

PACIFIC longshoremen's cases, involving appropriate unit, 91, 152–155
Packers and Stockyards Act, 223

Patternmakers' League, 90

Pecora, Justice, 209

Personnel relations, 132–133, 136

Picketing, legality of, 26, 28, 29, 30; mass, 172, 177

Pittsburgh Steel Co., 126

Politics, labor, 255–257

Preferential reinstatement, 13

President's committee on British labor relations, 183

Pressure politics, 247, 249, 250

Procedure, informal illustrated, 1–16; formal illustrated, 16–21; *see also* Courts, Evidence, Trial examiner

Professionals, group action of, 245; relation to government, 245

Propaganda, 48–49, 54, 55, 72, 75–76

Proportional representation, 86–87

Public Resolution No. 44, 42, 43, 46, 56, 85, 86, 222

RACKETEERING, union, 171, 172, 189, 193–197

Railway Labor Act, 159, 162, 166

R.C.A. Mfg. Co., case illustrating form of board elections, 93–95

Recognition, 99–100; strikes for, 130–131

Reed, Mr. Justice, 220

Refusal to bargain, illustrated, 18, 20

Regional director, 7, 12, 16

Regional office, 2, 6, 7, 10

Reinstatement, 60–61, 179–180

Remington Rand, case involving all forms of antiunionism, 73, 77, 80; corruption of union leaders, 198

Representation, proportional, 86–87; majority, 86–97

Republic Steel Co., case illustrating Mohawk Valley Formula, 75–77; board procedure, 223–226

Resolution No. 44, public, 42, 43, 46, 56, 85, 86, 222

Responsibility, union, 26, 29, 171, 189–193

Responsibility of management, 189–193

Restraint of trade, *see* Unions, legality of

Retail Clerks' Protective Association, 141

Roberts, Mr. Justice, 218

Roosevelt, Franklin D., 39, 40, 43

Roosevelt, Theodore, 27

Roosevelt administration, 38

Rubber Workers, United, 142, 147

"Rule of reason," 26, 28

Rules Committee of the House, 256

"Runaway" plants, 1–6, 55, 64–67

SAILORS' Union of the Pacific, 153

Sands Point Neckwear Co., fictionalized case involving adjusted charges, 10–13

Seamen's Union, International, 141

Section 7a, 38–42, 46, 56, 85, 86, 222

Securities Exchange Commission, 202

Sheet Metal Workers' Union, 141, 144

Sherman Antitrust Act, 27

Shoe machinery, 4–5

Shoe Workers' Union, fictionalized case illustrating dismissed charges, 1–6

Sloan, Alfred P., 190

Smith, Edwin S., 162

Socialist, 153

Stalinists, 87

Stay-in strikes, 172, 176–178

Steel Facts, 192

Steel Workers' Organizing Committee, 62, 96–97, 112–113, 161, 192

Stone Cutters' Union, 29, 141

Strikebreakers, 32; under Section 7a, 40; use illustrated, 124

Strikers, reinstatement of, 60–61, 179–180

Strikes, avoided through board action, 20, 126; legality of, 25–26; wave of, under Section 7a, 40; reduction expected under act, 118–119; strike statistics, 119, 120–121; causes of increase in 1937, 121; settlement through board action, 126–129; organizing, 128–129; causes of, 120–121, 129–132; for closed shop, 130, 172, 180, 182, 188–189; stay-in, 172, 176–178; jurisdictional, 166, 172, 180, 181, 182, *see* Conflict, interunion; against contracts, 172, 180, 182; social setting of, 180–181; prohibition of, 251–252

Suability of unions, 29, 43

Suit for breach of contract, 1

Supreme Court, United States, on constitutionality of N.L.R.A., 20, 44, 69, 120, 125, 171; self-reversal, 24; rule of reason, 26–27, 28; antiunion decisions, 29; decision against N.R.A., 43; support of board, 45; on injunction cases involving board, 122–123, 206–207; defiance of, 127; on procedure, 210, 212, 219, 220; on union liability, 195; on evidence, 220–222; Mr. Dooley on, 221; on intermediate reports, 223–226

Sympathetic strikes, 172, 180, 181, 182–185

Syndicalists, 30

Teamsters' Union, 141, 145, 153

Territorial representation, 247, 249

Textile Workers, United, 141

Tobacco Workers' Union, 150–151

Totalitarian government, 138, 248

Trade associations, 244–245

Trades Disputes Act, 183

Trial examiner, 17; intermediate report of, 17, 175, 223–226; on rules of evidence, 207–210; functions, 229–232

Unconstitutionality, of N.L.R.A., alleged, 20; of N.R.A., 43

"Unfair" practices of unions, 171–201; intimidation, 26, 171, 172–175, 177, 178–179; racketeering, 171, 172, 189, 193–197; irresponsibility, 171, 172, 189–193; violence, 171, 172–173, 177; mass picketing, 172, 177; stay-in strikes, 172, 176, 178; boycotts, 172, 177, 184; jurisdictional strikes, 166, 172, 180, 181, 182, *see* Conflict, interunion; sympathetic strikes, 172, 180, 181, 182–185; closed-shop strikes, 130, 172, 180, 182, 188–189; strikes in violation of contract, 172, 180, 182; corruption, 172, 189, 198–199; monopoly, 172, 186, 189, 197–198; autocracy, 172, 189, 199–201

Unions, legality of, 23–44; under common law, 23–27, 47; in restraint of trade, 23–24, 28–29, 43, 47, 198; picketing, 26, 28, 29, 30; intimidation, 26; under criminal law, 30, 43, 173–174; criminal syndicalism, 30; under local ordinances, 30, 43, 172, 173; suits for damages, 29, 43; boycotts, 24, 26, 27–28, 29; under injunctions, *see* Injunctions

Unions, methods of, 24, 25, 28, 29; responsibility of, 26, 29, 113, 171–172, 189–193; suability of, 29, 43; unfair practices of, 171–201; incorporation of, 195–197; as democracy, 246–248; in politics, 255–257; financial reports, 199; contracts, 1, 100–107, 111–116, 171, 172, 186–187, 189, 193; employer collusion, 104–106; *see also* Strikes, Interunion conflict, Unfair practices of labor

United Neckwear Workers' Union, 10–13

United Show Workers, 50

United States Chamber of Commerce, 47

United States Labor Department, 132

United States Stamping Co., case involving legal delays, 123–125

United States Steel Co., 28, 191

VIGILANTISM, 73–75
    Violence, union, 171, 172–173, 177

WAGES and Hours Act, 256
    Wages and Hours Bill, 256

Wagner, Senator, 40

Wagner Labor Disputes Bill, 41–42, 43

Washington, Virginia, and Maryland Coach Co., *vs.* N.L.R.B., case involving sufficiency of evidence, 219

Waterfront Employers' Association of the Pacific, 154

Way, Federal District Judge, 206

"We Don't Patronize" list, 24

Weirton Steel Co., case illustrating contempt of the board, 54

Welfare work, 49

White list, 32

Withdrawn charges, 9, 10, 16

YELLOW-DOG" contracts, 25, 32, 55, 63–64